THE ULTIMATE GUIDE TO
BUYING AND SELLING
CO-OPS AND CONDOS
IN NEW YORK CITY

NICE IDEA
PUBLISHING

The Ultimate Guide to Buying and Selling Co-ops and Condos in New York City
(Fourth Edition)

by Neil J. Binder

ISBN 0-9679249-1-5
1. Real Estate 2. New York City 3. Business

NICE IDEA
PUBLISHING

Published by Nice Idea Publishing, Inc.
936 Broadway, New York, N.Y. 10010

THE ULTIMATE GUIDE TO
BUYING AND SELLING
CO-OPS AND CONDOS
IN NEW YORK CITY

I wish to dedicate this book to all the salespeople of the Coldwell Banker Bellmarc Group. It has been the greatest honor of my life to have been associated with each and every one of you.

Acknowledgements

I have been greatly honored by the enormous success of my prior three editions of The Ultimate Guide; however, the accolades should not be mine alone to enjoy. Bellmarc's managers are also important to the quality of the final product. They are Janice Silver, sales manager for the East Side; Dan Berman, sales manager for Midtown; Veronica Raehse, sales manager for the West Side; Lisa Strobing, sales manager for Gramercy/Chelsea; Robert Cleary and Jennifer Roberts, sales managers for Greenwich Village; and Jo-Anne Sinnott, Executive Vice President and Communications Director. I also wish to thank the following experts, whose wisdom was invaluable to ensuring the accuracy and quality of the information in this book:

- Neil Garfinkel, Esq., Abrams Garfinkel Margolis Bergson, LLP
- Dan Levitan, Guaranteed Rate
- Laurence D. Pittinsky, Esq., Rosenberg & Pittinsky, LLP
- Stuart Jasphy, CPA, Harold Zoref, LLP
- John Janangelo, Douglas Elliman Property Management
- Ira Stechel, Esq., Wormser, Kiely, Galef & Jacobs LLP

Finally, I would like to express my continued gratitude to Nina Scerbo of Nina Scerbo Design, Inc. for her wonderful talents as my design director, and to Eve Binder for her meticulousness in editing this work.

Contents

Introduction

I am proud to say that I am a New York real estate broker. I founded Bellmarc with my former business partner more than 30 years ago in 1979. At the inception of the business, we began in a 12' × 15' office in Greenwich Village. We used phones with rotary dials and sat at desks that were purchased from the building superintendent. At the time, apartment ownership was a developing idea. Landlords were desperate, because New York City rent control laws limited their ability to pass on the increasing costs of operation to their tenants. The squeeze between rising interest rates, skyrocketing oil costs and inflation became a framework for stimulating conversions from rentals to ownership.

We too had tried our hand at buying real estate with investor money. As our own resources declined and our investors shied away from new opportunities, we knew that a new framework for moving forward was necessary. It is strange how recessions wash away the old and replenish the economy with new life. I have been through three recessions since the inception of Bellmarc and it is always the same cycle — denial, shock, pain, confusion and reinvigoration. I once heard a wise man say that God gives you a challenge because he thinks you're worthy of growing. I believe this. I believe that New York City and the residential real estate market have evolved over the years into an exciting, dynamic place to live and work. It has not been a steady climb, but nevertheless, today New York is a better city and a better place to live.

Bellmarc grew through a unique business model that focused heavily on training new agents, and I have played a central role in that function. My efforts began by sitting with recruits to discuss critical material. This evolved into a broader program, including audio tapes and examinations. Now there are Internet feeds, books and supplements, seminars, pretests and closed-book examinations. I still spend a tremendous amount of time working with trainees, developing new materials and guiding salespeople through issues on specific deals and in classes. I also spend a considerable amount of time studying and writing. I have written four books: three prior versions of *The Ultimate Guide to Buying and Selling Co-ops and Condos in New York City*, which is used as a general reference; *Selling Mechanics*, which is used as a guide for real estate brokers; *The Art of Selling: A Scientific Approach*, which focuses on selling and negotiating technique; and *Thinking about Selling*, which focuses on improving sales performance. In addition, I am the creator of Selection Portfolio, a patented business methodology for selecting properties and evaluating various alternatives.

In 2012, I undertook a new adventure by acquiring a rental company, AC Lawrence Real Estate, and formulating a new umbrella entity, The Bellmarc Group. The Bellmarc Group has since been invited to join Coldwell Banker, the premier residential brokerage franchise firm in the United States. Following the retirement of my original business partner, Marc Broxmeyer, I have been honored to have two new partners who have shown tremendous energy and creativity, Larry Friedman and Anthony DeGrotta.

The Bellmarc Group has developed a strong presence in the New York City residential market. It now consists of 10 locations predominantly focusing on Manhattan, with approximately 700 real estate agents, under the name of Coldwell Banker Bellmarc or Coldwell Banker AC Lawrence. For me it has all been a big adventure, a chance to make a difference by helping others become successful in their careers. For every salesperson it has also been a great adventure, a chance to help buyers make wise decisions about one of the most important investments of their lives, and a chance to help sellers achieve the financial rewards associated with home ownership. We are all proud of what we do and we are always seeking to do it better.

The last three versions of this book generated considerable positive attention, and each became a top seller on the subject in the marketplace. Real estate brokers, attorneys, appraisers and laypeople found that it was an easy-to-read and authoritative work. I have attempted to keep to that same standard. Thus, I have sought to reconfirm any and all legal, tax or technical matters with authoritative sources to ensure that the information is presented accurately. However, I have also sought to keep this book useful to all. There are often distinctions, exceptions or clarifications that may not be covered because they relate to technicalities rather than general practice, and I encourage those who are engaged in real estate transactions to rely on competent legal or professional advice on any specific "adventure" they may take.

The last time I updated *The Ultimate Guide* was in December 2005. I had initially planned to update the book every three years or so. Yet in 2008, the world changed. The stock market crash that plunged the country into its worst economic decline since the Great Depression also created an upheaval in the New York City residential market. Changes in the world of real estate were literally happening every day. Thus, I decided to wait for the dust to settle before I wrote a new version of this book. Now, in 2013, the light at the end of the tunnel has appeared. While there are many revisions throughout the book, I would like to point out some of the more material changes that have affected the New York City residential environment and accordingly the content of this guide:

The volatility in prices: For the first time in 30 years, a concerted decline in prices has occurred in the New York City market. In the past, there have been transitory price adjustment periods, particularly in 1990, but none has had the profound impact associated with the recession of 2008. This created a dramatic shift in strategies for purchasing and selling property. In 2013, the market materially rebounded due to a perception that the worst was over, resulting in a resurgence in prices with very low inventories of properties for sale.

The impact of the Internet: While using the Internet for real estate searches was possible years ago, the Internet is no longer an ancillary element to the real estate business; it is a core component. Now customers regularly access various websites to learn about product alternatives and gain a depth of information that was previously unavailable.

Disclosure requirements: New York State has sought to clarify the role that real estate brokers play in serving buyers and sellers. Real estate agents are now required to issue disclosure forms to each party divulging who the broker is working for.

Bank financing: In the past, financing the purchase of a home was a simple matter, where the rules were clear to real estate brokers. Those simple guidelines are no longer used by banks. Now financial institutions are applying a broader approach to reviewing applicants.

CHAPTER ONE

The Purchasing Journey

An Overview of the Process of
Buying a Cooperative or Condominium

Step 1: Submitting the Bid

Submitting a bid is not merely proposing a dollar figure to a seller. It also requires you to prove to the seller that you are qualified to purchase the property given your financial condition. So a seller, particularly one who is being represented by a real estate broker acting on the seller's behalf (also called the *exclusive listing agent*), will require that certain financial information accompany the bid to provide assurance to the seller that you are capable of meeting the co-op board's entry requirements.

In established condominiums, a review requirement is also common, since condominium bylaws normally provide the condo board with a *right of first refusal* on any offer made to purchase an apartment in the building. Condominiums have construed this right very broadly, and have demanded that prospective buyers fill out applications and provide documentation similar to that required in a co-op purchase. If the board decides in favor of your purchase, it will generate a *right-of-first-refusal waiver letter*, which is an essential document required by title companies as a precondition to insuring title to the condominium apartment. This letter is also normally required by banks as a condition to financing an apartment. If the condominium board does not approve, it will refuse to issue the waiver and you will have a difficult time completing the transaction.

You should be prepared to provide to the seller's agent the following information at the time of submission of a bid:

Reported income: You cannot obtain approval for the purchase (or the loan for the amount you may need) unless the income you are able to prove is adequate to support a loan as well as the monthly *maintenance* or *common charges* associated with the apartment. You normally must also disclose your employer or your source of income. If your source of income is commission-based, most cooperative boards will insist on seeing proof of at least two years of steady commission income to pass favorably on an application. Generally boards will look for no more than 30% of your income to be applied to the cost of carrying the apartment.

Cash investment: Almost all cooperative buildings have minimum cash investment requirements. This requirement is generally 25%, and in prestige buildings it is often 50%. If you are purchasing a condominium, there is no cash requirement. However, banks usually require at least a 10% cash investment, and you must still show the seller that you can support the resulting loan you intend to obtain to close on the transaction.

Net wealth: Many boards will insist that an owner possess a minimum *net worth*. While there are no specific standards, a board will look for signs that your wealth is adequate to support the lifestyle you intend to live.

Liquid assets, consisting of cash and marketable securities: Many co-ops require that you have adequate liquidity after the purchase of your new home. A good guideline is that you must have two years of your maintenance and projected loan cost in cash and cash equivalents (tradable securities). In prestige buildings this figure can be substantially higher, and could even exceed the cost of the apartment.

Liabilities: Banks will evaluate your ability to support a mortgage by ensuring that no more than 45% of your total income is being used for debt payments, including the payment of the loan you're proposing to obtain, and your monthly carrying charge. The carrying charge consists of the maintenance payment for a cooperative, or the real estate taxes and common charges for a condominium. A great many boards are quite reticent about approving applicants who are heavily indebted.

In addition, it has become common practice to submit a *preapproval letter* from a bank with an offer to purchase. This is different from a *pre-qualification letter*, which merely advises a prospective buyer at the beginning of his search that he is qualified to obtain a loan from the bank based on certain preliminary financial information provided to that institution. There is no specific property identified in a prequalification letter, while there is in a preapproval letter. A preapproval letter effectively provides the seller with some degree of assurance that the bank will approve the purchaser for the requested loan, subject to verification of documents, adequate *appraisal* of the property and the satisfactory condition of the building.

Other important features that must be disclosed to the seller include whether or not a guarantee for the loan is being provided by a third party, such as a parent or trustee; whether a portion of the cash investment is being provided as a gift; whether the residence will be the buyer's primary home or used for another purpose; and whether the buyer intends to have a pet. Many cooperatives have restrictions on these conditions, and the seller will want to make sure that no issues exist that he knows will be objectionable to the board of the building.

This information, along with the proposed bid, should be provided in written form as an *official offer.* The official offer specifies the amount offered, the amount you intend to finance and the amount of cash investment you propose to make.

The seller's broker is responsible for reviewing the information on the official offer to ensure that you are qualified to purchase the property. If you are not, the seller's broker should contact your broker to advise him that there is an objection. It is your responsibility to resolve the objection in order for negotiations to proceed.

If the official offer meets the requirements for board approval and financing, the seller's broker will submit the offer to the seller for guidance about how to respond. The seller's broker will then normally call your broker to engage in a conversation in order to resolve any differences and develop a framework for a final agreement. If there is a meeting of the minds, the seller's broker and your broker will create a *term sheet* or *deal sheet* expressing the finalized deal. This will usually contain the following:

- The price to be paid, the amount of cash investment to be made and the amount of financing to be obtained.
- Any personal property, such as furnishings, drapes or lighting, that will or will not be included in the sale.
- The party responsible for paying the transfer tax levied by the building against sales, if any.
- The proposed closing date, which is normally 90 days following the date of contract.
- Any other material terms to the deal, such as the right to have a pet, terms of occupancy, etc.

Once a final term sheet has been prepared that is agreeable to both the buyer and seller, a copy will be sent to the attorney representing each party. This is often sent by email.

As far as the seller is concerned, the sale price, in the vast majority of cases, is all cash. That means the seller will receive a check for the full amount on the day of the closing. About 75% of the time, the buyer will need a loan (*mortgage*) from a bank in order to have enough money to complete the transaction. If you need a loan, your offer is conditioned upon approval by a lending institution, and your proposed purchase is considered an offer *subject to financing*.

If you obtain a mortgage preapproval from a bank, always make sure it is in writing on bank stationery, and that it is not subject to any conditions you can't realistically meet. In some instances buyers may believe that if they make an offer with a preapproval letter, they don't have to condition their offer on obtaining financing. However, the current lending environment has considerable uncertainty, and there are often obstacles you might not be aware of that can impair your chances of obtaining a loan. This would include aspects of the building and its operation, your credit score and changes in bank policies. Therefore, you should be sure that you are on solid ground before proposing an offer without a *financing contingency*. This means that you should have the resources necessary to buy the apartment without a loan if you need to. While an all-cash, not-subject-to-financing offer does add value by reducing uncertainty to the seller, it adds considerable risk for you that something could go wrong. You could lose your *deposit* if financing doesn't go through and your cash resources are insufficient to close the deal. In fact, many attorneys are now including a funding contingency (not to be confused with the financing contingency) provision in contracts that stipulates that if the bank fails to provide the money at closing, the buyer can cancel the deal and have his or her *down payment* returned. There have been a number of occasions where even a *commitment letter* from a bank has not guaranteed that the bank will actually fund the loan.

Even if an offer is unconditional, the co-op contract still makes the transaction contingent on the co-op board's approval of the apartment purchase. In a condominium, a right-of-first-refusal procedure is normally required.

A verbal or official offer creates no legal obligation for either the buyer or the seller. Neither does a term sheet. Indeed, brokers normally send official offers and term sheets with a disclaimer stating that the official offer or term sheet does not represent an obligation of the real estate broker or the party he or she represents. Therefore, even if an official offer or term sheet has been submitted, you are free to change your mind until you sign a contract. It is important that the buyer, seller or broker not sign any of these documents, because doing so might create an unintended contract.

Some buyers are hesitant to make an offer that is significantly lower than the seller's asking price. Nothing is lost by submitting a low offer, and there may be much to be gained. A good real estate broker will tell you that in most instances, as long as there is reasonable justification for an offer, it will be seriously considered. However, if the offer is too low and cannot be justified by current market conditions, the seller may not think of you as a serious buyer and may decline to make a counteroffer. Accordingly, it is common practice for the buyer's broker to provide an *expression of interest* to the listing broker. This is merely a conversation between the two brokers to define possible parameters for an offer and explore levels of flexibility.

Step 2: The Contract Procedure

Once the basic terms of the deal have been agreed to and the term sheet prepared, the buyer and seller should immediately notify their attorneys. It is preferable that the attorneys have significant experience with real estate transactions in New York City. Recommendations from real estate brokers are helpful, but you should get more than one recommendation.

The contract is usually prepared by the seller's attorney and sent to the buyer's attorney, who reviews it along with the building's *prospectus* (also referred to as the *offering plan* or *black book*) and the last financial report for the cooperative corporation or condominium association. In addition, the attorney may wish to examine other pertinent documents, such as the minutes of the board of directors' meetings. The purchaser's attorney should ensure that all material issues are identified and properly addressed with the buyer. If the contract is acceptable, the buyer should then sign it and submit a check for 10% of the contract price as a deposit. Normally multiple copies of the contract are signed, so that both the buyer and the seller have original documents as do their respective counsels. Once the contracts are signed by the buyer, they are sent to the seller's attorney along with the deposit check.

The seller's attorney places the deposit funds into an *escrow* account (a special bank account held in trust for the parties to the transaction), and arranges for the seller's signature. The seller's attorney will then send one or more original sets of fully executed contracts to the buyer's attorney. A legally binding contract is now in full force, since it has been signed by each of the parties and delivered to both of them.

Step 3: Getting a Mortgage

A mortgage is a loan that uses real estate as security. If you don't pay the loan according to the terms of your agreement, the bank can take your real estate as an alternate form of repaying the debt (*foreclosure*). It is essential that you not borrow more than you can afford to repay.

In the case of a cooperative apartment, you are not buying real estate. You are buying stock in a corporation that owns the building, and receiving a *proprietary lease* entitling you to reside in a specific apartment. Since you own shares in a co-op, not real estate, your loan is not technically considered a mortgage. Rather, it is a *financing loan*. Notwithstanding this technicality, the general public, and even brokers, use the term "mortgage" to include a loan for a co-op apartment. Various types of mortgages or financing loans are available. They fall into two predominant categories: fixed-rate and adjustable-rate.

A *fixed-rate mortgage* has an unchanging payment and interest rate for the life of the loan, which is normally 15 or 30 years.

An *adjustable-rate mortgage*, also referred to as an ARM, permits the borrower to choose an initial fixed term (which can be one, three, five, seven or 10 years), after which the loan converts to a variable payment (adjusting annually, semiannually, monthly or semimonthly). Adjustable-rate mortgages normally offer lower initial interest rates than fixed loans. The loan payment amount varies based on market forces, but the interest spread between the payment on a fixed-rate mortgage and the payment on an adjustable-rate mortgage can be as little as 0.5% and as great as 4.0%. In addition, if the borrower selects a shorter initial fixed term (for example, one year instead of three years), the initial rate is often generally lower.

The interest rate variation on an adjustable loan is dependent on an index used as a benchmark. The most popular index is the *LIBOR*, which stands for the *London Interbank Offered Rate*, representing the interest rate offered by a specific group of London banks for U.S. deposits. The variation of the interest rate to this index is normally a premium of 2.25%. Adjustable-rate mortgages normally also have an interest rate ceiling, referred to as an *interest rate cap*. On one- and three-year initial-term loans, this cap is 2% for the first year after the fixed term (the second or fourth year), then 2% for any subsequent year, and a maximum of 6% over the life of the loan. For the five-, seven-, and 10-year initial fixed terms, the caps are usually 5% for the first year after the fixed term, 2% for any subsequent year, and a maximum of 5% over the life of the loan.

In deciding which loan type is preferable, a borrower should evaluate the difference in interest rates between the two loans and the length of time the buyer intends to own the property. Since the adjustable loan interest rate is generally 1.5% to 4% lower than the fixed loan, it becomes a more appealing choice in light of the initial lower cost and the cap on increases. In addition, at the time this loan converts from its initial fixed rate to the adjustable rate, the computation of the new payment is based on the reduced principal balance after the loan has been partially paid. Therefore, even if interest rates go up, the monthly payment may still be the same or possibly even lower. If the interest discount is less than 1.5%, then the fixed loan may be a better alternative, since this loan can be refinanced in the future without a prepayment penalty if interest rates drop, and if interest rates go up, the monthly payment is not affected.

Consumers often have questions about the APR, or *annual percentage rate*. This figure is intended to provide a means of comparing loan products from one financial institution with those of another, by combining the full cost of all elements associated with obtaining the loan into a single formula. Unfortunately, the APR formula is so complex that few people understand it. To make things even more confusing, some lenders calculate APR differently from others. The net effect is that the APR is a good comparative guideline but shouldn't be relied on religiously. It is recommended that you look at (1) the initial interest rate, (2) the upfront *points* and (3) the closing costs as the three critical elements of a loan. Points are an initial fee paid to the bank, stated as a percentage of the loan amount. For example, one point is equivalent to 1%. Points represent additional profit to the bank. Upfront closing costs include an application fee, an appraisal fee (to verify the value of the property), an underwriting fee (for processing the loan application), and the bank's legal fees (for preparing and processing the final loan documents).

Step 4: The Board Approval Process

A lot has been said in the press of what many New York City home buyers endure when purchasing an apartment in a co-op building — that is, the co-op board review process. In recent years, boards have been rigorous about reviewing the financial information of an applicant to make sure that he or she will qualify. If he does not, the board will reject the application without even arranging for an interview. If an interview is arranged, the buyer should make sure he takes a copy of his financial information with him and familiarizes himself with the contents prior to the meeting.

At your board meeting you should be prepared for questions relating to your financial condition. If your financial position is secure, the board will ask you questions about your intentions: Do you intend to make this your primary residence? Do you have a pet? The board is looking to make sure that you are buying a home first and making an investment second.

In performing a review of a buyer for a waiver of a condominium's right of first refusal, a condo board will primarily focus on your financial criteria. However, if you have a reputation — for example, you own another apartment in the building and you're litigious, or you've rented to tenants who have been controversial — the board may seek to impede your purchase. Other factors, such as pets and your reasons for purchasing, may also be important. Boards generally reject buyers for these reasons:

- You do not meet the minimum cash equity requirement for the building; your financial information does not show adequate income to support your purchase; you lack adequate liquidity after the purchase to meet the board's standards; or your overall financial condition and net worth look weak and uncertain.
- You have a pet and there is a no-pet rule.
- You have been dishonest in your application materials.
- You present yourself at the interview in an abusive, suspicious or offensive manner rather than as open and friendly.
- The price of the apartment is deemed excessively low, which may be perceived by the board as setting a bad precedent for the value of other apartments.

The following are documents normally required for a board package:
- An application with basic information about yourself and your family, including your financial condition.
- One or two years' tax returns.
- Two to four personal reference letters.
- Two to four professional reference letters from people you work with.
- One letter from a former landlord (if applicable) affirming that you were a good tenant.
- One letter from a bank verifying your balances and how long you have had an account with the bank.
- One letter from your employer verifying your length of employment and salary, including bonuses (if applicable).
- Your contract of sale.
- Your mortgage commitment letter.
- Documentation supporting your represented financial condition.

The buyer's real estate broker will customarily assist in preparing the board package. The broker should ensure that all the necessary material is gathered and complete, and should submit the completed documentation to the seller's broker to review. Thereafter, the seller's broker should send the package to the building's managing agent. Usually the board will not schedule an interview until after the board package, including all supporting documentation, has been deemed complete. Although buyers of condominiums cannot be "rejected," a board's failure to issue a waiver of its right of first refusal can be as powerful an impediment as a rejection. It is therefore important for a buyer to satisfy whatever application requirements are requested without reservation.

Step 5: Closing the Transaction

After you have been approved for a mortgage and by the board of the co-op or condominium, the closing will take place. The following people will normally be present: the buyer and his attorney, the seller and his attorney, a representative for the bank providing the buyer with a loan, a bank representative for the loan being paid off by the seller, the managing agent representing the building and the real estate brokers. If the purchase is a condominium, there will usually also be a representative from a title insurance company, who will ensure clear title to the property being transferred by the seller.

At the time of closing, the managing agent will issue to the bank a recognition letter permitting the bank to place a lien on the shares and proprietary lease, and recognizing the bank's right as a secured party. The buyer will sign the documents required by the bank to issue the loan. The bank will then give the loan amount to the buyer's attorney on his or her behalf, and the attorney will transfer it to the seller's attorney. In addition, the buyer will be requested to provide a bank or certified check, made payable to the seller, for the balance due (the purchase price minus the loan amount and the 10% initial deposit).

For example, say you are purchasing a home for $1 million. At the contract signing, you will give $100,000 (10% of the purchase price) to be placed in the seller's attorney's escrow account. The bank approves a loan of $750,000. At the closing, this amount will be given by the bank to the seller's attorney on the seller's behalf. The remaining amount of the purchase price, $150,000, must be provided to the seller at the closing. You will also be asked to make a payment for a portion of the building maintenance or common charges allocated for the remainder of the month. In the case of a cooperative, the stock and lease associated with the apartment will be given to the bank to hold as *collateral*. Your attorney should give you a closing statement in which he delineates the receipt of all money and the specific disbursement of funds. You should review this carefully: attorneys are not accountants and errors are made from time to time. As a last act, you will be handed the keys to your apartment. Congratulations!

Estimated Cooperative Closing Costs

The Buyer

Mortgage-Related Fees (If Financing)

Appraisal fee . . . . $ 450 *and up*

Credit report fee . . . . $ 75
approximate

Mortgage points . . . . $ 1,000
1% to 2% of loan, if any, (based on $100K loan)

Bank underwriting fee . . . . $ 350 *and up*

Bank legal fees . . . . $ 750 *and up*

UCC filing fee . . . . $ 100

Miscellaneous Expenses

Co-op board application . . . . $ 500

Buyer's attorney . . . . $ 2,500
approximate

Managing agent credit report . . . . $ 150

Move-in deposit . . . . $ 1,000
refundable in most cases

Move-in fee . . . . $ 300

UCC lien search . . . . $ 250

Lead paint disclosure . . . . $ 50

Prepaid expenses . . . .   ([1])
[1]*maintenance charge through end of month*

"Mansion tax" . . . .   ([2])
[2]*1% of sale price; applies to sales of $1 million or more*

Estimated Cooperative Closing Costs

The Seller

New York City transfer tax filing fee .... $ 50
plus...

Sales under $500K .... 1% *of sale price*

Sales over $500K .... 1.425% *of sale price*

New York State transfer tax .... 0.4% *of sale price*

Seller's attorney .... $ 2,500
approximate

Co-op flip tax .... $ (¹) *if any*
¹calculated as a percent of sale price, profit or cost per share; varies by building

Stock transfer tax .... $ 0.05 *per share*
computed by number of shares

UCC-3 .... $ 100

Mortgage pick-up/payoff fee .... $ 100 *to $500*

Managing agent fee .... $ 650
processing fees

Move-out deposit .... $ 1,000
refundable in most cases

Move-out fee .... $ 500

Estimated Condominium Closing Costs

The Buyer

Mortgage-Related Fees (If Financing)

Appraisal fee . . . . $ 400 *and up*

Credit report fee . . . . $ 75
approximate

Mortgage tax

   Sales under $500K . . . .   **1.8%** *of loan amount*

   Sales over $500K. . . . . **1.925%** *of loan amount*

Mortgage points . . . . $ ([1]) *if any*
[1] 1% to 2% of loan

Bank underwriting fee. . . . . $ 400 *and up*

Bank legal fees . . . . $ 750 *and up*

Application fee . . . . $ 500 *per application*

Miscellaneous Expenses

Condo board application. . . . . $ 500

Buyer's attorney. . . . . $ 2,500
approximate

Condo credit report. . . . . $ 75
approximate

Move-in deposit. . . . . $ 1,000
refundable in most cases

Move-in fee . . . . $ 250

Title search and insurance . . . . $ ([2])
[2] $0.5% to 0.8% of sale price

Recording charge. . . . . $ 200 *to* $750

Title closer fee . . . . $ 150 *to* $250

Prepaid expenses . . . . $ ([3])
[3] common charges through end of month plus real estate charges for up to six months

"Mansion tax". . . . .   ([4])
[4] 1% of sale price; applies to sales of $1 million or more

Estimated Condominium Closing Costs

The Seller

New York City transfer tax filing fee ....$ 50

plus...

    Sales under $500K................................   1% *of sale price*

    Sales over $500K .... 1.425% *of sale price*

New York State transfer tax......................... 0.4% *of sale price*

Seller's attorney ....$ 2,500
    approximate

Mortgage pick-up/payoff fee.......................$ 300 *to* $500

Managing agent fee.................................$ 650
    processing fees

Move-out deposit ....$ 1,000
    refundable in most cases

Move-out fee ....$ 500

Title charges.......................................$ 150 *to* $250

CHAPTER 2

Forms of Homeownership and Occupancy

Cooperative Ownership

Definition

A cooperative is a corporation that owns a building. Each apartment in the building is allocated a number of shares of stock, the sum of which equals all the shares outstanding of the corporation. These shares of stock are the evidence of ownership. In addition to the shares, each apartment receives a proprietary lease, which affirms the owner's right to occupy the specific apartment. Tenant-shareholders pay a monthly charge called maintenance, which covers their allocable portion of the cost of operating the building, the building's real estate taxes and the debt service on the building's mortgage (generally referred to as the underlying mortgage). Co-op owners are entitled to tax deductions for their portion of the building's real estate tax and their portion of the building's interest payment on its mortgage. They are also entitled to deduct the interest payment on the loan for their own apartment, with certain limitations.

General Overview

Cooperative corporations began as social clubs, and as a means of restricting who could move into a building. This form of ownership grew in popularity in the 1960s, 70s and 80s, not because of any exclusionary impulse but as a result of the restrictive rent laws in the city at that time. Though operating costs rose dramatically during that period because of inflation and exploding fuel costs, government limits on rent increases made it impossible for landlords to cover the increasing cost of operating their buildings. *Conversion* to cooperative ownership became a way to escape this burden, and was desirable for the following reasons:

- The New York State law regulating the conversion of apartment buildings to cooperative ownership (the *Martin Act*, Section 352, New York General Business Law, including added regulations) was relatively clear and had worked effectively in New York over many years.
- When co-op conversions were at their peak, banks were resistant to issuing new mortgages on rental buildings and charged extremely high interest rates when they did. But existing mortgages on many buildings had no restrictions on conversion to cooperative ownership, so existing low-interest-rate loans could be maintained. This proved enticing to landlords, because it permitted them to cash out of their economic predicament and at the same time offer a marketable product at a low monthly cost to the buyer.
- Co-ops were qualified to pass on to the individual tenant-shareholders the same federal and state tax deductions available for other forms of homeownership (with some limitations).

A bandwagon effect thus took place. Successful co-op conversions inspired emulation, which created a trend.

Advantages of Cooperative Ownership

The following are some of the advantages of cooperative ownership.

Tax deductibility: The owner is entitled to a tax deduction for a portion of the corporation's real estate taxes and mortgage interest under federal and state law.

Board approval: A co-op will normally require any prospective owner to go through an approval process. This ensures that the owner meets certain standards that the board of directors, as the representative of the apartment owners in the building, feels are appropriate. It allows the board to determine whether potential new members of the co-op are financially capable of supporting their home and carrying their share of the building's expenses. It also allows the board to screen out those who would not make desirable neighbors (subject to the requirement that co-ops follow all federal, state and local fair-housing and antidiscrimination laws). As a result of the board approval process, there have been very few foreclosures in co-ops, and the operations of these buildings have maintained extraordinary stability even during difficult times.

Popularity: Approximately 70% of all apartments owned in New York City are co-ops. Therefore, this form of apartment ownership offers a buyer the greatest selection of buildings to choose from.

Disadvantages of Cooperative Ownership

The following are some of the disadvantages of cooperative ownership.

Limitations of tax deductibility under certain circumstances: A cooperative corporation must meet certain legal criteria to qualify for state and federal tax advantages. If a building fails to meet these criteria, apartment owners will not be permitted to take the tax deductions otherwise allowed. This restriction doesn't exist for other forms of homeownership.

Board approval process: The approval process requires disclosure of significant personal and financial information, which some prospective buyers may prefer not to reveal. The process also makes the outcome of the purchase uncertain, since its successful conclusion is contingent on obtaining board approval.

Limited right to rent: Though most cooperative corporations do allow owners to sublet under limited circumstances and for a limited duration, it is often a cumbersome procedure that requires prospective tenants to go through an approval process prior to taking occupancy. Therefore, renting a co-op apartment is usually more difficult than renting a condo or single-family home. In addition, co-ops often charge a sublet fee, which varies in amount but can be material.

Equity requirement: While condominiums allow buyers to finance their purchases without limitation, co-op boards rarely permit this. Financing is commonly limited to 75% of the purchase price, and many cooperative buildings are even more restrictive. Indeed, some buildings require *all-equity cash purchases* (no mortgage).

Condominium Ownership

Definition

A condominium *is an apartment building in which each owner has a percentage ownership of the entire property, and each owner receives a unit deed evidencing his or her ownership to a particular apartment. Condo owners pay* common charges, *which are monthly payments covering their share of the costs of operating the building. Real estate taxes are paid directly to the city by each owner, and there is no underlying building mortgage. By legal definition, a condominium is considered real property, while a cooperative is considered personal property consisting of the stock and proprietary lease.*

General Overview

Condominiums as a form of homeownership originally appeared in the 1960s, when Congress passed legislation permitting the creation of housing associations as taxable entities. They first became popular in the Southern and Western United States, where large amounts of new housing were being created. Condominiums offer a means to maintain common property and provide common amenities within the framework of common ownership.

Today, practically all new construction projects and rental conversions are sold as condominiums. This is because seller-sponsors believe that condominium apartments offer buyers greater flexibility to rent or sell, so there is a wider audience of prospective buyers. In addition, foreign buyers generally are more interested in condominiums. In recent years established condominiums have sought to reduce the differences between cooperatives and condominiums, and have created mechanisms for the approval of both sales and rentals that have made both forms of ownership increasingly similar. In established condominiums it is now customary for the prospective buyer to fill out an application that requires substantial financial disclosure and personal information, similar to the approval process required by the boards of cooperatives.

If the board is unhappy with the buyer, it may similarly seek to impede the transaction by asking for more and more information and refusing to issue a waiver of its right of first refusal. Though there have been substantial protests by both sellers and buyers to the overreaching nature of this process, condominium boards have normally prevailed in insisting that their guidelines be respected.

Advantages of Condominium Ownership

The following are some of the advantages of condominium ownership.

Right to rent: In contrast to the restrictions on subletting commonly found in cooperatives, it is still common for condominium apartments to be rented, and when a board approval process is required it is normally not overly cumbersome.

Flexibility in purchasing: Newly constructed condominiums are easily purchased with no review requirement as long as financing can be obtained. Established condominiums, where the developer or sponsor is no longer a major participant in the building's affairs, have become more problematic. In these cases, the condo association has a right to refuse a prospective purchaser and buy the apartment on the same terms and conditions offered to the purchaser in a binding contract of sale. Due to this right-of-first-refusal provision in the condominium bylaws, a prospective purchaser may have to submit personal information, including financial data, to complete the review process. While this process can inhibit a transaction, brokers have generally found that completing the condo board's entry requirements is less challenging compared to completing those of a co-op board. Interviews in a condominium purchase are not customary, while they are typical in the purchase of a cooperative.

No equity requirement: In most cases, a purchaser is not restricted in the amount of debt he or she can assume to finance an apartment. By comparison, cooperatives normally require a minimum of 25% equity capital.

Controllable financing: Because there is no building mortgage (just the individual condominium owner's mortgage) and real estate taxes are paid directly to the city by the unit owner, common charges consist of operating costs only. Therefore, the monthly cost of ownership in a condominium can be lower than it would be in a comparable co-op apartment, since there is no debt service in the monthly payment to cover the building's underlying mortgage.

Disadvantages of Condominium Ownership

The following are some of the disadvantages of condominium ownership.

Transience: It is relatively easy to rent out a condominium apartment. As a result, there are likely to be more people moving in and out of the building. High turnover can diminish the sense of community among neighbors, and there may be more wear and tear on the building's common areas.

Control: Since the board approval process in a condominium is usually limited, it is much harder to restrict who moves in. When people with marginal finances fail to pay common charges, the cost of unpaid charges must be borne by the other unit owners. In addition, when an owner's behavior is disruptive, the condominium must seek to legally enjoin the behavior or else initiate a foreclosure procedure, which must be based on a violation of the unit deed or bylaws. In a cooperative, alternatives like eviction are available via the proprietary lease. Foreclosure in a condominium can be much more costly and time-consuming than in a cooperative.

Transaction costs: The closing costs for a condominium are significantly higher than for a cooperative. This is due in large part to the deed and mortgage recording costs and title insurance required for real property transactions, which are not applicable to co-ops (which are personal property transactions).

Lien risk: When purchasing a condo, the buyer may obtain a mortgage on real property. If the common charges are unpaid, this obligation becomes a *subordinate lien* to the recorded first mortgage and to any unpaid real estate taxes. This effectively means that the condo association is last in line with respect to repayment of its unpaid common charges. In the event of foreclosure, the condo association runs the risk that the proceeds received will not be enough to cover the first mortgage, the unpaid real estate taxes and the legal fees incurred in the foreclosure process. In such a case, the condo's claim for unpaid common charges can be effectively wiped out, and the association will never be reimbursed for payments made on behalf of the delinquent unit owner.

This is not the case with a co-op, where buyers obtain financing secured by shares of stock and a proprietary lease, not by real estate. Should a co-op owner fail to pay the maintenance, the claim of the cooperative corporation continues as set forth in the proprietary lease. Any action of foreclosure on the stock does not adversely affect the cooperative's rights under the proprietary lease.

To sum up, a cooperative corporation's right to make a claim for unpaid monthly charges takes precedence over the rights of a lending bank. In a condominium, it's the other way around: the condo association's right to monthly charges is subordinate to that of the bank. If these common charges are not received, the missing income will eventually have to be made up by *assessments* against the condo owners.

Tenancy in Common

Definition

A tenancy in common *is an agreement in which each apartment owner has proportionate ownership of the total building and exclusive use of a specific apartment. Each owner pays maintenance to cover operating costs, real estate taxes and any mortgage on the entire building. There is no stock or proprietary lease, and there is no unit deed. The legal rights of the owner are derived solely from the deed to the property and the tenancy-in-common agreement.*

Advantages of a Tenancy in Common

The following are some of the advantages of a tenancy in common.

Informality: Buildings owned under a tenancy-in-common agreement are usually small. This helps to create a sense of informality and flexibility in solving building problems. In contrast, cooperatives and condominiums have larger and more formalized organizational structures, which usually means that decisions take longer.

Formation cost: The legal fees required to form a tenancy in common are lower than those required to form a condominium or cooperative.

Sense of community: In a tenancy-in-common building, everyone contributes to the common good. All the affairs of the building are addressed and resolved by all the owners together.

Disadvantages of a Tenancy in Common

The following are some of the disadvantages of a tenancy in common.

Informality: Informality in managing the building can lead to misunderstandings and disputes that can seriously affect the building's operation and condition.

Lack of professional management: Many tenancy-in-common buildings are self-managed, which means that the owners, not a professional management company or building staff, are responsible for the maintenance of the building, including basic functional duties and regular upkeep.

Lack of market: Only a small number of buildings are structured as tenancies in common because acceptance of this as a form of homeownership has been limited. This lack of popularity can significantly reduce the resale value of the property unless the entire building is sold at one time.

Lack of financing: It is very difficult for a buyer of an apartment under a tenancy-in-common agreement to get financing from a bank. Financing must normally be offered by the seller, or the apartment must be purchased with all-equity cash.

Liability: As a result of the building's joint ownership, actions taken by one member create obligations for all the owners. This can lead to situations in which one owner makes commitments inconsistent with the wishes of others. Each owner can be legally responsible for the full amount of any obligations incurred.

Single-Family Property

Definition

A single-family property is a building for which the owner has the deed to the property and is solely responsible for all costs and maintenance of the entire property. In New York City, particularly in Manhattan, this is often characterized by the townhouse market.

Advantages of a Single-Family Property

The following are some of the advantages of a single-family property.

Controllable environment: The costs associated with running the property are solely the responsibility of the owner, and there can be no assessment or other charge levied by a vote of a board of directors or other group of managers.

Discretionary use: The use of the property is not subject to rules and conditions set by a board or other external authority, apart from local zoning ordinances.

Space: Single-family properties usually offer more interior space, as well as amenities not frequently found in cooperative or condominium apartments, such as backyards, basements, roofdecks and extra storage.

Privacy: Single-family homeowners don't have to share private information, such as the details of their financial affairs, with their neighbors. If they wish to make alterations to their property, they don't have to ask a board of directors for permission.

Disadvantages of a Single-Family Property

The following are some of the disadvantages of a single-family property.

Security: There is less control over who enters the premises of a single-family property than there is in cooperative and condominium buildings. Co-ops and condos usually have employees in regular attendance or other common-area security measures, which are not always feasible for a single-family property.

Maintenance: The duty of overseeing the property and ensuring that it is maintained in good working order rests fully on the owner.

Cost: Purchasing a single-family home, particularly in Manhattan, is cost-prohibitive for many people.

Real estate taxes: In condominiums and cooperatives, the real estate assessed value is determined at the building level, and there is no change in the assessment of real estate taxes when an apartment changes hands. However, in a single-family property, the sale price of the property could result in a reassessment of the taxable value, which in turn could increase the yearly tax liability. As an offset, New York City restricts the increase in a townhouse owner's tax obligation to no more than 20% in any five-year period. The tax rate is also lower than the rate applied to cooperative or condominium buildings.

Rental Property

Definition

Rental *property provides for occupancy rather than ownership. There is a lease prescribing the occupant's use and possession of the property under defined terms and for a limited duration.*

Advantages of a Rental Property

The following are some of the advantages of a rental property.

No risk of ownership: The increase or decrease in real estate values is not an issue for renters, since they have no real investment at risk.

Limited duration: Renters can limit the duration of time they wish to inhabit a property without worrying about selling it upon departure.

Broader service: More services are usually provided to a tenant in a rental property than to a unit owner. For example, in a rental, if appliances need repair or the walls need to be painted, the landlord is typically responsible, while in a cooperative or condominium these are the responsibility of the apartment owner.

Liquidity: The renter's financial assets remain available for other investments, which may be more profitable than owning a home.

Disadvantages of a Rental Property

The following are some of the disadvantages of a rental property.

No economic gain: Over the long term, real estate has proven to be an excellent investment, offering attractive economic returns and favorable tax treatment when the property is sold. These financial benefits are not available to renters.

No tax advantages: The tax deductibility of mortgage interest and real estate taxes frequently makes it cheaper to own than to rent.

Aesthetics: Renters are usually reluctant to make significant improvements in their apartments, since they know their investment won't bring them any financial return. Indeed, many landlords prohibit alterations to the property. Therefore, it is not easy to customize a rental property to fit the lifestyle of the tenant.

No permanence: A renter is subject to the terms of a lease, which include limits on the duration of his or her occupancy. The tenant may have to move at the end of the lease term.

CHAPTER 3

Evaluating the "Rent vs. Buy" Alternative

Understanding the costs of renting versus ownership is a beginning point in deciding which choice to make. However, choosing to rent or buy is not just an economic decision. Other important factors must be evaluated.

Considerations

Permanence

Some people are reluctant to make a long-term commitment to a specific apartment or geographic area.

According to Bellmarc records, the average length of time a home-owner stays in a Manhattan apartment is seven years. People living in large apartments, particularly if they have children in school, stay somewhat longer, while people in smaller apartments, particularly if they are young and single, tend to stay for a shorter term.

Consider a young person moving into the first home he or she has ever owned — probably a studio. Before long, salary increases allow a move to a larger apartment, possibly a one-bedroom. With marriage and dual incomes comes a nicer one-bedroom apartment or a two-bedroom. Within a few years, children arrive, and the young couple feels pressured to move to an even larger home. This whole process frequently happens within a period of 10 years!

Permanence is a state of mind with most buyers. Very few actually stay in their apartments for the long term. Rather, the home they buy is merely the right apartment for the moment, until a better opportunity or a change in lifestyle warrants a new alternative.

Fear

The responsibility of homeownership and the magnitude of the decision can be intimidating, especially to those with no prior experience in the matter or those who have had a negative experience.

Fear is a legitimate reason for not buying an apartment, especially considering the size of the investment and the potential risks. Almost everyone experiences some degree of anxiety when faced with the prospect of buying a home, but it is usually lack of knowledge that precipitates fear and uncertainty.

Acquiring even a bit of knowledge about the advantages and disadvantages of homeownership can make you feel a lot more confident about making a wise decision. One useful idea is to perform a full rent vs. buy analysis (see page 47). This will enable you to better understand the economic consequences of each alternative. Whatever your decision, by doing a rent vs. buy analysis, you will know that your options have been carefully and logically considered.

One mistake some buyers make is to seek a "needle in the haystack": an apartment that outshines all others. These buyers view enormous numbers of properties without making any offers. It is as if they are afraid to commit themselves because they believe that the "special one" is just around the corner. If you find yourself in this position, I propose that you take a second look at apartments that you rejected. Is there a lower price — even if that price is substantially lower — at which one of those apartments could meet your needs? If so, put in a low offer and think about reasons to justify your offer. Create an appropriate rationale as to why your bid is a reasonable figure to consider. Sometimes these bids end up in great deals.

A good exercise is to mentally create the apartment you desire and determine a price you would be willing to pay for it. Then look on the Internet. Is the price you imagined consistent with prices listed for comparable properties? Ask a broker if the apartment and price you are seeking are achievable. If the broker says no, ask him or her to give you supporting information. It is essential to be informed. Knowledge of the market will give you the confidence to put in bids in order to take advantage of opportunities. If you are serious about property-hunting, a real estate broker should be able to give you supporting information related to values, and explain to you the relative cost of different components of value.

Economic Trends

Some buyers may view the risks and returns of buying a home as uncertain in light of economic trends.

Real estate remains the single biggest and best investment most families have ever made. The key is to view it as a long-term investment that is subject to cycles. While there is a possibility that the cycle may go up or down, a review of long-term trends in real estate prices shows that each peak has surpassed the previous one.

Consider this: According to the standard rules used by banks for mortgage lending, up to 45% of your income can be applied to the cost of carrying a home (along with other debt). Therefore, for each dollar your salary increases, your ability to carry a loan increases by about 45 cents. Importantly, this is the cost to carry the loan portion, not the principal amount. The principal is determined by dividing this extra money by the available interest rate. For example, if the rate is 5%, this additional 45 cents can support an additional loan amount of $9. Simply stated, for every dollar your income goes up, you can afford to borrow $9 more. More income equals a bigger mortgage, which in turn equals higher values.

The conclusion to be drawn is clear. Even if everything stayed the same and supply and demand were in balance, the long-term effect of an appreciating economy would naturally increase prices because of the leveraging effect of borrowing. While the economy has had quarters when the Consumer Price Index has declined, these have been relatively unique events.

Life Objectives

For some buyers, buying a home may be viewed as inconsistent with one's current life objectives.

Everyone has his or her own set of priorities. It is not surprising that some people don't look upon homeownership as one of their life objectives. But homeownership provides many benefits beyond the obvious. If you believe homeownership is inconsistent with your goals, it may be because you are not looking at all the possible opportunities owning a cooperative or condominium apartment can offer. The following are some key points that should be taken into consideration:

- A home is the epitome of security. It is the one place you can feel safe from outside pressures and influences.
- In terms of personal growth and development, homeownership is frequently considered "the next step."
- For most people, a home is the best financial investment they will ever make — one that will provide their greatest source of wealth accumulation.
- Many banks prefer to lend to homeowners rather than renters because the real estate they own represents a significant and tangible asset, which is valuable collateral. At present, accounting rules require that the value of your home be listed on your personal financial statement at its current fair market value rather than its initial cost. This means that your home is accumulating tangible wealth in the form of increased creditworthiness without your having to sell it.

Liquidity

To some people, liquidity is like an insurance policy against the effects of future uncertainty. Using one's available cash to buy a home may eliminate this protection.

There is no question that if you use your money to purchase a home, you have made a commitment that cannot be quickly altered. If the funds you are thinking about investing in real estate are essential to maintaining your lifestyle, you should think twice. On the other hand, purchasing a home is often the first step toward creating wealth. You build equity through your home's appreciation, the reduction over time in the amount of your mortgage, and your yearly tax savings.

You can also use your home to get cash by means of an *equity credit line*. This is a bank line of credit that uses your equity value, including the appreciation you have built up in your home, as security for the loan. Funds can be borrowed and paid back at will, and interest is charged only on the balance outstanding. The rate of interest on an equity credit line is normally very attractive, and the interest charge is tax-deductible as homeowner interest as long as the borrowed principal amount does not exceed $100,000. An equity credit line allows you to tap into the accumulated wealth in your home as funds are needed. Equity credit lines are available from most major banks or from mortgage brokers at no (or minimal) cost.

Using the Rent vs. Buy Analysis Chart

This section is designed to help you evaluate the economic advantages and disadvantages of ownership versus renting. There are two parts to this analysis: determining the cost of carrying a home, and comparing the returns on real estate with those of alternative investments. The following are directions for using the worksheets that start on page 53.

Part 1: The Cost of Carrying a Home

The question you will be answering is: on a monthly after-tax basis, is it cheaper to rent or to own an apartment?

In order to answer this question, you must:

- Select a prospective apartment to buy.
- Select a prospective apartment to rent.

- Determine the tax rate applicable to your highest earned dollar by combining the federal, state and city rates (pages 203 and 204). Make sure to adjust your New York State and City rates by your federal rate, since state and local taxes are deductible on your federal tax return. To do this, multiply your state rate by 1.0 minus your federal rate. For example, if your income is $200,000 and you are married, filing jointly, you are in the 35% federal tax bracket and the 11.75% state and local tax brackets. This would compute to an after-tax state and local rate of: 11.75% × (1.00 − 0.35) = 7.64%. Thus, you have a combined total rate of 42.64% (35% federal plus 7.64% state and local taxes after adjustment).

- Find the maintenance charge on the apartment you have selected as a prospective purchase and determine the tax-deductible portion. You should be able to obtain this figure easily by asking the broker or the seller. In the absence of specific information, brokers generally use 50% of the maintenance fee to approximate the deductible portion.

Procedure

Step 1. On the worksheet on page 50, enter the amount charged for renting the prospective apartment in Section I: Rent Alternative (A).

Step 2. In Section II: Tax Liability, enter the annual maintenance charge for the prospective purchased apartment on the first line (Maintenance). (The annual maintenance charge is the monthly amount multiplied by 12.) Then put the percent associated with the tax-deductible portion — consisting of the real estate tax and underlying mortgage interest as a percentage of the gross maintenance payment — next to the annual maintenance charge in the second column. Finally, multiply the annual maintenance charge (gross amount) by the tax-deductible percent to compute the yearly tax-deductible amount, and put that figure in the last column.

Step 3. Multiply the proposed purchase price of the apartment by

75% (0.75). This is the assumed amount to be financed. Then go to page 135 and consult the Debt Service Payment Table. Select the *interest rate factor* you think would be applicable to your loan, and identify the yearly payment per $1,000 of loan. This payment consists of the interest charge on the funds borrowed as well as the principal repayment based on a 30-year amortization schedule.

Multiply the yearly payment per $1,000 of loan by the mortgage amount you calculated above (75% of the purchase price). This figure is your yearly loan payment and should be entered on the second line (Debt Payment) in the first column.

To determine the tax-deductible interest amount, multiply the financed amount by the pure interest rate (the interest rate excluding any principal amortization). The product of this calculation is the figure to place in line two of the third column of the Debt Payment line, the Tax-Deductible Amount. For example, if you borrow $300,000 at 10%, your annual tax-deductible interest payment would be $30,000.

Step 4. Total the figures in the Gross Amount column (B). Then total the figures in the Tax-Deductible Amount column.

Step 5. Add the Federal Tax Rate (page 203) and the State and Local Tax Rates (page 204) adjusted for federal taxes (page 48) to determine the Total Tax Rate. Multiply the Total Tax-Deductible Amount by the Total Tax Rate to arrive at your Computed Tax Effect (C). The Computed Tax Effect is the cash value of the tax deduction you receive from ownership of the prospective property.

Step 6. In Section III, subtract (C), the Computed Tax Effect, from (B), the Total Gross Amount, to determine (D), the After-Tax Ownership Cost. Divide (D) by 12 to determine (E), the After-Tax Monthly Cost.

Step 7. Subtract (E), the After-Tax Monthly Cost of ownership, from (A), the Rent for the Apartment. The difference between the two figures is (F), Rent vs. Ownership: Monthly Cost. If (F) is a positive number (i.e., the rental number is higher than the ownership figure), then ownership will cost you less each month than renting.

Rent vs. Buy Analysis

Part 1: Analysis of Monthly Effect

Section I: Rent Alternative

Rent for the apartment $_____(A)

Section II: Tax Liability

Description of Payment (Annual)	Gross Amount	Percent Deductible	Tax-Deductible Amount
Maintenance	$_____	____%	$_____
Debt payment	$_____	Interest portion	$_____
Total	$_____ (B)		$_____

Federal tax rate   _____%

State & local tax rate   *plus* _____%

Total tax rate[1]   *equals* _____%

Computed tax effect $_____(C)

Section III: Rent vs. Buy Comparison

After-tax ownership cost *(B minus C)* $_____(D)

After-tax monthly cost *(D divided by 12)* $_____(E)

Rent vs. ownership: monthly cost *(A minus E)* $_____(F)

Therefore:

The purchase of an apartment is less/more expensive than a comparable rental by _____ per month.

[1]*Net of federal tax effect*

Part 2: Evaluating Alternative Investments

If you buy real estate, the return on your investment is a function of the appreciation of your property. If you do not buy real estate, your equity is available for some other investment opportunity. This section will show you how to evaluate the relative returns for each investment, so that you can decide which is the best alternative.

The question you will be answering is: which yields a better return, the appreciation on a home or another investment?

To help you answer this question, use the worksheet provided on page 53 and follow these instructions:

- Identify an alternative investment in which you would place your funds if you decided not to purchase a home. For comparative purposes, assume that the amount you would invest is the same amount you would use to make a down payment on a home — 25% of the purchase price.

- Estimate the Investment Yield, which is the annual rate of return you expect on this investment in the foreseeable future.

- Estimate the Rate of Inflation/Appreciation you expect for residential real estate in New York City. To do this, you can consider the prior year's rate of return, or you can ask real estate brokers, mortgage brokers, mortgage banks or others whose opinion you respect what they anticipate. You can also use the level of increase in the local Consumer Price Index (CPI) if you believe prices will not increase beyond the level of inflation.

Procedure

Step 1. In Section I: Investment, enter the amount you would invest in your alternative investment (25% of the purchase price of a home) on Line 1, Invested Funds.

Step 2. Enter the estimated Investment Yield on Line 2.

Step 3. Compute your Yearly Investment Return (Line 3) by multiplying your Invested Funds by your Investment Yield.

Step 4. Apply your Total Tax Rate, determined in Step 5 of Part 1, to the Yearly Investment Return (Line 3) to determine your Tax on Investment Income (Line 4). Subtract this amount from the Yearly Investment Return (Line 3) to determine your investment's Net After-Tax Return (A).

Step 5. In Section II: Homeownership, enter the Purchase Price of Home on Line 1.

Step 6. On Line 2, enter the Rate of Inflation/Appreciation you estimate to be applicable to your home.

Step 7. Multiply the Purchase Price of Home (Line 1) by the Rate of Inflation/Appreciation (Line 2) to determine the After-Tax Yearly Appreciation Benefit (B). This is after-tax because the profit from the sale of a home is free from tax on the first $250,000 for a single person (or $500,000 for a couple). The excess is taxed at the capital-gains rate of 15%, or at 20% if your income exceeds $400,000 (see page 159).

Step 8. Subtract (B) from (A) to determine the Relative Yearly Benefit of homeownership.

In evaluating investment returns, remember that homeownership has the advantage of substantial leverage, which is effectively interest-free because interest has already been considered in determining the relative monthly cost of owning versus renting.

Rent vs. Buy Analysis

Part 2: Analysis of Investment Return

Section I: Investment

(1) Invested funds $_____

(2) Investment yield   _____%

(3) Yearly investment return $_____

(4) Tax on investment income (rate _____%) $_____

Net after-tax return $_____(A)

Section II: Homeownership

(1) Purchase price of home $_____

(2) Rate of inflation/appreciation   _____%

After-tax yearly appreciation benefit[1] $_____(B)

Relative yearly benefit *(B minus A)* $_____

Therefore:

The economic return on an investment in the home offers a more/ less favorable return than an alternative investment by _____ (before transaction costs).

[1]*In the event of a sale, the proceeds will be tax-free because current tax laws exempt up to $250,000 in profit from taxation for individuals, or $500,000 per couple.*

Example of the Rent vs. Buy Analysis

John Evans is considering renting an apartment for $3,000 per month. He is evaluating it against the cost of buying a similar cooperative apartment for $500,000 that has a monthly maintenance charge of $1,650, which would be $19,800 per year. The broker has advised Mr. Evans that the tax-deductible portion of the maintenance is 50% and that financing is currently obtainable at 5% interest for 75% of the purchase price ($375,000).

In looking at page 137, Mr. Evans determines that for a loan with 5% interest, his monthly payment rate per $1,000 would be $5.37, or $64.44 per $1,000 per year. He can take the principal sum he would borrow, $375,000, and multiply it by 0.06444 to get the yearly payment required to carry the proposed mortgage, $24,165. To determine the interest portion of his yearly payment, he takes the amount of the loan, $375,000, and multiplies it by the pure interest rate, 5%, to get $18,750. The total cost to carry the apartment is $43,965, and the total tax-deductible amount is $28,650.

Mr. Evans, who is married, earns $150,000 per year. Using the tables on pages 203 and 204, he determines that his federal tax rate is 28% for the upper portion of his income and that his combined state and local tax rate is 11.75%. State and local taxes are deductible on his federal return, so his net tax rate for state and local taxes is actually 8.46%. This is computed by taking the combined state and local tax rate and multiplying it by 1.00 minus the federal rate. In this example, 11.75% × (1.00 − 0.28) = 8.46%. Mr. Evans's total tax rate is 36.46% (federal plus state and local tax rates). The total computed tax effect is 36.46% × $28,650 = $10,445, resulting in an after-tax ownership cost of $33,520. Accordingly, based on his after-tax ownership and monthly costs, he determines it is $207 a month cheaper to buy than to rent.

If Mr. Evans does not purchase a home but decides to rent, he will put his savings in an alternative investment with a yield of 2%. He believes that real estate values will increase by 1.5% per year over the next five years.

Mr. Evans has the $125,000 down payment to invest in the apartment. In light of this information, he performs the following analysis, and concludes he will see a better return if he buys a home than if he pursues an alternative investment.

Rent vs. Buy Analysis:
John Evans

Part 1: Analysis of Monthly Effect

Section I: Rent Alternative

Rent for the apartment $_____3,000[1]__(A)

Section II: Tax Liability

Description of Payment (Annual)	Gross Amount	Percent Deductible	Tax-Deductible Amount
Maintenance	$____19,800____	____50_%	$____9,900____
Debt payment	$____24,165____	Interest portion	$____18,750____
Total	$____43,965__(B)		$____28,650____

Federal tax rate   ____28_%
State & local tax rate   plus   ____11.75_%
Total tax rate[2]   equals   ____36.46_%

Computed tax effect $__10,445____(C)

Section III: Rent vs. Buy Comparison

After-tax ownership cost (B minus C) $__33,520____(D)
After-tax monthly cost (D divided by 12) $____2,793____(E)
Rent vs. ownership: monthly cost (A minus E)   favorable $____207____(F)

Therefore:

The purchase of an apartment is less/more expensive than a comparable rental by ____$207____ per month.

[1]All numbers are rounded to the nearest dollar
[2]Net of federal tax effect

Rent vs. Buy Analysis:
John Evans

Part 2: Analysis of Investment Return

Section I: Investment

(1) Invested funds	$ _125,000_
(2) Investment yield	_2_ %
(3) Yearly investment return	$ _2,500_
(4) Tax on investment income (rate _36.46_ %)	$ _912_
Net after-tax return	$ _1,588_ (A)

Section II: Homeownership

(1) Purchase price of home	$ _500,000_
(2) Rate of inflation/appreciation	_1.5_ %
After-tax yearly appreciation benefit[1]	$ _7,500_ (B)
Relative yearly benefit *(B minus A)*	$ _5,911_

Therefore:

The economic return on an investment in the home offers a (more/ less favorable return than an alternative investment by __$ 5,912__ (before transaction costs).

[1] *In the event of a sale, the proceeds will be tax-free because current tax laws exempt up to $250,000 in profit from taxation for individuals, or $500,000 per couple.*

CHAPTER 4

The Science of Buying an Apartment

Purchasing an apartment is a major decision, so wouldn't it make sense to evaluate your options using a tested method? The following technique is based on a business methodology I developed and patented entitled Selection Portfolio, which has been used successfully by Bellmarc salespeople for years.

Every purchasing decision has an underlying buying formula — a recipe made up of the critical components involved in the evaluation process. The first step in buying an apartment is to identify these criteria, and then to understand the relative importance of each in your decision-making process. I have found several recurring qualities that buyers seem to care most about. They fall into two categories. The first category, referred to as the *primary motivators*, relates to the specific location of the building, the quality of the building and its services, and the air, light and space in the apartment. The second category encompasses economic factors and relates to cash down payment and monthly cost. These are referred to as the *financial motivators*.

Understanding the Primary Motivators

It is important not merely to understand what you want in an apartment in a general sense, but also to create a means of evaluating various choices by specific criteria. These criteria should serve as benchmarks by which each choice is measured and prioritized against others.

Measuring the merits of your criteria allows you to create a *buying formula*, which is your delineated statement of what you would like to buy. Within your buying formula there are certain elements that are more fundamental than others, which are your primary motivators. These consist of the following:

Location: The aesthetics, quality and reputation of the place you want to live.

Building: The building's reputation, quality and services.

Air: A sense of the openness of the layout and its functionality for your purposes.

Light: The apartment's height from the street and the quality of the view.

Space: The usable footage, with an emphasis on the size of the living room (which includes the dining room) and master bedroom.

In order to guide you in this process, I have created a system to rate these various elements, which you should evaluate to find your comfort zone. For each primary motivator, the ranking you check represents your minimum acceptable value for that criterion.

Evaluating the Primary Motivators

Location

What is your minimum location requirement?

___ **10.** Overlooking Central Park, near world-renowned buildings and landmarks

___ **9.** Internationally prestigious, residential, near Central Park or overlooking a park

___ **8.** Exceptionally beautiful and charming residential street, near a park or river

___ **7.** Quiet and charming residential street

___ **6.** Commercial or residential street without notable features, with good demand

___ **5.** Commercial or residential street with growing potential and active buyer interest

___ **4.** Emerging area with few local services, restaurants, etc.

___ **3.** Minimal aesthetics, less convenient to transportation and shopping

___ **2.** Street with low market demand

___ **1.** No preference

Building

What is your minimum building requirement?

___ **10.** Internationally recognized, architecturally significant, high-end services, top condition

___ **9.** Excellent local reputation, architecturally significant, high-end services, top condition

___ **8.** Very good local reputation, great amenities, at least two lobby attendants

___ **7.** Doorman, good-quality amenities

___ **6.** Doorman, average amenities

___ **5.** Either an intercom, top condition or a doorman, needing renovation

___ **4.** Low- or mid-rise, intercom, average condition

___ **3.** Low- or mid-rise, intercom, condition issues

___ **2.** Low- or mid-rise, intercom, substantial renovations needed

___ **1.** No preference

Air

Are there any layout elements that are critical to you?

___ Formal dining room

___ Eat-in kitchen

___ Alcove studio

___ Maid's room

___ Spacious entry

___ Separation between master and other bedrooms

___ Other _____

Light

Is there a minimum floor that you require?

___ No preference

___ Third floor and above

___ On or above the ____ floor

View

What is the minimum direct view you require out of the living room?

___ **10.** Sweeping views of Central Park and grand cityscape views

___ **9.** Grand cityscape views with river and/or park

___ **8.** Grand cityscape views without a river or park

___ **7.** Basic skyline views, basic river views or beautiful courtyard views

___ **6.** Street views into buildings but bright

___ **5.** Street views into buildings, moderate light (middle floor)

___ **4.** Street views into buildings, limited light or basic courtyard views

___ **3.** No views but bright

___ **2.** No views, moderate light

___ **1.** No preference

Space

What is the minimum amount of space you desire for the following rooms?

Living room _____ × _____

Master bedroom _____ × _____

Secondary Amenities

Are there secondary elements that are important to you?

___ Garage in building

___ Fireplace

___ Health club

___ Pool

___ Laundry room

___ Terrace/outdoor space

___ Pets

___ Washer/dryer

___ Prewar building

___ Specific neighborhood(s) _____

___ Other _____

Identifying the Financial Motivators

In addition to aesthetic considerations, there are economic criteria that every buyer uses in making a decision, which are the financial motivators. Contrary to what many people believe, the listing price is not the most important element in evaluating the economics of buying an apartment. Rather, it is overall cost. Overall cost consists of both the cash down payment and the cost per month of carrying the home. The following explanation outlines how to analyze your financial motivators.

(A) Cash Down Payment

The amount of cash a buyer uses to purchase an apartment varies depending on his or her resources, cooperative board rules and bank lending requirements. However, none of these factors initially matters when you are deciding between apartments. Rather, the important element is relative cost. To determine this, it is essential to create an "apples-to-apples" comparison, so that all apartments are hypothetically considered on equal terms. Therefore, for comparative purposes, I propose that you use a down-payment percentage of 25% for all apartments.

Some people have problems understanding the need to create this hypothetical down-payment percentage. Consider an example of two apartments. In one, the price is $500,000 and the maintenance is $5,000 per month. In the other, the price is $1,000,000 and the maintenance is $500 per month. Which is the better deal? Obviously, you need to create a common ground for comparison to draw a conclusion.

Assuming 25% down, it is clear that the down payment on the lower-priced apartment is half as much as that of the higher-priced apartment: $125,000 versus $250,000. However, in terms of the monthly cost (debt payment plus maintenance), the lower-priced apartment costs $7,013.75 per month, while the higher-priced apartment costs $4,527.50 (assuming 5% interest for the debt on each apartment, page 136). The difference in cost is $2,486.25 per month, or $29,835 per year. If you divide that amount by the difference in cash down payment ($125,000), the net result is a cost of funds of approximately 23%. This is excessive relative to the amount banks are charging to borrow money. Therefore, the higher-priced apartment is the better deal because its cost is lower.

(B) Cost Per Month

The monthly cost of the apartment consists of the maintenance charge plus the monthly loan payment for a cooperative, or the common charges, real estate taxes and mortgage payment for a condominium.

As with the cash down payment, the monthly carrying cost must be defined in a way that allows an "apples-to-apples" comparison with other apartments. Therefore, the mortgage principal amount is presumed to be 75% of the purchase price of the apartment. Determine your monthly debt service payment by multiplying this principal by the interest rate percentage (page 136). if you are considering only a condominium, you can do your "apples to apples" evaluation using 10%, which is the minimum cash investment banks require. However, you should also consider that the interest rate will be 0.5% to 1.0% higher, and you will probably have an upfront fee (referred to as points) of approximately 4%.

As a guideline, no more than 45% of your gross income should be used for carrying the monthly cost of your home and all other debt you are currently obligated to pay. This is called your *debt-to-income ratio*. Co-op boards will also use a rule that no more than 30% of your income can be directly applied to the cost of carrying the home, excluding unrelated debt. Other debt would include car loans, consumer loans, credit cards, alimony or child support, other mortgages and similar types of obligations. Typically, even if you pay off your credit card obligation on a monthly basis, banks will still take the average loan balance over the last three months and assume that you will pay it over 60 months, and will add this as additional debt. Banks do not include insurance premiums as part of current debt.

Evaluating the Overall Cost of an Apartment
Using a Mortgage to Calculate Housing Cost

(A) Cash Down Payment
Non-borrowed cash you want to use to purchase
an apartment $_____

(B) Cost Per Month
Compute your ideal monthly payment below:

Reported monthly income $_____

Coverage rate   × 45%
   as defined by all banks

Maximum monthly debt payment   *equals* $_____

Total of other debts you currently pay   *minus* $_____

Cash available for covering the monthly cost
of your home   *equals* $_____ (A)

Mortgage $_____
   assume 75% of the purchase price

Monthly interest factor for ____ % = _____
   see debt service payment table on page 135

Monthly mortgage payment   *equals* $_____ (B)

Available for monthly housing cost[1]   *(B minus A)* $_____

---

[1]*Maintenance for a cooperative; common charges and real estate taxes for a condominium. The average maintenance charge for the type of property you are looking for can be ascertained by going to Bellmarc.com and clicking on Survey Our Inventory. The system will then display by type of property and price category the average monthly cost for that type of apartment. For a cooperative it shows the maintenance charge; for a condominium it shows the monthly common charges and the real estate tax allocation to the apartment.*

Example of Using a Mortgage to Calculate Housing Cost

Gerald Jones wants to determine how much he can afford to pay for an apartment. He currently makes $200,000 per year in income, which equals a monthly amount of approximately $16,667. He owns a car for which he pays $350 per month, and has a credit card with a current balance of $5,000, which a bank will automatically prorate over 60 months for a monthly rate of $83. Thus, his total monthly debt is $433. Importantly, in evaluating potential borrowers, banks generally require that no more than 45% of total income be allocated to the cost of paying outstanding debt, including mortgage debt. For purposes of this evaluation, Mr. Jones therefore has available income of 16,667 × 45% = $7,500 − $433 = $7,067.

Mr. Jones has $300,000 in cash and investments that he is prepared to use as a down payment, which (assuming a standard down payment of 25% is required) would enable him to purchase an apartment for up to $1,200,000. He will therefore need to borrow $900,000, which he can do at an interest rate of 5%. Using the interest rate factor corresponding to 5% (page 135), Mr. Jones determines that his monthly mortgage cost is $900,000 × 0.00537 = $4,833. Out of the $7,067 available to him for debt payments, he therefore has $2,234 left to cover his monthly maintenance or common charges.

Evaluating the Overall Cost of an Apartment
Using a Mortgage to Calculate Housing Cost

(A) Cash Down Payment
Non-borrowed cash you want to use to purchase
an apartment $ _$300,000_

(B) Cost Per Month
Compute your ideal monthly payment below:

Reported monthly income $ _16,667_

Coverage rate   × 45%
  as defined by all banks

Maximum monthly debt payment   *equals* $_7,500_

Total of other debts you currently pay   *minus* $_433_

Cash available for covering the monthly cost
of your home   *equals* $_7,067_ (A)

Mortgage $ _900,000_
  assume 75% of the purchase price

Monthly interest factor for _5_ % = _0.00537_
  see debt service payment table on page 135

Monthly mortgage payment   *equals* $_4,833_ (B)

Available for monthly housing cost[1]   *(B minus A)* $_2,234_

---

[1]*Maintenance for a cooperative; common charges and real estate taxes for
a condominium. The average maintenance charge for the type of property
you are looking for can be ascertained by going to Bellmarc.com and clicking
on* Survey Our Inventory. *The system will then display by type of property
and price category the average monthly cost for that type of apartment.
For a cooperative it shows the maintenance charge; for a condominium it
shows the monthly common charges and the real estate tax allocation to the
apartment.*

Given a specified monthly housing cost, it is also possible to determine the amount of mortgage that a buyer can sustain given his available income. Calculating your implied mortgage can be useful if you've already found an apartment with certain maintenance or common charges, and you want to know if you can support the ongoing cost. The procedure for this calculation is similar to determining monthly housing cost based on a given mortgage payment, but requires a slightly different formula, as illustrated in the following chart.

Buying Formula Worksheet:
Evaluating an Apartment Purchase
Using Housing Cost to Calculate an Implied Mortgage

(A) Cash Down Payment
Non-borrowed cash you want to use to purchase
an apartment $_____

(B) Cost Per Month
Compute your ideal monthly payment below:

Reported monthly income $_____

Coverage rate   × 45%
   as defined by all banks

Maximum monthly housing cost   *equals* $_____

Total of other debts you currently pay   *minus* $_____

Cash available for covering the monthly cost
of your home   *equals* $_____ (A)

Monthly maintenance payment   *minus* $_____ (B)

Available for monthly mortgage payment $_____ (B–A)

Current monthly interest factor for ___%   *divided by* _____ %
   page 135

Implied mortgage that can be sustained $_____

Implied maximum purchase price for a co-op $_____

Example of Using Housing Cost to Calculate an Implied Mortgage

Gerald Jones finds a cooperative apartment that he likes. The apartment's monthly maintenance charge is $3,000, which is higher than the housing cost of $2,234 he can afford under a $900,000 mortgage at 5%. Given the bank's 45% coverage rule, paying more for housing each month means he will have less money available to cover his mortgage and any other debt, so he will need to recalculate the implied mortgage he can carry.

By dividing his cash available for mortgage payment by his monthly interest rate factor, Mr. Jones can determine the total amount he would be able to borrow under the bank coverage rule. A monthly cost of $3,000, combined with his other debts, means he will have $4,067 available to pay his mortgage every month, which yields a total mortgage of $757,355. With his $300,000 in cash and investments, Mr. Jones can afford a maximum purchase price of $1,057,355.

Buying Formula Worksheet:
Evaluating an Apartment Purchase
Using Housing Cost to Calculate an Implied Mortgage

(A) Cash Down Payment
Non-borrowed cash you want to use to purchase
an apartment $ _$300,000_

(B) Cost Per Month
Compute your ideal monthly payment below:

Reported monthly income $ ___16,667___

Coverage rate   × 45%
  as defined by all banks

Maximum monthly housing cost   *equals* $ ___7,500___

Total of other debts you currently pay   *minus* $ ___433___

Cash available for covering the monthly cost
of your home   *equals* $ ___7,067___ (A)

Monthly maintenance payment   *minus* $ ___3,000___ (B)

Available for monthly mortgage payment $ ___4,067___ (B–A)

Current monthly interest factor for _5_% *divided by* ___0.00537___ %
  page 135

Implied mortgage that can be sustained $ ___757,355___

Implied maximum purchase price for a co-op $ _1,057,355___

The Step-by-Step Process to Create a Buying Formula

A buying formula consists of your criteria for comparing and evaluating apartments in order to select the best one. It may be useful to refer to the worksheets at the end of this chapter to help you understand each step of this process. An example of applying the strategy is provided in the next chapter.

Step 1: Developing Parameters for Each Primary Motivator
The first step in buying a home is to develop a clear statement of your preference level for each primary motivator. You can do this by reviewing the lists starting on page 59 and checking the appropriate line that represents your minimum desirable standard for each criterion.

Step 2: Identifying Secondary Factors
So far, you have analyzed the basic elements of an apartment and your feelings about them. There may, however, be other factors that still call out to you, like outdoor space or fireplaces. If so, these should be added to the buying formula. But these *secondary factors* should be considered only after the primary motivators have been rated. They are rarely integral to selecting an apartment and become important only after a desirable apartment has been found. You do not buy a terrace with an apartment; you buy an apartment with a terrace.

It is useful to identify the cost associated with each secondary factor. Try to find an apartment with that feature and a similar apartment without it. Knowing how much the secondary factor will cost may impact your evaluation process.

Step 3: Understanding Cash Down Payment
On the Buying Formula Worksheet (page 79) you are asked to write down the equity cash you plan to invest. Don't put down all the money you have invested or in the bank. There are transaction costs, move-in costs and incidental charges that must be taken into account before

you determine the amount available to invest in an apartment. In addition, many cooperative boards are hesitant to approve applicants who appear illiquid. You should maintain a cash balance (or cash equivalents) after your down payment of at least 10% of the purchase price.

Once you have identified the down payment sum you can afford, you can compute an approximate apartment price by dividing by 0.25 or 0.10 depending on how much down payment you intend to make (see the debt-to-equity ratio rule on page 119).

Step 4: Understanding Cash Per Month

On your Buyer Formula Worksheet, you are asked to fill in the amount you want to spend monthly. A bank would compute the maximum appropriate amount by multiplying your gross income by 45%, then dividing this amount by 12. This amount is called the *back-end ratio* and represents the maximum sum the bank will lend to you to carry the monthly cost of your home as well as any other monthly debt you have incurred. Most cooperatives will limit your monthly carrying cost to what is referred to as your *front-end ratio*, which cannot exceed 30% of your gross income. I recommend that you figure out all of your debt payments beforehand to give you a fuller impression of your borrowing power.

Next, determine the *implied mortgage* amount you can borrow (see Debt Income Ratios on page 114). Take the monthly amount computed above as your back-end ratio and subtract all your other debt payments. Then divide this remaining sum by the debt service payment factor relating to the current market interest rate (page 136). You can determine prevailing interest rates by looking on the Internet (a simple way is to Google current mortgage rates).

You can determine your approximate maintenance expense by visiting Bellmarc.com and accessing *Survey Our Inventory*. The system will compile all the listings for sale by neighborhood in price categories, and will display the average monthly cost for each. Given this information, the approximate price you wish to pay and the mortgage that you can carry, you can understand the economic limitations of your search.

Having evaluated your primary motivators and financial motivators, you can now complete the Buying Formula Worksheet. This worksheet is your initial statement about the kind of property you would like to buy and what you can afford, both in terms of purchase price and monthly maintenance. Now that you have this fundamental information, you can begin the process of considering various apartments.

One cautionary note: banks have been rigorous recently about reviewing applicants for loans. It is suggested that you use the standard 30-year fixed-rate mortgage for evaluation purposes, regardless of your preference for a cheaper adjustable-rate mortgage, to give yourself a cushion. It is also suggested that you determine your current credit score. This can be easily done via the Internet, where a number of sites, like freescore.com or nextadvisor.com, offer you the opportunity to learn your credit score at no charge. You are entitled by law to one free credit report a year. Generally, banks obtain three scores from three different reporting agencies; however, the one credit score you will receive from this free report is still a good point of reference to identify whether you will have any problems. If your credit score is above 740, you are likely to be A-rated. If your score is under 640, you are considered a high-risk borrower and you will have more difficulty getting a lender to approve you at a favorable rate. If you are unsure, go to a mortgage broker or mortgage banker and get a pre-qualification letter to help you gain greater clarity about your lending parameters.

Searching for Apartments

Apartment searches should be performed by using the Internet, reading newspapers and contacting real estate brokers. There is a wide selection of websites that have significant amounts of useful information (see page 263). I also suggest that you contact a number of different brokerage companies for their input and insight. Visit apartments based on their recommendations, and explore your choices by actually seeing what the market has to offer.

Selecting Properties

I usually advise prospective buyers to start by going online and looking at a number of websites for properties. This can be easily done by putting in your price range parameters. You should be able to quickly size up the components of value in your buying formula, so that you can understand how the cost of an apartment varies based on changes in the aesthetics of the apartment. I caution buyers against putting in advanced search options for their initial review, which can limit the selection to only apartments with secondary amenities like fireplaces, terraces, health clubs, etc. For your first evaluation, focus on the qualities associated with the primary motivators in order to develop an impression of what the apartment will cost with respect to these fundamentals. After you have gained a clear impression of the apartment that you feel is desirable, you can add additional criteria to fine-tune your evaluation. I highly recommend that you go to brokerage websites in order to get the most up-to-date information from each brokerage company on their promoted properties.

Communicating With a Broker

When you call a real estate broker, you will normally be asked for your name and telephone number to ensure that you are registered with the firm. If you are calling about a specific property, you should ask questions in order to find out more about it. If it sounds interesting, make an appointment to see it at the earliest possible time. If you delay, it may be sold by the time you get there. Do not assume that because you feel the market is soft, the property you might be interested in is waiting for you. If a property looks exciting to you, it is probably also interesting to others. In addition, describe your buying formula to your broker and ask him or her to recommend other possibilities. Ideally, you should see between three and five apartments when a broker takes you out, so you have some points of comparison.

Going Out on Showings

When you visit an apartment, try to picture yourself living in it. Imagine that you just bought it and are moving in. Where would you eat? Where would you sleep? How would you utilize the space? After you envision the environment, ask yourself, "Would I be happy here?" Do not view it as a price issue; it is a lifestyle decision. If the apartment doesn't work for you and the way you want to live, then it doesn't matter what the price is — it is not a candidate.

If you consider the apartment viable, you should go through a checklist of its strengths and weaknesses using the criteria you defined in your buying formula. Don't expect to find the perfect apartment. Consider the value of variations within your degree of flexibility. For example, one apartment may have a better location than you specified in your buyer formula, but it may be slightly smaller than you desire. Consider all the pros and cons to find properties that best fit your overall needs. After you have seen a number of apartments, several candidates should stand out as worthy of serious consideration.

Going to Open Houses

A common practice used by many brokers is to conduct an open house. The broker will announce a specific date and time when he or she will be present at the property to help any inquisitive parties view it without an appointment. Open houses are typically listed on brokerage websites and other sites such as StreetEasy.com and NYTimes.com. Buyers often like the idea of being able to step in and see a property without the pressure of an appointment. Many buyers will create a list of properties and open house times, and then spend a leisurely afternoon going from one property to another to get a feel for the market. You should be aware that some buildings are very restrictive about open houses, so the broker will announce that the open house is "by appointment only." In this case, you need only to call prior to coming to ensure that the broker can make arrangements for you to visit consistent with the building's open house requirements.

Comparing Alternative Properties

Take your list of candidates and create a concise worksheet to compare them (see page 79). If one or more is a condominium, investigate whether you can obtain an interest rate that is lower than it would be for a cooperative. Some banks will reduce the rate for a condominium by 0.5% if the equity cash down is 20% or more. From this final analysis, you should select one apartment as your top choice. This is the apartment on which you should bid. If there is more than one apartment that you think satisfies your needs, I would recommend that you place bids on both to see which apartment offers you the best financial opportunity.

Bidding on an Apartment

The first step in making a bid is determining what the apartment is worth to you — not the seller's asking price, but your sense of its value based on your impression of the market, the degree to which it meets your needs and your economic limitations. When you have a figure in mind, you should consider making a bid below the asking price in order to negotiate the most favorable terms.

I suggest that you ask the broker about the flexibility of the seller. Then develop a justification for your offer that the broker can use to communicate the legitimacy of your proposal. If the seller responds with an unacceptable counteroffer, ask the broker to obtain the seller's justification. If the response is reasonable, increase your offer if you can afford to. If the seller is not reasonable, renew your search.

I often say to buyers that good deals are not found, they are made. Don't reject apartments because they appear overpriced. However, bear in mind that sellers are not naïve. They know they are selling an asset of great importance, and normally they have carefully considered how they are marketing their property based on relative sales, current offerings in the marketplace and their perception of future trends in the market. Sellers are sometimes also motivated by economic need, resulting in pricing that reflects their personal goals. For example, a seller might be looking to buy a larger apartment and knows he cannot afford the bigger home unless he achieves a certain price. Obviously, comparable sales will not be an adequate motivation for him to reduce his price, because it doesn't afford him the funds to fulfill his objective. However, time causes many people to change their points of view. Don't consider an apartment that has been on the market for an extended length of time as a limited opportunity. Indeed, the length of time an apartment has been on the market may be a reason for the seller to have a change of heart, while the owner of a newly listed property might be overly optimistic.

It is also important to be aware that New York City isn't merely one market, but a conglomeration of different markets. You may find that in one neighborhood prices are soft for a given type of property, say studios, while for another, say three bedrooms, they are very firm. You may also notice that there is considerable variation by type of property. A seller of a studio may be willing to drop his price, while a two-bedroom seller in the same building may not.

Buying Formula Worksheet:
Comparison Analysis of Selected Apartments

	Buying Formula	Selected Apartments A	B	C
Address		_____	_____	_____
Location grade	_____	_____	_____	_____
Building grade	_____	_____	_____	_____
Air	_____	_____	_____	_____
Light				
View grade	_____	_____	_____	_____
Minimum floor	_____	_____	_____	_____
Space				
Living room sq. ft.	_____	_____	_____	_____
Master bedroom sq. ft.	_____	_____	_____	_____
Secondary amenities	_____	_____	_____	_____
Price	_____	_____	_____	_____
Monthly charge[1]	_____	_____	_____	_____
Cash down	_____	_____	_____	_____
Cash per month	_____	_____	_____	_____

[1]*For co-ops use maintenance payment; for condos use common charges and real estate taxes.*

CHAPTER 5

The Applied Science of Buying an Apartment

Applying the strategy described in the preceding chapter will provide a clearer sense of the method in action.

Gina and Alan Green are thinking about buying an apartment. They want to start a family. They both work, giving them a combined income of $200,000, and they have accumulated $275,000 in cash savings. They undertake the following procedure.

Location: They decide that they are willing to accept an active commercial street with moderate demand but they want it to look appealing, so they select a minimum location grade of 6.

Building: They decide that they definitely need a doorman, and they would like to live in a high-quality building. They choose a minimum building grade of 7.

Air: They have no special layout requirements.

Light: A street view is acceptable as long as it is bright, which translates into a minimum view grade of 5. They would like to have an apartment that is on or above the fifth floor.

Space: The amount of space in the apartment is of high importance. In looking at various other apartments available for sale in their price range, they decide that they would like a living room of at least 20 × 12 and a master bedroom of at least 16 × 11.

Cash Down: Since they know that they need to have savings after the closing, they decide that ideally they would like to use no more than $200,000 for the down payment. Therefore they estimate that, based on putting 25% down, they can afford an apartment of $800,000.

Cash per Month: The Greens know that they can only use 45% of their reported income to pay their housing costs and other debt. They have a car that costs $200 per month in loan payments. They have credit cards that they pay in full monthly, but the banks will still make an adjustment equal to 1/60th of their average monthly balance. They pay approximately $3,000 per month for their credit card balance, which means that the bank will take off an additional $50 per month. They are able to report on their tax return an adjusted gross income of $200,000, which means their monthly income is $16,667. Thus the computation is as follows:

Monthly gross income .... $ 16,667

Allowable percentage .... × 45%

Funds available .... *equals* $ 7,500

Other debt payments............................ *minus* $ 250

Available for housing .... *equals* $ 7,250

Evaluating the Primary Motivators:
Alan and Gina Green

Location

What is your minimum location requirement?

___ **10.** Overlooking Central Park, near world-renowned buildings and landmarks

___ **9.** Internationally prestigious, residential, near Central Park or overlooking a park

___ **8.** Exceptionally beautiful and charming residential street, near a park or river

___ **7.** Quiet and charming residential street

_X_ **6.** Commercial or residential street without notable features, with good demand

___ **5.** Commercial or residential street with growing potential and active buyer interest

___ **4.** Emerging area with few local services, restaurants, etc.

___ **3.** Minimal aesthetics, less convenient to transportation and shopping

___ **2.** Street with low market demand

___ **1.** No preference

Building

What is your minimum building requirement?

___ **10.** Internationally recognized, architecturally significant, high-end services, top condition

___ **9.** Excellent local reputation, architecturally significant, high-end services, top condition

___ **8.** Very good local reputation, great amenities, at least two lobby attendants

_X_ **7.** Doorman, good-quality amenities

___ **6.** Doorman, average amenities

___ **5.** Either an intercom, top condition or a doorman, needing renovation

___ **4.** Low- or mid-rise, intercom, average condition

___ **3.** Low- or mid-rise, intercom, condition issues

___ **2.** Low- or mid-rise, intercom, substantial renovations needed

___ **1.** No preference

Air

Are there any layout elements that are critical to you?

___ Formal dining room

___ Eat-in kitchen

___ Alcove studio

___ Maid's room

___ Spacious entry

___ Separation between master and other bedrooms

___ Other _____

Light

Is there a minimum floor that you require?

___ No preference

___ Third floor and above

_X_ On or above the _5th_ floor

View

What is the minimum direct view you require out of the living room?

___ **10.** Sweeping views of Central Park and grand cityscape views

___ **9.** Grand cityscape views with river and/or park

___ **8.** Grand cityscape views without a river or park

___ **7.** Basic skyline views, basic river views or beautiful courtyard views

___ **6.** Street views into buildings but bright

_X_ **5.** Street views into buildings, moderate light (middle floor)

___ **4.** Street views into buildings, limited light or basic courtyard views

___ **3.** No views but bright

___ **2.** No views, moderate light

___ **1.** No preference

Space

What is the minimum amount of space you desire for the following rooms?

Living room _____20_____ × _____12_____

Master bedroom _____16_____ × _____11_____

Secondary Amenities

Are there secondary elements that are important to you?

___ Garage in building

___ Fireplace

___ Health club

___ Pool

___ Laundry room

___ Terrace/outdoor space

___ Pets

___ Washer/dryer

___ Prewar building

___ Specific neighborhood(s) _____

___ Other _____

The Greens go to Bellmarc.com and click on *Survey Our Inventory*. This presents them with various price brackets by apartment size. They decide to look at one-bedroom apartments between $800,000 and $900,000 and at two-bedrooms in the same range. They find there are currently 256 one-bedrooms in Manhattan available for sale in this category, with an average monthly maintenance cost of $1,324. For two-bedrooms, they determine that there are 151 apartments for sale in Manhattan in their category, and that the average monthly mainte-nance cost is $1,524. They also decide to focus on the Upper East Side, where the average monthly maintenance cost is $1,586 for a one-bedroom and $1,882 for a two-bedroom. With this information, they conclude that the maximum maintenance they will use for their search is $2,000. Thus, by subtracting the maintenance component from the monthly funds, they conclude that they are able to apply $5,250 toward their monthly debt payment. At the current time, the rate of interest for a 30-year fixed mortgage is 5%. So by taking $5,250 and dividing it by 0.00537 (which is the monthly interest rate factor for 5% as expressed on the Debt Service Payment Table on page 136) they are able to determine that their maximum potential borrowing power using the debt-to-income ratio is $977,653. In applying a debt-to-equity ratio of 25%, the Greens determine that they can buy a co-op for $800,000, and can comfortably borrow approximately $600,000. If they purchase a condominium, they can borrow more, and if the monthly common charges are substantially less on the condominium they will have even more funds available to cover their debt payment. Therefore, they decide that their search range for condominiums will be $800,000 to $1,000,000. The Greens then check their credit score, and confirm that they have a score of 740. This means that they are qualified to obtain a loan at favorable rates.

Buying Formula Worksheet:
Evaluating an Apartment Purchase
(assuming a given monthly housing charge to determine an implied mortgage)

(A) Cash Down Payment

Non-borrowed cash you want to use to purchase
an apartment $___*$200,000*___

(B) Cost Per Month

Compute your ideal monthly payment below:

Reported monthly income		$ _16,667_
Coverage rate		× 45%
as defined by all banks		
Maximum monthly housing cost	*equals* $	_7,500_
Total of other debts you currently pay	*minus* $	_250_
Cash available for covering the monthly cost of your home	*equals* $	_7,250_ (A)
Monthly maintenance payment	*minus* $	_2,000_ (B)
Available for monthly mortgage payment	$	_5,250_ (B–A)

By dividing the cash available for mortgage payment by the interest factor (as shown on page 135), you can obtain the total amount you are potentially able to borrow under the bank coverage rule.

The bank equity leverage rule is 25% cash down. Thus, the lesser of this rule or the bank coverage rule creates the limitation on your purchasing power and your maximum mortgage.

Cash available for monthly mortgage payment	$ _5,250_
Current monthly interest factor for _5_ % *(page 135)*	_0.00537_ %
Implied mortgage that can be sustained	$ _977,653_
Implied maximum purchase price for a co-op	$ _800,000_

Purchase range: $800,000 for a co-op to $1,000,000 for a condo.

Developing Parameters for Each Primary Motivator

The Greens complete the primary motivator worksheet by filling in their buying formula. They then go to various websites and begin searching for properties that meet or exceed their buying formula requirements. They go on a number of apartment showings, and conclude that there are three candidates worth serious consideration.

Apartment A: Property A is located in the mid-50s on the West Side of Manhattan in a busy location. There are many poorly maintained buildings nearby, but the apartment is two blocks from Central Park South. In judging the various location grades, they decide that the closest grade that conforms to this property is a 5. The building is a prewar in good condition with a doorman. The building grade they give the property is a 7. The apartment is on the 18th floor and has panoramic cityscape views facing south, which they give a view grade of 8. The living room is 25' × 12', and the master bedroom is 18' × 12'. There is an eat-in kitchen. The asking price is $850,000, and the maintenance is $1,750 per month.

Apartment B: Property B is located on the Upper West Side of Manhattan in the 80s. It is on West End Avenue, an area that has an appealing residential character. The Greens decide on a location grade of 7. The building is a prewar doorman building in good condition. Thus the building grade is judged as a 5. The apartment is on the 10th floor. It is bright but the view is of the apartment building across the street. The view grade is judged as a 6. There is a large 28' × 12' living room, and the master bedroom is 18' × 12'. There is an eat-in kitchen. The asking price is $880,000 and the maintenance is $1,560 per month.

Apartment C: Property C is located in the 80s on East End Avenue. The area is quiet; Carl Schurz Park is across the street. The subway is five blocks away, the supermarket four. Even though the location would normally be rated at 7, the Greens decide to lower the grade to 6 because it is slightly less convenient. It is in a new condominium building with a doorman and the Greens assign it a building grade of 7. Since it has views of the East River but also views into other buildings, they assign it a view grade of 7. The apartment is on the sixth floor. It has a living room of 24' × 12' and a master bedroom of 17' × 11'. The asking price is $950,000, and the common charges are $850 per month, with real estate taxes of $700 per month, for a total monthly cost of $1,950.

Buying Formula Worksheet:
Comparison Analysis of Selected Apartments

	Buying Formula	Selected Apartments A	B	C
Address		Apt A	Apt B	Apt C
Location grade	6	5	7	6
Building grade	7	7	5	7
Air qualities		Eat-in kit	Eat-in kit.	
Light				
View grade	5	8	6	7
Minimum floor	5	18	10	6
Space				
Living room sq. ft.	240	300	336	288
Master bedroom sq. ft.	192	216	216	187
Secondary factors		Prewar	Prewar	New
Price	$800,000	$850,000	$880,000	$950,000
Monthly charge[1]	$2,000	$1,750	$1,560	$1,950
Cash down	$200,000	$212,500	$220,000	$237,500
Cash per month[2]	$7,250	$5,173	$5,104	$5,776

[1]For co-ops use maintenance payment; for condos use common charges and real estate taxes.

[2]Asssuming a 5% interest rate.

The Greens' Decision

By evaluating these three alternatives in light of their buying formula and their financial limitations, the Greens can come to some conclusions. It is important to remember that their decision might be different from yours. Every buyer is unique.

Apartment A: Apartment A is favorable in all respects except for the location grade, where the building is designated as a 5 compared to the Greens' minimum location grade of 6. They decide that even though the apartment has ample space and is in a nice building, the location is definitely an issue here. They judge that the value to them of this negative feature is $100,000. However, the better view is worth $50,000 to them. So to the Greens, the apartment is worth about $750,000 compared to the standard of what they want to pay. This is a lesser choice.

Apartment B: The Greens like the location. They also like that there is more space than in the other apartments they are looking at, although the building is a little tired and this somewhat offsets the favorable qualities of the location. They think the price at their standard of $800,000 is worth it, and because of the low monthly charge they decide that they would pay up to $850,000 if they need to. They figure they have enough cash and income to qualify with the co-op board even at the higher figure. This is their first choice.

Apartment C: The Greens like the building and are satisfied with the location. The floor and the view are also acceptable. The space in the living room is adequate, and the bedroom space is a little less than they would desire but not material. They also like that everything is new. The cash down is more than they want to spend, and the common charges and real estate taxes are considerably higher than those of the other properties they have seen. They decide that the property isn't worth more than $900,000 to them. This would reduce their down payment to $225,000. Since it is a new condo, they don't have to worry about board approval. This is their second choice.

The Greens decide that their first offer will be $800,000 for Apartment B. If this is rejected, they will make a higher offer for Apartment B and will also make an offer of $900,000 for Apartment C.

CHAPTER 6

Understanding the Contract

Disclaimer

This chapter contains a summary of the material provisions of the Standard-Form Cooperative Contract, normally referred to as Blumberg Form M123 (or New York State Bar Association form 7-2001). Blumberg contracts are the predominant forms used in New York City for the transfer of cooperative and condominium apartments. The features that distinguish this contract from the one used for condominiums, Blumberg Form 146, are discussed at the end of this chapter.

This outline is not intended to be legally authoritative. Rather, it is an encapsulation of the material issues presented in the contract. Anyone buying or selling property should use a lawyer for professional guidance. Make certain that he or she has experience with cooperative and condominium transactions, which are different from other forms of real estate transactions.

Basic Information

On the first page of the contract, the buyer and seller make a number of representations. These include:

- Identifying the buying and selling parties and their attorneys
- Identifying the apartment being sold
- Identifying the party who will hold the contract deposit (referred to as the escrow agent; normally the seller's attorney)
- Identifying the broker
- Stating the current maintenance fee (or common charges and real estate tax in the case of a condominium)
- Disclosing any open assessments levied on the apartment. If there is a transfer charge levied by the cooperative corporation

(referred to as a *flip tax*), the party responsible for making that payment will be noted. The contract stipulates whether or not the purchase is contingent on the buyer obtaining financing, and if so, the amount of that loan.

· Identifying the proposed occupants and any pets.

A number of these points deserve further consideration. The first relates to the escrow. Contract deposit funds are normally held in a regular checking account and do not bear interest. This is because the State of New York does not permit an escrow agent to commingle funds from different clients into a common interest-bearing account. If the client specifies that the escrow account should be interest-bearing, the escrow agent must open a separate account specifically for that purpose. Normally the cost of the time and effort involved exceeds the benefits, unless the contract deposit is unusually large or the length of time between the contract and the closing is unusually long. In those rare instances when an interest-bearing account is used, the interest on the escrow funds usually accrues to the benefit of the buyer, although this can be a point of negotiation.

Another issue is the flip tax. The name is deceptive, since it isn't a tax and nothing is necessarily being "flipped." A flip tax is basically a charge levied by the co-op corporation or the condo association on the transfer of ownership of an apartment, and serves as a means of generating income for the building. The seller customarily makes the flip tax payment, but the contract is silent on this point in order to permit flexibility in negotiations between the parties. The flip tax is normally a percentage of the sale price, usually ranging from 1% to 3%.

Pets are a touchy issue in many co-ops and condos. If an owner is allowed to keep a pet in the apartment, it should say so clearly in the contract, particularly since many buildings do not permit pets. Don't assume because you have seen a resident with a dog in the lobby that the building permits pets. It may have been grandfathered in under an old rule, and new owners may not be entitled to the same privileges.

The term "pet" does not refer only to dogs, but also to cats, birds and any other type of animal.

The occupants of the apartment should be spelled out in the contract, especially if they are not the owners. There is bound to be controversy if the prospective owners are interviewed and accepted into the building as residents but then someone else (a relative, for instance) occupies the apartment instead. This is an issue that should be resolved at the earliest possible moment with the board of directors and/or the building's managing agent.

In Clause 2 of the standard contract, the price of the apartment is stated and the terms of payment defined. The terms are normally a 10% deposit due upon signing the contract, with the balance due in certified funds on the closing date, usually 60 to 90 days after the contract is signed. Often banks take a considerable length of time to process mortgage applications, and many attorneys for buyers seek automatic extensions for as long as 180 days. If there is no language added to the contract about extensions, then a buyer can usually get a 30-day extension of the closing date without fear of adverse consequences under protections afforded through New York State law. If the contract specifically states that "time is of the essence," no extensions will be permitted to the buyer, and he or she must close by the stated date.

During the period between the signing of the contract and the closing, the buyer must obtain board approval, arrange for financing and finalize any other open issues related to purchasing the apartment.

There are things in the apartment, referred to as *personal property*, that are customarily transferred as part of the purchase. The legal definition of real estate is "land and anything permanently affixed thereto," while personal property is everything "not permanently affixed thereto." Accordingly, the contract will typically state that items of personal property — such as kitchen appliances, cabinetry, air conditioners, lights and wall-to-wall carpeting — are included. If there are a washer and dryer, the contract will state that these should also stay. If the windows have screens and window treatments, these are included as well. Even hardware such as doorknobs, doorstops, handles and bells are typically specified as part of the deal.

The contract stops there. Nothing else will be transferred to the buyer unless specifically provided for in the contract. This includes, for example, any special built-ins, furnishings or pictures. It is not uncommon for disagreements to arise regarding what is and what is not included in a deal. In many instances, the seller may wish to remove items that the contract form stipulates are included. A wise buyer should assume that nothing is included unless the contract expressly says it is. All understandings should be spelled out in the contract in clearly defined terms.

Representations and Promises

The contract calls for the seller to make certain representations about the nature of his ownership. The seller must represent that he is the sole owner and that he is in good standing with the cooperative corporation. The seller must also affirm that he has the right to sell the apartment and will do so free of any liens or encumbrances. Furthermore, the seller must represent that there will be no money owed on the apartment at the time of transfer. Finally, the seller must assert that he has done nothing wrong during his tenancy that would adversely affect the subsequent owners, and that he has not received any notices about assessments or increases in the maintenance.

The buyer, in turn, must assure the seller that he has looked at all the documents necessary to make his decision or that he waives examination of those documents as a condition of the transaction.

Required Approval

In cooperative corporations, the sale of any apartment is subject to approval by the board of directors. The contract states that the buyer must submit an application and any other required documents to the board within 10 days of signing the contract, and that within three days of receiving a loan commitment the buyer must submit proof of the commitment.

These deadlines are sometimes difficult to meet. Preparing the application and gathering financial reports, reference letters and supporting documents could take a substantial amount of time. In addition, if the deal is subject to financing, boards will rarely accept an application for review without a commitment letter from a bank. It is therefore suggested that if the application is not subject to financing, the term for submission of the application should be extended to 30 days from the signing of the contract. If the contract includes financing, the term for submission should be 10 days after receipt of the loan commitment letter. (Receipt of the commitment letter has specific date limitations.) Make certain that the application is complete, because the board will not review incomplete applications.

In a cooperative apartment transaction, in addition to submitting the application and supporting documents, the buyer normally must attend a board interview. Many prospective buyers fear the interview process, but in the vast majority of cases boards are respectful, friendly and even welcoming. Indeed, many buyers become more committed to the purchase after having met the board and having seen who their neighbors will be. However, there are at least a few buyers with war stories to tell, so it's a good idea to consider the following before attending a board interview:

- Don't be angry or indignant.
- Don't use the meeting as a forum to espouse any social or political philosophy.
- Don't tell the board what you dislike about the building or what you want to change when you move into the building.
- Dress in business attire and look professional.
- If you are asked a question that you think is inappropriate, try to remain diplomatic in your response. If you have strong feelings about the question, it might be appropriate to address the issue

with a board member on an informal basis after you have closed the sale and moved into the building.

- Review your application, including financial documents, before the meeting so that you can answer any questions that may be posed about them intelligently, and don't contradict yourself. It is useful to take your documents with you to the board meeting so that if someone refers to them you can actually look at the documents being discussed.
- Be yourself. Don't try to be overly impressive or humble.

Most boards will not interview a purchaser until they are satisfied with the application, which means that the likelihood of rejection is significantly reduced if the interview is scheduled.

Risk of Loss

The contract typically states that the apartment is to be sold "as is," that it will be delivered "broom clean," and that the appliances will be in working order.

In the event that damage occurs in the apartment prior to the closing, it is the responsibility of the seller to fix it. Sometimes the damage is substantial. In this case, the seller can elect to restore the apartment within 60 days after notifying the buyer, or the buyer can accept the apartment in its current condition and receive any insurance proceeds relating to the damage. If there has been significant damage and the seller refuses to repair it, the buyer can opt out of the agreement. In the event that the buyer, or anyone responsible to the buyer, performed the act that caused the damage, the risk of loss is borne by the buyer.

The risk-of-loss provision covers some serious issues. What happens if, when moving out, the seller's movers damage a wall, the floor or some other part of the apartment? Customary practice is that a sum of money representing a reasonable estimate of the cost of the repair remains in escrow. The buyer then makes the repair and submits the bill to the seller's attorney for reimbursement. If the amount of the bill is less than the amount held in escrow, the balance goes to the seller. If the amount of the bill is greater than the amount in escrow, the buyer must absorb the shortfall.

The Closing

The location of the closing will normally be designated by the co-op corporation's managing agent.

The seller shall deliver the following at closing:
- The seller's shares of stock and proprietary lease
- A statement permitting the transfer of the shares, signed by the appropriate representative of the cooperative corporation
- All necessary tax documents associated with the transfer
- Other documents as specifically noted and required under the contract
- The keys to the apartment

The buyer shall do the following at the closing:
- Deliver a certified check for the remainder of the funds due.
- Execute loan documents and deliver the new stock and propri-etary lease (or assignments of the existing stock and lease) to the bank funding the purchase.
- Provide tax documents and any other documents that are re-quired under the contract.

In addition, at the closing an apportionment of maintenance for the current month is paid by the seller for the period running through the prior day. If an assessment is due, the contract states that if the due date is prior to closing, it will be paid by the seller, and if it is subse-quent to closing, it will be paid by the buyer. Then, usually by separate agreement, the real estate brokers will be paid their commissions.

Defaults, Remedies and Other Limitations

If either party breaches the agreement, the remedies are clear:
- If the buyer defaults, the seller can keep the buyer's 10% deposit.
- If the seller defaults, the buyer can either bring an action at law to compel performance under the contract or sue for monetary damages.
- The parties to the sale and to the purchase indemnify each other against breaches of contract made by one or the other. This means that any claim made by a third party adversely affected by the breach is the exclusive responsibility of the violating party.

In addition, other limitations exist:
- The contract stands as the total agreement. No oral statements made by either party can be enforced unless they have been placed in writing in the agreement.
- The agreement cannot be assigned to another party.
- Nothing represented in the agreement survives the closing unless expressly stated in the contract.
- The buyer can inspect the apartment within 48 hours of the closing.
- The parties agree to act in good faith.

Financing Contingency

A financing contingency is the right of the buyer to obtain a loan from a bank to purchase a property. If financing is a condition of the agreement, the buyer must diligently apply for a loan within seven days after the contract is executed. The contract can be canceled, and the buyer's deposit returned, if any of the following three conditions occur:
- A loan commitment letter is not obtained by the date specified in the contract.
- The bank is unable to obtain a letter from the cooperative cor-

poration recognizing its secured interest under terms the bank finds satisfactory.

- The closing is extended by the seller or the co-op corporation by more than 30 days, the commitment letter expires during this period, and the buyer cannot get an extension without making an additional payment. However, this provision can be overcome if the seller agrees to make that payment on the buyer's behalf.

If the buyer seeks to cancel the contract, he or she must give legal notice within seven days of the date that the right of cancellation initiates. Legal notice must be in writing and delivered by hand or overnight mail, or by certified or registered mail, to the seller and the seller's attorney.

It is extremely important that the conditions under the financing contingency be carefully monitored. In the event that the commitment date on the contract passes and the buyer has not provided legal notice to the seller and the seller's attorney, the contract is no longer subject to financing, and the buyer must perform under the terms of the contract or lose his or her deposit. The dates are critical, as well as the form of giving notice.

Attorneys have been adding another provision, referred to as a *funding contingency*. A funding contingency is the right of the purchaser to a return of his deposit and the voiding of the contract if the bank subsequently decides after issuing a commitment letter that it will not actually fund the loan at closing because conditions have changed. These conditions include changes in bank policies, unfavorable financial conditions in the building that are revealed after the commitment is released, or material changes in the borrower's financial condition that are identified before closing. This has created a new level of risk for borrowers, which attorneys now seek to address by including language in the contract that requires not only the delivery of the loan commitment letter from the bank, but also funding by that bank of the loan proceeds at the time of the closing.

Features That Distinguish the Condominium Contract from the Cooperative Contract

Attorneys involved in a condominium sale normally use Blumberg Form M146. This contract is substantially similar in content to the contract described above except for the following items:

Condominium unit deed: A condominium buyer receives a deed rather than a lease and stock. Additionally, the seller must identify the real estate taxes on the unit, as these taxes are paid separately by the condominium unit owner. Furthermore, the monthly charge is referred to as a common charge rather than as a maintenance charge.

Approval: Normally, no condominium board approval is required for purchasing a condominium. However, a right-of-first-refusal procedure is common. This permits the board to review the contract and request information about the purchaser. On many occasions this review can be as extensive an inquiry as that required by a cooperative board. If the condominium board objects to the purchaser, it may refuse to permit the sale. However, the condominium is then compelled to buy the unit under the same terms and conditions as expressed in the rejected contract.

Title insurance: Since a condominium is real estate, it is important that the title be free of claims by third parties. A review of the title must be performed, and insurance obtained, to protect against any claims of which the buyer is unaware. The title search is done by a title abstract company, which, for a fee, will also issue title insurance that guarantees the new owner protection from any future claims made by third parties against the title.

CHAPTER 7

The Prospectus

Part 1:
The Standard Procedure for Converting a Building to Cooperative or Condominium Ownership

Forms of Ownership

Buildings generally change to unit ownership through conversion of existing rental property, new construction or rehabilitation. In its simplest terms, a cooperative or condominium conversion is the sale of a building to a newly formed corporation or housing association, respectively. In a cooperative, the original owner, the landlord, becomes the *sponsor*, and initiates the process by creating an offering plan promoting the sale of stock in the new corporation. The purchaser gains residency rights by means of a proprietary lease relating to each specific apartment that is appurtenant to the stock ownership.

In a condominium, the offering plan proposes the partition of the building's ownership into unit interests. Each purchaser acquires an apartment and receives a unit deed. In addition, a master deed and the condominium bylaws describe the rights and obligations of both the condominium association and the unit owners to the building's common areas and services. Condominiums in New York State are governed by Article 9-B of the New York Real Property Law, also known as the New York Condominium Act.

The Offering Plan

The offering plan, also known as the prospectus or black book, is prepared by the owner of a building being converted to co-op or condo ownership. It is intended to assist buyers in making an informed decision about a prospective apartment purchase. Before it can be distributed to the public, the offering plan must be reviewed by the New York State attorney general's office to ensure that the information is complete and accurate in accordance with New York State legal requirements.

Once the attorney general's office determines that the offering plan is in compliance, it is accepted for filing and can be distributed to prospective buyers. However, the mere fact that an offering plan meets minimum legal standards of disclosure should not be construed as an endorsement of its terms, conditions, accuracy or offering prices by any government authority. Therefore, *caveat emptor* — "let the buyer beware" — are still the watchwords for any potential purchaser.

During the course of the conversion, it is not unusual for the sponsor to make alterations in the price and/or terms of the offer. In such a case, the sponsor must file an amendment to the plan, which must also be approved by the New York State attorney general's office. These *amendments* are an integral part of the offering plan and should be reviewed by buyers.

Amendments may be filed even after the date of conversion to cooperative or condominium ownership if the sponsor has a continuing economic interest in the property and proposes a revised offer for selling apartments to tenant-occupants. Additionally, the attorney general requires ongoing yearly disclosure by any party having a material interest that exceeds 10% of the shares of the corporation, whether it be the sponsor or a third-party investor. This yearly disclosure must include financial information about that party.

If a building was converted to cooperative or condominium ownership prior to 1970, it will not have an offering plan.

The Martin Act

The law in New York State regulating the process of conversion to cooperative and condominium ownership is called the Martin Act and can be found in Sections 352-eee and 352-eeee of New York State's General Business Law. Under the provisions of this act, a building may be converted to cooperative ownership if 15% of the shares of stock in the new corporation are subscribed to and transferred. In the case of a condominium, a similar percentage of unit-deed interests must be transferred.

The law also provides for an alternate conversion form, referred to as an eviction plan, wherein 51% of the tenants in occupancy must subscribe and the nonsubscribing tenants must leave their apartments at the end of their lease terms. Years ago, the threshold percentage for an eviction plan was 35%, and eviction plans were common. Under current rules, eviction plans are rarely employed.

The law mandates that shares of stock in a cooperative corporation, or unit interests in a condominium, be allocated to specific apartments and that this allocation of shares (i.e., the percentage of the total number of shares for the building assigned to each specific apartment) be rational and reasonable. Therefore, the 15% rule effectively mandates transfer of property ownership of approximately this same percentage before an offering plan can be declared effective. By law, each cooperative apartment must receive, along with the shares, a proprietary lease that gives the shareholder the right to occupy a specific apartment. In a condominium conversion, the deed covering the entire property is partitioned into unit interests, and each apartment is allocated a percentage of the whole (including a percentage of the common elements), also on a rational and reasonable basis.

The law requires the sponsor to offer tenants in occupancy the first right to purchase the shares allocated to their units. As a result, landlords frequently offer tenants a discounted price to encourage them to buy the apartments they have been renting. However, the tenant has no obligation to purchase. Under a 15% non-eviction plan, if the apartment is covered by New York State rent regulations, the tenant may continue to live in it for as long as desired, and the lease must be renewed. This remains true even if the apartment is sold to a third party.

At times a group of people will acquire a building and each investor will be allocated an apartment, with no units being offered to outside buyers. On these rare occasions, the New York State attorney general's office will issue a no-action letter permitting the conversion to cooperative ownership without the filing of an offering plan. Any later purchaser will not be able to review a plan, since none was developed.

Declaring the Plan Effective

At any time after the 15% subscription threshold is met, the sponsor can issue a declaration of effectiveness. This is the sponsor's pronouncement that statutory requirements have been met and that the conversion is now in effect, subject to final closing on all subscription contracts for the purchase of stock (or unit deeds in the case of a condominium) and the transfer of funds. When all subscription agreements are closed, the cooperative corporation will pay and transfer the funds to the sponsor/landlord in exchange for the deed to the property. When apartments remain unpurchased, the landlord takes the *unsold shares* as additional payment to conclude the transfer of ownership of the property. In a condominium the procedure is essentially the same, except the landlord is given condominium unit interests instead of shares and leases for the unsold apartments.

Therefore, even if a landlord or sponsor continues to have an economic interest in the property, all apartments have been transferred to the co-op corporation or condo association for the purpose of effecting the conversion. All of the apartments have equal rights and obligations subject to their respective share allocation or their unit-deed percentage interest.

A Summary of the Conversion Process

In a nutshell, the conversion process goes like this:
- A *preliminary offering plan*, often referred to as a *red herring*, is issued to all tenants; it is an informational book advising them

of the prospective offer. (For new construction there is no red herring, as there are no existing tenants.)

- The state attorney general's office reviews the proposed prospectus and accepts the plan for filing. Thereafter, the offering plan is officially issued.

- Negotiations on price and terms begin between the landlord and the tenants. Amendments are filed with the state attorney general's office to advise of any changes in the initial offering terms.

- Subscriptions (contracts to purchase) are signed by tenants in occupancy and outside parties for shares of stock (co-ops) or condominium unit interests (condo). A minimum of 15% of the apartments must be sold to declare the plan effective.

- All tenants and outside parties fully pay up their subscription, and receive stock in the cooperative corporation and a lease to a specific apartment (in the case of a co-op) or a unit deed (in the case of a condo).

- For co-ops, the deed to the entire property is transferred to the cooperative corporation. The landlord or sponsor receives the cash from the sale of all subscribed shares, as well as the unsold shares on apartments not purchased in a co-op or unit deeds on unpurchased apartments in a condo.

Part 2:
Material Components of the Prospectus

Schedule A: Share Allocations or Unit Interests

Each apartment is allocated shares of stock. The shares of the apartments, in total, comprise the full number of outstanding shares in the cooperative corporation, or unit percentage interest in the case of a condominium. The actual number of shares allocated to any specific apartment has limited meaning. Rather, it is the apartment's fractional interest to the total shares outstanding that is relevant. Section 216 of the U.S. Internal Revenue Code and the New York State Martin Act require that a cooperative's allocation of shares to each apartment bear a reasonable relationship to the total. The term "reasonable relationship" is open to interpretation, but generally it means that the allocation of a co-op's shares is based on the relative fair market value of the apartments. In condominiums, since the ownership is of real estate, Section 216 does not apply, but the Martin Act still requires that unit interests be allocated reasonably, which is typically based on square footage and other factors meaningful to value. Under the Martin Act, the share allocations for a cooperative or unit percentage interests for a condominium must be certified as rational and reasonable in an opinion letter by an independent expert. This opinion letter, referred to as a *letter of reasonable relationship*, is normally prepared by a real estate broker familiar with values in the area and can be found in the offering plan.

The share or unit interest allocation for each apartment is given in Schedule A of the offering plan. Schedule A normally includes the apartment number of each unit, the number of rooms, the allocated number of shares or unit percentage interest, the portion of the underlying mortgage of the building allocated to the unit, the initial maintenance charge or common charges (if applicable), the allocated portion of the real estate taxes on the building and the allocated portion of the building's tax-deductible interest.

Schedule B: First-Year Operating Budget

An offering plan must present an operating budget for the building's first year of operation. This budget, outlined in Schedule B of the offering plan, estimates an amount for each expense item, along with accompanying notes explaining how these amounts were determined. In newly constructed buildings, generous expense estimates are the norm since they are based on input from outside engineers and consultants, who tend to overestimate operating costs out of caution. The sponsor may also favor generous estimates, since under current state regulations he or she may be held responsible if the building has an economic shortfall.

When a building is converting from rental to ownership, the state requires that the offering plan include audited financial statements for prior years. Since rental buildings are often run more frugally than co-ops and condos, it is common for projected maintenance charges expressed in Schedule B to be lower than the actual amount owners will eventually pay. This is somewhat ameliorated by a provision found in many offering plans restricting the right of the cooperative corporation to increase services and amenities during the initial stages of the conversion without the sponsor's consent.

Under New York State law, an expert must certify that the proposed operating budget is adequate to cover the first year's operation. A property management company familiar with the costs of operation in the local area normally prepares this *letter of adequacy*, which is also found in the offering plan.

Tax Opinion Letter

Under Section 216 of the Internal Revenue Code, tenant-shareholders of cooperative corporations are entitled to deduct on their personal tax returns their allocable portion of the real estate taxes and interest paid by the cooperative corporation. However, there are certain qualifying criteria that the cooperative corporation must meet in order for tenant-shareholders to be able to take these deductions. These criteria are:

- The corporation must have only one class of stock outstanding.
- Each stockholder must be entitled, solely by reason of ownership of stock in the corporation, to occupy, for dwelling purposes, an apartment in the building owned by the cooperative corporation.
- No stockholder of the corporation may be entitled to a distribu-

tion not out of earnings and profits, except in complete or partial liquidation of the cooperative corporation.

- Eighty percent or more of the gross income or space of the corporation each year must be derived from the tenant-shareholders, and 90% of the income must go to benefit the shareholders.

In condominiums, owners can deduct the interest they pay on their mortgages and real estate taxes in the same manner as any other homeowner without regard to Section 216.

In addition to federal tax advantages, New York City offers certain tax programs to qualifying buildings. The nature of and qualifications for these programs vary, but are primarily as follows:

421a: This program is for newly constructed buildings and permits a phase-in of real estate taxes either over a 10-year period, or over a 25-year period for designated areas (the tax increase of the newly constructed property is abated for 21 years, and then the full tax is phased in during the subsequent four years). The program is still available in certain areas of the outer boroughs, but not in Manhattan. However, there are many previously qualifying properties in now-excluded areas that are still in their phase-in periods.

J-51: This program is for buildings undergoing substantial rehabilitation. The program provides for an abatement of real estate taxes for a certain term, and then an exclusion from additional taxes for an additional term based on the change in property use and the level of improvement. The level of adjustment is determined by a formula set by the city, which changes from time to time. The program is still available in certain areas of the outer boroughs, but not in Manhattan. However, there are many previously qualifying properties in now-excluded areas that are still in their phase-in periods.

In the prospectus, a tax opinion letter, prepared by a tax expert or attorney, must define the rights of each co-op tenant-shareholder to the benefits prescribed by Section 216 of the Internal Revenue Code, as well as any benefits associated with state tax programs. For condominiums, the tax opinion letter describes the tax features specific to condominium ownership.

Engineer's Report

An engineer must evaluate the condition of the building and issue a certified engineer's report, in which all physical aspects of the building are commented on and any building code violations specifically identified. It is not necessary for the sponsor to correct any of the reported deficiencies unless they are extremely serious. Rather, the report must provide full disclosure. In addition, the engineer must estimate the cost of correcting any identified problems.

In a building converting from rental to ownership, the tenants will often hire their own engineer, whose findings may vary significantly from those of the sponsor's engineer. Each report is likely to differ on the nature of defects and the appropriate remedies, usually reflecting the bias of the party it represents. When two reports are prepared, the attorney general may require that both be presented in the offering plan.

Although the engineer's report is extremely important in the conversion process, its usefulness is of limited duration, since the evaluation reflects the condition of the property only at the time of inspection. Repairs and/or additional defects could have occurred since the date of the report. Generally a report that is more than five years old is considered obsolete. If the report is less than five years old, it should be evaluated in conjunction with other documents, such as the minutes of the board meetings and the financial statements of the co-op or condo, which would outline changes since the engineer's report was generated.

Identification of the Parties

The attorney general requires that the party initiating the offering plan, the sponsor, be clearly identified. This identification must include the individuals, owners, partners and material investors who are the responsible parties. In addition, the experience of these parties in performing conversions and/or other real estate experience must be disclosed. The identification of these parties is material, because if there are complaints or lawsuits, those responsible will not be able to hide behind a veil of corporate anonymity.

Financing and Lease Arrangements

The nature of the underlying financing on the property must be fully disclosed in the section regarding financing arrangements. This includes the name of the financing institution as well as the terms of all mortgages — the monthly payment amount, the interest rate and the maturity date. If there is a land lease on the property, the name of the owner of the land must be disclosed along with the terms of the lease, including the amount of the monthly payment, any renewal or purchase options and the maturity date. Normally the attorney general's office does not accept land leases for filing if the term is less than 50 years. In addition, the mortgage should have a minimum term of five years.

Rights of Tenants in Occupancy

Tenants who live in a building in the process of conversion to cooperative ownership are normally offered special inducements to purchase their apartments. These tenant rights are defined by tenant class — rent-controlled, rent-stabilized or uncontrolled free-market — and each class is provided with its own unique terms and conditions.

Rights Under a Proprietary Lease or Unit Deed

Rights and Obligations of the Landlord

After the date of conversion, the cooperative corporation effectively becomes the landlord/lessor, and the board of directors represents its interests. The board has the right to set rent (referred to as maintenance), to ascertain the cash requirements of the building, to levy assessments and to issue additional shares when appropriate. The cooperative corporation is also responsible for maintaining the common areas of the building and common services, including elevators, heating, common lighting, hot and cold water and air-conditioning (if there is central air-conditioning), and for the hiring and supervision of building employees, including the selection of a managing agent. It is also responsible for maintaining any standard building equipment: gas, steam, water or other types of pipes or conduits within the walls, ceilings or floors, as well as air-conditioning and heating equipment for the building.

Rights and Obligations of Tenant-Shareholders and Unit Owners

Owners of cooperative apartments are called *tenant-shareholders*, while in condominiums they are called *unit owners.* They have the right to reside in their designated apartments and must pay maintenance or common charges on a periodic basis, usually monthly. They may not transfer their interest or sublet their apartments without the consent of the board of directors, or without obtaining a right-of-first-refusal waiver from the condominium.

Tenant-shareholders and unit owners are responsible for the interior of their apartments, including the maintenance, repair and replacement of plumbing, gas and heating fixtures and appliances. They are also responsible for exposed gas, steam and water pipes extending from the wall to the fixtures, and any special pipes or equipment they may place in the walls, ceilings or floors. Tenant-shareholders and unit owners must also maintain, repair and replace electrical circuits, fixtures and appliances running from the junction box at the riser through the apartment, including meters, fuse boxes and circuit breakers.

Bylaws

Bylaws are the basic rules by which a cooperative corporation or condominium association operates. They specify the number of members on the board of directors, the nature of the officers and their duties, and the manner in which they are elected. Furthermore, the bylaws define the requirements of the annual shareholders' meeting and the voting rights of each owner. They also set forth the corporate responsibilities of the co-op.

House Rules

Almost every cooperative or condominium has rules that govern acceptable practices and behavior of owners and guests. These *house rules* cover a broad array of subjects, including limitations on pets, permitted times for construction, and behavior and decorum in the building's common areas.

CHAPTER 8

Qualifying for a Mortgage

A bank lending money has two objectives: to earn a return on its investment and to get its money back on time. Guidelines for qualifying for a loan are directed toward protecting lenders against defaults and, when defaults occur, ensuring that the invested money can be recouped. These guidelines fall into three categories:

1. Your income, as expressed by your housing cost ratio.
2. Your assets, as expressed by the amount of your down payment, including closing costs and reserves.
3. Your credit, as expressed by your credit score.

The amount of the loan you can get and the rate you are charged are based on the bank's evaluation of all three components. If you are strong in one component it can offset weakness in another.

Qualifying Rules

Debt-to-Income Ratio

If a bank made a loan such that repayment ate up 100% of the borrower's yearly income, he or she would certainly default. Obviously, no bank would do this. Generally the *housing cost ratio* (also known as the debt-to-income ratio) rule that lenders use is that the cost of carrying all your debt, including your housing cost, should not exceed 45% of your income. Housing cost is defined as follows:

Single-family home: Debt service (regular payment of interest and principal on the borrowed funds), real estate taxes and adequate property and casualty insurance.

Condominium: Debt service, common charges and real estate taxes.

Cooperative: Debt service and maintenance payments.

Normally, bank mortgages require that a portion of the original loan be returned with each payment for the duration of the loan. For a variable-rate loan or a 30-year fixed-rate loan, the monthly payment will completely repay the original amount in 30 years. In the case of a 15-year fixed-rate loan, the loan will be entirely repaid in 15 years. Loans with a repayment schedule are called *amortizing* loans, and the amount of interest plus the loan repayment portion is called the *debt service* payment. A loan that has no principal repayment schedule (i.e., no amortization) is an interest-only loan, often called a *standing mortgage*.

The table on page 136 shows the debt service payment per $1,000 for differing rates of interest on a standard 30-year amortizing loan. Using this table, you can figure out the size of a mortgage a bank would give you based on your income at the prevailing rate of interest. If you apply for a variable-rate loan, the bank will often qualify you at their fixed-rate level even though your starting rate will be lower. There are certain cases, though, in which selected banks will apply the lower starting rate though their interest rate is generally slightly higher. It is also common for many mortgage brokers and banks to provide mortgage calculators on their websites that permit you to identify the various products they offer and their current interest rates.

Example of Loan Application: Single-Family Home

Ian Byrnes has an income of $100,000. He intends to purchase a home for $800,000 and apply for a 30-year fixed-rate mortgage of $600,000. The interest rate on the loan is 5%. By looking at page 136, he determines that he will pay a total of $64.44 per $1,000 of loan per year. This equals $38,664 per year ($30,000 interest plus $8,664 principal repayment). In percentage terms, this is 5% interest plus 1.444% principal amortization. In addition, Mr. Byrnes must pay real estate taxes of $5,000 per year on his new home. The bank requires that he insure the house, which will cost approximately $1,000 per year. We can now analyze whether or not Mr. Byrnes is likely to get his desired mortgage:

Debt service	$	38,664
Real estate taxes *plus*	$	5,000
Insurance *plus*	$	1,000
Total housing cost *equals*	$	44,664
Gross income *divided by*	$	100,000
Total housing cost percent *equals*		44.66%

This is 44.66% of Mr. Byrnes's gross income, which is within the 45% back-end ratio requirement. However, if Mr. Byrnes has other debt that he must pay, this will increase the ratio and he may not qualify. For example, say Mr. Byrnes has a car and makes a monthly payment of $300 for his auto loan ($3,600 per year). This would make his back-end ratio rise to $48,264, which is 48.26%, and he would not qualify for his mortgage.

Example of Loan Application: Condominium Apartment

Janet Rodriguez wants to buy a condominium. Her gross income is $150,000. The price of the apartment is $800,000. She intends to invest $212,500 and obtain a loan for $587,500. The common charges on the condominium are $850 per month, or $10,200 per year. The real estate taxes are $500 per month, or $6,000 per year. The interest rate is 5% on a fixed-rate 30-year amortizing loan. By looking at page 136, she determines that the interest rate factor is $64.44 per $1,000 of loan per year, which yields a total of $37,859 per year. Thus, she can figure out her annual housing cost as follows:

Debt service	$	37,859
Common charges *plus*	$	10,200
Real estate taxes *plus*	$	6,000
Total housing cost *equals*	$	54,059
Gross income *divided by*	$	150,000
Total housing cost percent *equals*		36.04%

Since her total housing cost is 36% of her $150,000 income, she is qualified to buy the home. If Ms. Rodriguez had a charge card that she was paying off at $300 per month ($3,600 per year), as well as a consumer loan of $200 per month ($2,400 per year) and an auto loan of $450 per month ($5,400 per year), her total loans would be as follows:

Debt service		$	37,859
Common charges	plus	$	10,200
Real estate taxes	plus	$	6,000
Credit card	plus	$	3,600
Consumer loan	plus	$	2,400
Auto loan	plus	$	5,400
Total housing cost and debt	equals	$	65,459
Gross income	divided by	$	150,000
Total housing cost percent	equals		43.64%

This is still less than 45% of her income, so she would still be qualified to get the loan.

Example of Loan Application: Cooperative Apartment

Matthew and Suzanne Smith have a combined gross income of $150,000 and wish to buy a cooperative apartment for $1,000,000. The minimum cash down payment required by the board of directors of the cooperative corporation is 25%, or $250,000. They have applied for a 30-year amortizing loan at 5% for $750,000. Accordingly, by looking at page 136, they determine that their yearly debt service payment would be $48,330. They also have a vacation home that has a monthly mortgage payment of $1,800 per month ($21,600 per year), and an auto loan of $250 per month ($3,000 per year). They have no other monthly debts. The maintenance on the apartment is $1,600 per month ($19,200 per year). We can calculate their housing cost as follows:

Debt service		$	48,330
Maintenance	plus	$	19,200
Vacation home	plus	$	21,600
Auto loan	plus	$	3,000
Total housing cost and debt	equals	$	92,130
Gross income	divided by	$	150,000
Total housing cost percent	equals		61.42%

Since the Smiths have a combined gross income of $150,000, their housing cost would be 61.42% of their gross income. This ratio is too high and the Smiths would be denied their loan.

Debt-to-Equity Ratios

Debt/equity ratio rule: While banks will typically lend up to 80% of the value of an apartment (or 90% through their heavy-leverage loan programs, involving mortgage insurance, a higher interest rate and high up-front fees), most co-op boards allow a maximum debt-to-equity ratio of 75%/25% (i.e., 75% debt and 25% equity). A higher debt-to-equity ratio can be used in purchasing a house or a condominium.

A lender will want to lend less than 100% of the value of the collateral (the home or apartment) when issuing a mortgage. There are a number of reasons for this.

Personal loss: The bank perceives that if a borrower invests money along with the lender, the borrower will have a greater interest in maintaining the property because his or her own funds can be lost. Meanwhile, if the borrower has no personal investment and things go wrong, the borrower can theoretically abandon the home without taking a loss.

Foreclosure costs: When a borrower defaults on a loan and the lender must foreclose, there are costs associated with obtaining control of the property. These include legal fees, real estate tax arrears (which always take precedence over the defaulted mortgage) and the lost income in unpaid interest after the point of default. The lender needs enough cushion in the asset value that, in the event of a foreclosure, the eventual resale value will pay for all these costs as well as for the loan principal.

Market risk: Borrowers often default when the economy is bad, which is usually also a time of declining property values. By requiring that the borrower have a substantial equity investment, the lender creates a cushion. If the value of the property declines, the owner's equity will be wiped out before the lender's invested amount is affected.

Distressed-sale price: Foreclosure sales are frequently distressed sales, which often result in bargain prices. If a borrower has an investment in the property, the transaction loss is first borne by him or her, and not by the lender.

Example of Debt-to-Equity Ratios

Bill Arnold is thinking about buying a cooperative apartment for $1,000,000. He has a yearly income of $500,000, but only $100,000 in cash. He would be able to obtain a loan for this apartment even with his low cash down payment, because it meets the bank's minimum requirement of 10%. However, it is unlikely that he will be approved by the board of directors, since most co-ops have a minimum cash requirement of 25%.

Understanding Heavy Leverage

90% Financing Transactions

In the case of a condo or a single-family home, financing programs offering 90% debt and 10% equity are readily available. These are called *heavy-leverage* or *deep-leverage* loans. The interest rate on such heavily leveraged loans is usually about 0.5% above the interest rate on conventionally financed condo mortgages. Typically, under Fannie Mae rules, there is a maximum mortgage of $417,000, although in some cases a loan can be obtained of up to $645,300 if the borrower has strong credit and the property is viewed by the bank as a higher-quality asset. In issuing heavy-leverage loans, the lender normally obtains mortgage insurance from an insurance company for the excess over the conventional 8% ceiling. Therefore, extra leverage ends up being extremely expensive money, as the following example illustrates.

Consider two $100,000 loans. One has a conventional 80% debt-to-equity ratio and an interest rate of 5%. The other has a 90% heavy-leverage debt-to-equity ratio and a 5.5% interest rate. The breakdown of costs for each of these loans is as follows:

	80% Conventional	90% Heavy Leverage
Purchase price	$ 100,000	$ 100,000
Mortgage amount	$ 80,000	$ 90,000
Private mortgage insurance (PMI) "points"	$ 5,000	
Interest rate	5%	5.5%
Yearly cost (page 136)	$ 5,155	$ 6,019

Difference in yearly cost = $864

Applicable interest rate on additional $10,000 loan = 8.64%

Therefore, the additional $10,000 costs 72.8% more (8.64% versus 5%) than conventionally borrowed funds.

In some cases, particularly for single-family residences, banks offer *piggyback loans* that consist of a conventional loan of 80% and a secondary loan of 10% structured as a home equity loan. The use of a piggyback arrangement can eliminate the need for mortgage insurance.

Understanding Mortgage Associations

Historical Development

At the turn of the century, mortgages were provided by local banks, which got their funds from their communities and surrounding regions. Unfortunately, this resulted in an uneven distribution of capital. Some regions had ample capital, while others had qualified borrowers unable to obtain loans because of a shortage of bank funds. As a result of this inequitable distribution of money, in the 1930s Congress passed legislation forming a number of mortgage associations under government control and direction. The Federal National Mortgage Association (Fannie Mae) was one. The Federal Home Loan Mortgage Corporation (Freddie Mac) was another. The purpose of these associations was to provide single-family-home financing nationwide by developing consistent criteria and creating a national market for mortgage securities.

For years these two associations were independent corporations acquiring mortgages from banks and selling them to the markets with implicit guarantees from the federal government. However, the recession of 2008 created enormous losses for these entities as a result of the dramatic decline in the real estate values, excessive lending risks and the volatility of the mortgage market. Today they have both been taken over by the United States government, which seeks to maintain stable markets for homeowners in an otherwise uncertain environment. Generally banks still continue to place qualifying loans with either Fannie Mae or Freddie Mac. (The underlying guidelines of these two organizations are similar, so for convenience, bankers and mortgage brokers refer to the guidelines of both entities as *Fannie Mae guidelines*.)

There has also been a bifurcation of lenders since 2008. Larger banks are primarily focused on conforming to Fannie Mae guidelines and are selling a substantial portion of their business to these entities, while smaller regional banks seem to be taking a broader position, providing greater flexibility and more liberal terms. These banks are using their own resources to fund loans, or are selling them to other financial institutions directly. They are generally referred to as *portfolio lenders*.

While Fannie Mae/Freddie Mac lending is still predominant, portfolio lenders play an important role in the marketplace today. In light of this variation in approaches, a prospective borrower should strongly consider using the services of a mortgage broker, or search an array of banks offering a range of options to meet your borrower's specific need.

Another increasingly popular loan source is the Federal Housing Authority, or FHA. This government agency offers special programs to first-time homebuyers and those with a need for low-equity investment (as low as 3%). FHA programs are only available for approved condominiums. Unfortunately, FHA processing procedures are cumbersome, and the time to complete the underwriting process and receive financing could be excessive to many buyers.

Fannie Mae Limiting Criteria

Loans today fit into four tiers:

1. **Conforming loans:** Fannie Mae loans for $417,000 or less.

2. **High-balance or agency jumbo:** Fannie Mae loans for between $417,000 and $625,500. The interest rates are approximately 0.25% higher for these loans than for conforming loans.

3. **Jumbo:** Fannie Mae loans ranging from $625,500 to $1,100,000. *Jumbo loans* have interest rates that are 0.25% higher than those of high-balance loans.

4. **Super jumbo:** Loans offered by portfolio lenders that exceed Fannie Mae limits. These normally require up to 20% down for loans of up to $1,500,000, and 35% to 45% down for loans in excess of this amount.

Documentation

A borrower needs to provide a number of pieces of information in a bank application in order to qualify for a loan.

If employed, the most recent of the following:

- Two pay stubs
- Two years of W-2 tax forms
- Two years of tax returns
- Two months of bank statements
- Two months of brokerage statements (if applicable)
- Two months of retirement statements (if applicable)

If self-employed, the most recent of the following:

- Two years of personal tax returns
- Two years of K-1 tax forms
- If the party owns more than 25% of the business, two years of corporate returns
- Year-to-date profit and loss statement on the business
- Two months of bank statements
- Two months of brokerage statements (if applicable)
- Two months of retirement statements (If applicable)

If there are joint borrowers, both parties must submit tax returns. In addition, the bank will request that a building questionnaire be filled out relating to the building's financial affairs and other pertinent matters.

Borrowers Who Own Their Businesses

If a borrower owns 25% or more of a business, a bank will normally require both personal and business tax returns. The bank wants to ensure that the business generates adequate income to provide the personal resources necessary to carry the loan. If there is a question about this matter, it can be resolved by an accountant's letter adequately explaining the sources of the borrower's money. For example, a taxpayer's corporation may display limited taxable income but the borrower may also receive interest, royalties and dividends from the company, which may be the cause of the minimal reported income. The business might also have deductions, such as depreciation, that don't affect the company's cash flow. An accountant's letter explaining this will normally suffice to give the bank proper assurance about granting the loan. In large measure, loans to business owners are heavily geared toward evaluating credit history and assets.

Stated-Income/No-Documentation Loans

There are cases in which an applicant can get a loan without tax returns. Normally the application will merely require that the applicant state his or her income without the bank verifying this figure. Generally the borrower must have a credit score of 740 or better.

However, in some cases a borrower with a low credit score can obtain a loan if he or she can prove that the actual use of credit was satisfactory. Typically the borrower must put down 35% equity, and can only purchase a condominium. In addition, certain levels of wealth to debt are necessary.

Equity Requirements

Most banks require a minimum down payment of 20% at closing for any cooperative loan or condominium loan. If the loan exceeds $1,000,000, it's likely that the bank will insist on a minimum of one third down, unless the borrower has a lending relationship with the bank (which will require that a substantial bank balance be maintained). Loans for sums above $3,000,000 are difficult to obtain without a personal banking relationship. No equity funds may be borrowed. If the borrower is receiving a gift for the down payment, it must be sourced and documented. If the applicant borrows 401(k) retirement funds, Fannie Mae rules do not treat this as a loan and it is acceptable as an equity source. In addition to the down payment, the borrower must also prove sufficient funds for covering all closing costs, and must have free reserves equal to two to 24 months of the monthly housing cost, depending on the size of the loan.

Back-End Rules for Housing Cost Coverage and Credit Scores

One consideration in obtaining a loan is the ratio of the owner's monthly cost of ownership to his or her income (debt-to-income ratio). This rule historically provided that the minimum ratio was 30%, called the front-end ratio. However, banks quickly realized that this was insufficient. Borrowers with debt from second homes, personal loans, credit cards and credit lines, auto loans and other sources could easily find themselves in trouble even if the lending ratio on the purchase appeared favorable. Thus, banks now focus on the back-end ratio, which subtracts all debt carried by the borrower to determine whether the applicant qualifies for the loan. The back-end ratio used by banks is that no more than 45% of your income can be utilized for any debt you may have, including the cost of carrying your home.

Credit Scores

All banks now use FICO credit scoring as the third major element in evaluating an applicant for a mortgage. The complicated scoring system is based on an algorithm that incorporates over 150 variables. The report normally generates three separate scores from three different reporting agencies: Experian, TransUnion and Equifax. Each has a different formula that will generate slightly different results. Fundamentally, your credit score is derived from your payment history, your utilization of credit lines and any public records that display liens and encumbrances on your name.

For a good credit score, a borrower's credit history should be clear of delinquencies for the prior 24 months. In utilizing credit, it is recommended that if you have multiple credit cards, you use no more than 50% of the available credit on each card for the preceding 90 days. It is better to distribute your use of credit cards, rather than concentrate on one card and risk exceeding the 50% threshold while the other cards are underutilized.

Credit card companies grade cardholders using an eight-tier system that rewards timely payments and penalizes tardy payers. It is important to maintain a good payment history, so that your grade is at a high level. A payment score of 740 or better is A-rated credit, offering the applicant the best rates available by the bank. A credit score below 640 is considered a high-risk level, at which a loan will be more expensive or unavailable. An applicant can quickly determine his or her credit score by visiting a website like annualcreditreport.com. If you have a low score, there are ways to improve it using various credit services. These can be identified by a mortgage broker.

Ownership Concentrations

New Condominiums

Fannie Mae guidelines define new condos as properties existing for two years or less from the date of first occupancy. The general rule is that 70% of the apartments must be in contract for sale by buyers who intend to use the property as their principal or second home. However, a waiver is available to reduce the requirement to 50% after a review process undertaken by Fannie Mae. For a buyer seeking to purchase an apartment in a condo where the minimum threshold has not been met, the loan must be obtained from a portfolio lender and the rate of interest will be slightly higher.

Established Condominiums

Fannie Mae guidelines define established condos as any building in existence for more than two years, and in which 90% of the apartments are sold to purchasers who are using them as a primary residence or a second home. If this threshold is not met, the building will require a building waiver, which involves a full review of all building documents consisting of two years of financial statements, insurance policies, the current budget and a building questionnaire. If the investor concentration in the building exceeds 10%, the building will not qualify for Fannie Mae lending, and a portfolio lender must be used unless a waiver is granted.

Cooperatives

Cooperative buildings must be at least 51% sold and owner-occupied. It is possible to obtain a waiver if this threshold is not met, provided the co-op building meets all other Fannie Mae guidelines.

In the past, banks were indifferent to the affairs of the building in which a borrower was making a purchase. This is no longer the case. Banks have become acutely aware that the financial health of the building is intimately connected to an apartment's value. A great concern centers on the heightened level of risk associated with a high concentration of investor ownership. This has been defined as a situation in which 10% or more of the building's apartments are investor-owned. Banks are concerned that such a large concentration of investors might exert influence over the building's affairs. Banks are also anxious that if an investor with a large ownership position has financial difficulties or defaults, the impact on the financial health of the entire building could be substantial.

Another bank concern focuses on new construction. In these cases, banks are unwilling to lend if the sponsor or developer's ownership position exceeds 30%, though in some cases, with a special waiver, this can rise to 50%. The biggest reason for their hesitancy is the uncertainty surrounding the ability of the sponsor or developer to sell the remaining apartments. If the sponsor fails to meet his financial obligations, it can create significant exposure for existing owners. There are numerous stories of newly constructed buildings whose sponsors left the unit owners high and dry without covering maintenance costs on the remaining unsold apartments, or used the building's funds or resources to complete or renovate the sponsor's own apartments. This can place a significant financial burden on the other unit owners to cover the cost of operations.

10% Capital Improvement Fund Replenishment

Historically, cooperatives and condominiums have accumulated funds in order to maintain the physical condition of the building over time. However, it has often been the case that the amount accumulated has been insufficient to actually accomplish its intended purpose. Thus, it is common that additional funds must be collected through assessments. These assessments have proven to be of great concern to banks, since they are not predictable and are not considered in evaluating the borrower for a loan unless the assessment has been previously announced or is being paid at the time of the appraisal. In order for building finances to more accurately reflect the true nature of the long-term cost of running a property, banks are now requiring that buildings allocate 10% of yearly maintenance collections for their reserve/capital replacement funds (although exceptions are made for buildings that have large reserve funds already in place).

This new allocation requirement has created a number of significant issues for buildings, particularly because most typically seek to increase their reserves by about 3% a year on average. If a building does not have an adequate reserve fund in place and has been utilizing this lower figure, it may be compelled to increase maintenance or common charges to accommodate the bank's lending requirement. An adequate reserve fund should consist of at least $5,000 per apartment in the building.

There are certain steps a building can take in order to alleviate this financial burden. Banks will accept a professional evaluation of a building's condition that more accurately portrays its level of obsolescence, and have been willing to adjust the 10% requirement upon an indication that a lesser sum would be adequate to address the building's needs.

The positive side of this new requirement is that buyers will be able to evaluate the ongoing costs of ownership more accurately, since there will be a reasonable assurance that the necessary amount to cover operating costs and future improvements is being regularly collected.

Blacklisted Buildings

Fannie Mae guidelines now require that banks review the cooperative or condominium building of interest as an additional prerequisite for offering a loan to a prospective buyer. A full building review consists of the following:

- Completion of a building questionnaire
- Two years of audited statements or two years of tax returns
- The current budget for the building
- The building's insurance certificate

It is now common for managing agents to fill out a building questionnaire as a condition to a prospective buyer getting an apartment loan. If the bank learns that there are adverse conditions, it will not only deny the borrower a loan, but also blacklist the building for anyone else. The following are reasons that a building may be blacklisted:

Land leases: If the lease term on the building is shorter than the term of the apartment loan, then the loan is unlikely to be approved.

Litigation: If a building has onerous litigation, it can impair its ability to secure financing at the apartment level.

Unusually high homeowner arrears: When the amount of maintenance or common charges owed to the building exceeds 15% of the monthly collected rent, the bank will normally refuse to lend on the building.

Unacceptable insurance: Banks will only lend on buildings that maintain adequate insurance to cover the replacement cost of the property, and will insist that the insurance provider be at least A-rated. If applicable, the bank will also require adequate flood insurance and fidelity coverage equal to 25% of total revenue collected by the building. In addition, the building cannot have an insurance deductible greater than $25,000.

Excess commercial use: If non-homeowner commercial sources account for more than 20% of the building income or footage, a bank normally will not lend on the property.

Building code violations: If there are material building code violations, a bank will insist that these be remedied prior to lending on the property.

Mechanics' liens and property encumbrances: If there is a material delinquency in meeting building obligations — for instance, mechanics' liens, real estate tax delinquencies or recorded judgments — a bank will normally refuse to lend on the property.

Negative cash flow: A building that has a negative cash flow equal to or exceeding 5% of its revenue for two years will not qualify for Fannie Mae lending until the building can present a financial statement showing positive cash flow.

This is only a partial list of items that banks have used as reasons to deny loans on a property. In many instances it is a subjective evaluation. Suffice it to say that banks and mortgage brokers have regularly advised real estate brokers to call them about pending deals prior to the buyer signing a contract, in order to make sure that the building being considered is on the "approved" list. In the event that a bank denies an applicant a loan based on building conditions, the borrower should apply to a portfolio lender to get financing.

Investor Loans

Few lenders will provide an investor loan on a cooperative apartment, even if there is no board approval requirement and the owner has the right to rent. Investors are still regularly able to obtain financing on condominiums, but the terms have become more conservative. Fannie Mae investor loans will only be offered in amounts of up to $625,000, and for loans above $417,000, Fannie Mae will require a minimum cash investment of 40%. In addition, in order to qualify for an investor loan, the applicant must be able to prove a prior history of collecting rental income. For any financing above $417,000, a borrower can do better with a portfolio lender, where the cash equity requirement is generally a minimum of 35%.

Banks typically will not permit a second mortgage on the property, so you can't rely on the seller or private sources to supplement the bank's loan proceeds in order to reduce your invested capital. In addition, banks are anxious to ensure that the rent being collected on the property is more than sufficient to cover the full cost of ownership, including common charges, real estate taxes and monthly loan debt payments. If this cannot be done, then the investor must contribute a larger level of equity.

Normally, investor loans are issued at an interest rate premium of 0.05% to 1.5% over the home-owner rate. The difference depends on the nature of the property, the financial strength of the investor and his or her banking relationship.

Heavy-Leverage Loans (90% Financing)

There still is a market for borrowers looking to obtain 90% financing on the purchase of condominium apartments (not co-ops). This financing is accessible by obtaining *private mortgage insurance*. The borrower must thus engage in the dual arrangement of obtaining a loan from the bank, and securing insurance protecting the bank's position for any amount borrowed above conventional lending limits. The cost of this insurance adds 5 to 6 points at the time of closing in order to prepay the first year's insurance premium. Thereafter, the borrower will have to pay approximately 0.5% more on a monthly basis for the following year's insurance premium. Many banks will agree to include the first year's premium as an add-on to the loan principal, but the borrower must have a strong credit score and be able to adequately cover the loan payment based on back-end ratio rules. Qualifying for private mortgage insurance is often more difficult than qualifying for the underlying loan.

The Federal Housing Administration has become a new source for low-equity loans, but at the current time their procedures are fairly onerous, and banks and mortgage brokers have used them hesitantly. However, most of them believe that the FHA will be an increasingly important lending source for condominium purchases in the future, particularly for first-time homebuyers.

Buying Down the Rate

A bank makes a profit on a mortgage by charging points and fees when the loan is issued. It also makes money on the *interest rate spread*, which is the difference between the retail interest rate, paid by the borrower, and the wholesale interest rate, which is an additional profit to the bank when the loan is sold in bulk to Wall Street buyers. For example, if wholesalers demand a 5% rate from the bank, the bank may charge you 6% and make a profit from the difference. A borrower can usually lower the interest rate on his or her loan by offering additional upfront points to the bank. The rule of thumb is that a payment of one additional point will result in an interest rate reduction of 0.25%.

For example, Mr. Solomon is taking out a loan for $100,000, which is being offered at 6% interest with one point (which is equal to 1%). He will have to pay $1,000, one point, at the time the loan is issued and will have a yearly debt cost of $7,200 (page 136). If he increases the amount he pays upfront by three points, to $4,000, the interest rate on his loan will be reduced by 0.75% to 5.25%. His yearly debt payment cost will be lowered to $6,384.

Appraisals

In order for a home to receive a loan, a bank will normally require that an independent party evaluate the property to ensure its worth. These *appraisers* will normally inspect the property and perform an evaluation of comparable properties that have sold within the last 90 days as a basis for determining the market value. In the past, appraisers were selected by the borrower from an approved list provided by the bank. However, as a result of instances of abuse, this procedure has changed, and now banks form *appraisal pools* consisting of appraisers who participate in a bidding program to perform property appraisals for the bank. This sometimes results in appraisers being selected who are not intimately aware of values in a selected neighborhood, and brokers occasionally find that the determination of value by the appraiser is inconsistent with their own conclusions. It is therefore important that the broker accumulate comparative properties to give to the appraiser at the earliest possible time. The appraiser is usually willing to look at all information supporting value, and is often anxious for the broker's input.

A borrower should also be aware that since the appraiser is now selected by the bank, the appraisal can only be used by that lender. If another application is placed with another bank, a separate appraisal and a separate appraisal fee will be required.

Interest-Only Loans

Interest-only loans are now available at some banks based on adjustable-rate products, and to a limited degree on fixed-rate products. These generally have an interest rate that is approximately 0.125% higher than that of a fully amortizing loan. The benefit of this loan is that the payment is lower, since you are not paying any principal reduction, and your tax deduction in most cases is the full amount of your payment. On the negative side, the loan is never extinguished.

This is a favorable choice if:

- Your time horizon is short-term.
- You have high fluctuations in your income. You can make a minimal payment as required, and as you gain substantial cash infusions from bonuses or elsewhere, you can elect to pay down the loan. Each time the loan is paid down, the interest charge and succeeding monthly payments are correspondingly reduced.

12 MAT Index Loans

12 MAT Index loans are appealing to buyers who wish to borrow large sums for their purchase and seek the greatest flexibility and lowest possible monthly payment. 12 MAT stands for *12-Month Average Treasury*, and is an index based on a 12-month moving average of United States one-year Treasury rates. Since the measure includes historical experience and therefore lags the market, in a time of rising interest rates it offers a lower payment than a currently adjusting index.

Generally, a margin of 2% to 3% is added to the 12 MAT index to reflect what is referred to as the *fully indexed rate*. Banks normally offer borrowers a fixed introductory one-month to six-month rate, which then converts to a monthly adjustable that is measured against the 12 MAT index. Each month, the borrower can elect to make a payment in one of three ways:

Option 1: A payment consisting of the 12 MAT index rate, plus a sum to fully amortize the loan balance over 30 years. The difference between the minimum payment and the fully indexed rate is then added as *negative amortization* to the outstanding loan.

Option 2: An interest-only payment, which is based on the fully indexed rate.

Option 3: A full payment, consisting of interest at the fully indexed rate and a principal payment to amortize the loan balance over 30 years.

For example, at the time of this writing, the 12 MAT index is 1.23%. Given existing loan programs, a borrower can expect a margin of about 2.77%, which would result in a fully indexed rate of 4%. The borrower can currently obtain an introductory rate for the first month at 1.5%, or for six months at 1.75%. Thereafter, subsequent monthly payments would conform to the 12 MAT index and would vary each month.

Assume that $1,000,000 is borrowed and that the rate increases by 0.02% in the first month after the introductory period.

Given these facts, if the borrower chooses Option 1 after the introductory period, the monthly payment he or she would make is $3,332.52. This consists of $1,041.67 in interest (which is based on the new 12 MAT index of 1.25% and represents a 0.02% rise after the initial period as noted in the example) and $2,290.85 for principal amortization. Even though the payment was initially computed with principal amortization, the bank will redefine the payment as all interest. The difference between the fully indexed rate of 4.2% and this amount is $167.40, which will be treated as negative amortization and added to the loan balance.

If the borrower decides to pay using Option 2, which is interest only, he or she would pay only the fully indexed rate of 4.2%, which computes to a monthly payment of $3,500.

If the borrower chooses Option 3, the full payment, he or she would add principal amortization in the amount of $1,390.17 to the fully indexed rate, which would total a monthly payment of $4,890.17.

Normally negative amortization accumulated under Option 1 cannot exceed 10% of the original loan for a term of five years before payments against this excess must be made.

Each month the 12 MAT index changes, and the borrower is given a different set of parameters with which to evaluate his or her options.

Negative Pledges

Condominiums generally do not restrict the level of mortgage financing placed on an apartment. However, in a number of cases, condominiums have instituted a *negative pledge*, which alters the condominium bylaws and unit deed to limit the permissible ratio of loan to apartment value. In this case, when an owner seeks to finance a condominium apartment with more than the prescribed debt percentage, the board has the right to foreclose against the owner in order to compel compliance.

Debt Service Payment Table

Your mortgage schedule is the monthly or yearly amount of payment per $1,000 of loan that must be made at varying levels of interest to fully amortize a loan over 30 years. If you wish to convert the figure in the following chart to a percentage, you would move the decimal point three spaces to the left. Thus, an interest rate of 4% gives a monthly interest rate factor of 4.77 and a yearly factor of 5.724, which yields a monthly percentage of 0.00477% and a yearly percentage of 0.05724%. You can then multiply these numbers by the full amount of your loan to get the amount of payment that you will be required to make every month or year, respectively, at the given interest rate.

By going to www.amortization-calc.com, you can input any mortgage principal amount and determine the complete mortgage schedule for your loan.

Debt Service Payment Table — Per Thousand
(to fully amortize a principal balance at a
given rate of interest over a term of 30 years

Interest Rate (%)	Per Month ($)	Per Year ($)
2.00	3.70	44.40
2.25	3.82	45.84
2.50	3.95	47.40
2.75	4.08	48.96
3.00	4.22	50.64
3.25	4.35	52.20
3.50	4.49	53.88
3.75	4.63	55.56
4.00	4.77	57.24
4.25	4.92	59.04
4.50	5.07	60.84
4.75	5.22	62.64
5.00	5.37	64.44
5.25	5.32	63.84
5.50	5.68	68.04
5.75	5.84	70.08
6.00	6.00	72.00
6.25	6.16	73.92
6.50	6.32	75.84
6.75	6.49	77.88
7.00	6.65	79.80
7.25	6.82	81.84
7.50	6.99	83.88
7.75	7.16	85.92
8.00	7.34	88.08
8.25	7.52	90.24
8.50	7.69	92.28
8.75	7.87	94.44

Debt Service Payment Table (Continued)

Interest Rate (%)	Per Month ($)	Per Year ($)
9.00	8.05	96.60
9.25	8.23	98.76
9.50	8.41	100.92
9.75	8.59	103.08
10.00	8.78	105.36
10.25	8.96	107.52
10.50	9.15	109.80
10.75	9.33	111.96
11.00	9.53	114.36
11.25	9.71	116.52
11.50	9.91	118.92
11.75	10.09	121.08
12.00	10.29	123.48

Short Sales

As homeowners have been confronted with the challenge of being unable to meet their mortgage commitments, they have increasingly turned to *short sales* to head off foreclosure. With this increased interest in short sales has come a corresponding rise in misinformation on what short sales are and how they work. Here is a primer of sorts to help you understand the ins and outs of short sales.

What Is a Short Sale?

A short sale occurs when a property sells for a price that is insufficient to pay back the mortgage or mortgages encumbering a property. A property owner must obtain the consent of his or her lender(s) to satisfy the debt for less than the actual amount due. If a short sale arrangement is not agreed to by the lender, the owner must give the bank the difference between the funds provided by the sale and the total amount owed to the bank, which is generally referred to as the *deficiency amount*. Lenders will agree to short sales because they are concerned that they might lose even more money if they foreclose on the borrower. Factors considered by the lender in acquiescing to a short sale include the following:

- Time to foreclose and sell the property compared to the short sale alternative
- Attorney fees and court costs
- Property condition, including damage
- Carrying costs
- Resale transactional costs
- Lowered value of the property

Qualifying for a Short Sale

A precondition for entering into a short sale arrangement is that the owner cannot afford to maintain the property given his current financial state. The mere fact that an owner wants to sell his home quickly to avoid making mortgage payments doesn't qualify.

How Does a Seller Start the Short Sale Process?

Each lender has unique requirements that must be met in order to consider a property for a short sale, and every lender is different. However, in general, the home must be worth less than the amount owed, and the homeowner must be under financial stress. It is very important that the borrower maintain the loan as current. If the loan becomes delinquent, most banks won't consider it for a short sale and will presume it will be going through foreclosure.

What Is the Process to Get Lender Approval for a Short Sale?

The seller, his attorney or his broker negotiates with the loss mitigation, pre-foreclosure or workout department of the bank, not the collection or customer service department. The homeowner must submit an application to the bank; if possible, a proposed or signed contract of sale; an appraisal; a closing statement (preliminary HUD-1); and a personal financial statement to prove hardship.

Most lenders will start the approval process in advance of having a signed contract of sale, which can make the process move more quickly once a buyer is found.

Normally the bank will want the following:

Hardship letter: This letter should focus on describing what happened, how the current situation is being handled and why this situation will not be changing in the near future.

Statement of financial position: A statement of all assets and liabilities at the current time. Some banks may also ask for supporting documentation, such as bank statements, pay stubs and brokerage statements.

Pro forma source and use of funds: The bank must understand what is being done with income received, whether it be salary, dividends or interest.

Real estate broker exclusive agreement: The bank will normally want to approve any exclusive agreement with the broker to ensure that the terms and compensation are acceptable.

Does the Buyer of the Property Have to Know?

Yes. It may take three to six months to negotiate the short sale with the lender. The contract of sale must be subject to all necessary third-party approvals. The sale must occur absolutely as is, because there is no more money to make adjustments at the closing. The buyer may insist on a provision allowing him to get out of the deal if the lender does not approve the sale within a certain period of time, or if the deal doesn't close by a certain date.

After the Short Sale, What Happens to the Seller?

The lender may forgive the portion of the debt not covered by the home sale, or the lender may require the seller to sign a promissory note for the unpaid loan balance. Normally the IRS treats a cancelled debt as taxable income even if the home is a principal residence and if the debt was used to purchase or improve it. The short sale will adversely affect the seller's credit rating by 100 to 180 points (compared to a foreclosure, which reduces the credit score by up to 300 points). It is possible to obtain another mortgage in one to three years.

What About Other Lien Holders, Like a Home Equity Lender?

If other lien holders are being asked to accept less, then they must also approve the short sale. The second mortgage lender usually has to absorb a bigger loss. In addition, if the mortgage has been securitized, the entity that holds the security must approve the short sale. These lien holders are likely to agree because in a foreclosure they will probably get nothing. Real estate taxes, income taxes and transfer taxes cannot be reduced.

Who Pays the Closing Costs?

The seller's closing expenses (including broker's commission) are paid at the closing out of the proceeds of the sale.

How Should Apartments Be Priced?

Apartments being sold through short sales should be priced at close to fair market value. Most lenders are willing to accept a sale price of 20% to 30% below that of comparable properties, though this depends on the nature of the market at any given time.

What Should the Attorney or Real Estate Broker Serving the Seller Do?

The attorney or broker should make sure that the short sale request is credible by determining that the seller is truly in a difficult financial position. A seller who wants to get out of the home just because he or she made a bad investment won't get the bank's cooperation.

The attorney should make sure that the seller prepares all required financial documents, including the hardship letter, as soon as possible.

The attorney or broker should communicate directly with the loss mediation representative at the bank about the property's value. Be accommodating: the more they like you, the more they will help you in the process and let you know where you stand.

Once the broker or attorney advises the bank of his or her opinion of value, don't be surprised if the bank later insists that its appraisal came in at a higher value. Banks are notorious for overstating values in order to motivate the seller and the broker to maximize their efforts. You should do whatever you can to convince the bank that the value is consistent with the evaluation: the more the bank recognizes that a full effort has been made, the better.

The broker or attorney should make sure that the property is properly promoted and advertised for maximum impact. You must ensure that you can show the bank that you made a concerted effort to sell it.

The broker or attorney should forward any offers on the property directly to the bank. If the bank rejects the offer, the seller should be hesitant to proceed.

The attorney should review the hardship letter, the financial information and any related documents that will be evaluated by the bank. The attorney will typically also submit a HUD settlement statement, which specifically identifies all the costs associated with the closing and the net proceeds expected to be received by the bank against its mortgage balance. The contract should have a short provision stating that it is subject to consent by the lender. The settlement statement will also include the broker's fee and the attorney's fee, so that all the parties who are expected to be compensated are specifically identified in the document and paid out of the sale proceeds.

After the contract and related documents are submitted in their entirety to the bank, the bank will hire another appraiser to affirm the value of the property as stated in the contract. If the value is consistent with that expressed in the contract, and if the documents confirming hardship are in order, the bank will issue a decision letter authorizing the short sale.

Conclusion

Short sales can be very arduous to a seller. Banks are notoriously slow in making decisions. Attorneys can also be reticent about engaging in a short sale transaction, because if the seller's request is not accommodated and the deal falls through, the seller may not have money to pay counsel.

On the other hand, a broker can be a critical cog in making short sale mountains move. The broker's role is often an active one: to keep all the parties focused on a successful conclusion.

Foreclosures

When a homeowner fails to make a payment on his mortgage for 90 days, the loan is placed into foreclosure proceedings. Legal papers are normally filed in court for the purpose of gaining legal right to and control over the property. The length of time that it will take the bank to present its case in New York City is probably somewhere between six and nine months.

How Does a Foreclosure Sale Work?

After a judgment is entered, the bank must arrange for the property to be sold on the courthouse steps or a court-designated alternative location. An announcement must be filed and a date specified. At the discretion of the bank, a *minimum upset price*, which is the starting point for the auctioneer, may be set.

If there is a bidding war, the bank has the right to bid up to the full amount of its mortgage. If the value of the property has declined significantly, the bank's bid is often the winner. In instances where the value of the property is greater than the bank's loan, a third party can enter a bid that exceeds the bank's claim and can become the successful bidder. In these cases, it is conceivable that the bidder might be able, depending on the level of attendance at the auction, to achieve a good deal.

What Are the Common Alternatives to Foreclosure?

There are two important points that influence a bank in its decision to proceed with a foreclosure against a property. One is time and the other is expense. While it is necessary for the bank to take all prudent steps it can to protect its interest, it is rare that a bank won't make some attempt to work out payment terms with a borrower.

One common work-out proposal is a reduction in the monthly payment for a limited term, in order to give the borrower breathing room to resolve his affairs. Another is placing the foreclosure proceedings on hold through a stipulation agreement, whereby the owner agrees to sell the property and the bank agrees to forebear any claim above the sale proceeds, or to enter into a payment arrangement for the deficiency after the sale. The property is then sold at the best possible terms through a broker, who often doesn't even know that there has been an arrangement with the bank until the closing takes place.

How Are Foreclosed Properties Disposed of?

In instances where foreclosure has taken place and the bank has taken title to the home, the bank will generally manage the property through its *Real Estate Owned* (REO) department. This department is responsible for evaluating what to do with the property in the context of current market conditions. Often they will either sell the property at market value, or rent the property hoping for a future turnaround in the market.

Can I Use Foreclosure Sales to Make Money?

Many people wonder why there are few opportunities in foreclosure sales in New York compared to other markets, such as Las Vegas and Florida. The difference exists for a couple of reasons.

In depressed markets, the level of foreclosure is so severe that workouts with owners are often unable to provide fruitful results. Additionally, prices in these markets have gone down so severely that lenders do not see another path to resolving their problem, other than to accept bids below the amount of their mortgage in order to bail out of the properties they own.

Unlike Las Vegas or Florida, New York is not perceived as a severely depressed market, and the current level of buyer activity has eliminated the likelihood that foreclosure prices will be meaningful benchmarks for new lows on prices. Accordingly, banks are bidding their full mortgage value at auction and then promoting the sale of these properties through the conventional market.

The approval process in cooperatives and the condominium right-of-first-refusal requirement have largely limited the number of owners who have marginal qualifications, and have increased the level of equity in home purchases. These requirements dramatically reduced the number of homeowners who were at risk when negative economic conditions arose.

The firming, and at times appreciation, in prices over the last few years has satisfied most investors that they still own a viable investment, and has permitted them to obtain rents that are capable of covering their monthly obligations.

The points of greatest risk exposure are the homeowners who purchased properties with high leverage just prior to the recession, as well as owners who had significant financial reversals (such as job loss). Some of these buyers are incapable of supporting their properties, and have limited motivation to protect their assets because their values are less than the mortgages. This results in a high likelihood that the bank will foreclose and auction off the properties for less in order to bail out of these interests. Very few banks are reporting significant amounts of properties in the foreclosure pipeline for Manhattan. However, properties in the outer boroughs are more likely to undergo foreclosure.

Development sites are a second area of concern. A large number of sites have ceased construction due to a soft economy. Properties that were recently completed or are nearly complete are finding that their initial sales projections are not supportable given current demand. Many sponsors are hesitant to make adjustments to their prices for fear that other buyers will seek to renege on their agreements.

There have been a number of lawsuits in which buyers have sought the return of their deposit; so far the outcomes of these lawsuits have been mixed. Thus, sponsors are anxious to give away free amenities and upgrades before they make any price concessions. This creates a phenomenon called the "squeeze and bleed." The "squeeze" is the demand from the bank on the sponsor or developer to start delivering loan paydowns, though he is unable to sell his product; the "bleed" is the continual outflow of mortgage interest and other costs that deplete reserves.

There finally comes a time when the bank sees the handwriting on the wall, and the parties undertake a workout to resolve their difficulties. More often than not the resolution is to convert unsold apartments to rentals. Then, quietly, the developer and the bank seek to market large blocks of apartments at a significant discount to third-party investors.

The New Consumer Financial Protection Bureau

Setting up Guidelines for "Ability to Repay" and Qualified Mortgages

In 2010, Congress passed the Dodd-Frank Wall Street Reform and Consumer Protection Act, generally referred to as Dodd-Frank, in order to address the many issues identified as causes for the recession of 2008. Among other things, this law authorized the formation of the Consumer Financial Protection Bureau (CFPB), whose role is to regulate consumer financial products and services like mortgages and credit cards in order to ensure fairness and transparency. On January 10, 2013, the new CFPB set forth regulations for a new underwriting standard for home lending called a *qualified mortgage*. The purpose of this standard is to ensure that "a creditor [has made] a reasonable and good faith determination based on verified and documented information that the consumer has a reasonable ability to repay the loan according to its terms." In other words, lenders must now meet certain standards of rigor in evaluating loan applicants. If a lender meets these standards, it will be considered compliant and granted legal protection from consumer lawsuits. There are eight factors that the regulations require as minimum underwriting standards:

1. **Current or reasonably expected income or assets:** The lender must verify the income of the applicant, and must document any assets or cash flows that are integral to supporting the loan.

2. **Current employment status:** The lender must verify the employment of the borrower and confirm the wages or other sources of income used to carry the loan.

3. **Monthly property expenses:** The lender must confirm the cost of carrying the home in terms of the common charges and real estate taxes for a condo or the monthly maintenance charge for a co-op. This would include any assessments levied on the unit.

4. **Monthly cost of any simultaneous transaction financing:** If the borrower intends to obtain additional financing from outside sources for the purchase of the property, this additional cost must be included in determining whether the applicant is qualified.

5. **Monthly payment and mortgage-related obligations:** The lender must confirm the amount of interest and principal associated with the proposed loan. This requires basing the loan on a 30-year monthly self-amortizing schedule, or in the case of an adjustable-rate mortgage, on the highest payment rate proposed during the first five years.

6. **Other debt obligations:** The lender must determine the cost of carrying other loans or obligations held by the borrower, including credit cards, lines of credit, alimony and child support.

7. **Monthly debt-to-income ratio or residual income:** The lender must confirm that the borrower has a permissible ratio of debt to income, and that his residual income after paying all monthly

obligations is sufficient to support his lifestyle. The general benchmark for an acceptable debt-to-income ratio is 43% based on the highest cost of the loan during its first five years (as opposed to the current general rule of 45%).

8. **Credit history:** the lender must ensure that the borrower has good credit as evidenced by his or her current credit reports.

Qualifying criteria outlined by the CFPB are in some instances slightly different from the current criteria delineated by Fannie Mae and Freddie Mac for conforming mortgages in their programs, which currently constitute approximately 90% of all home loans. However, there is a strong likelihood that these lending organizations will quickly update their own guidelines to meet these new regulations, which are officially scheduled to go into effect in January 2014.

The CFPB has also proposed restrictions on certain other products and practices, including:

1. **Unconventional loans:** Interest-only loans, reverse mortgages, loans that carry a balloon payment over a limited term or loans with terms of more than 30 years will be discouraged.

2. **Teaser rates:** A mortgage whose interest rate starts low (at what is known as a *teaser rate*) and increases over time will only be qualified if the loan is based on a fully indexed rate without reference to the teaser. The guideline for these loans is its average percentage rate (APR) plus 3.5%.

3. **Points:** Loans cannot have points and fees that exceed 3% of the borrowed amount.

4. **Documentation:** Loans lacking sufficient documentation are not permissible. A borrower who merely represents his income or provides limited verification of his financial worth will not qualify.

The new guidelines are more than 700 pages in length and are burdened with exceptions and conditions that make them challenging to fully appreciate. However, there are a few key takeaways that can be discerned. Assuming they meet the standards set forth by the CFPB, banks now have a mechanism to minimize their exposure to legal action. However, the new rules in no way restrict the ability of banks to make unconventional loans; they only limit the level of legal assurances offered by the government. There still will be lenders offering "creative" products and services without taking advantage of the additional legal protections offered by the CFPB.

Mortgage brokers believe that the new regulations will give comfort to large banks, many of which have been obligated to make major payments to settle lawsuits and claims. Since the regulations are currently only proposals and are not scheduled to take effect until January 10, 2014, additional changes to the rules are expected. One matter that will likely be addressed is the meaning of "residual income," which is not clearly understood in the context of underwriting for a residential loan.

The creation of the CFPB has also given consumers a helpful new mechanism for filing complaints when they believe they have been treated unfairly by a lender. An aggrieved borrower can go to www.consumerfinance.gov and click on *Submit a Complaint* to report improper lending practices.

CHAPTER 9

Putting Together an Effective Board Packet

General Purpose

After the buyer has signed a contract to purchase a cooperative apartment (or a condominium, if there is a right of first refusal), the next important step is to prepare the board packet. The purpose of the board packet is to provide a profile of the buyer for the board of directors, so they can determine whether or not the buyer meets their criteria for admission to the building.

The key qualifications for admission are rarely put in writing. However, certain evaluation procedures are commonly undertaken. The first thing a board looks for is whether or not the prospective buyer is financially qualified to own the apartment. The qualifying rules for a cooperative apartment are frequently far more rigorous than those of a bank. In addition, the board — consciously or not — always screens a potential neighbor for indications of a troublesome personality. Therefore, personal references may carry some weight in the board's decision. Co-op boards usually try to form an overall picture of their prospective neighbor, in order to reassure themselves that the buyer will enhance the building's congeniality and reputation and not be financially detrimental or unpleasant to live with.

Duties of the Broker

Under New York State law, a real estate broker earns his or her commission by finding a ready, willing and able buyer and by being the *procuring cause* in bringing about a meeting of the minds on the material terms of the deal. Even so, the real estate industry generally assumes that the broker's responsibilities also include assisting in the success-ful conclusion of the transaction. To that end, the buyer's broker is expected to do the following:

- Obtain from the buyer and/or assist in compiling all documents necessary for completion of the board packet.
- Monitor, advise and assist in the completion of applications and forms.
- Review and verify all documents, making sure that they are com-plete and correct and that the proper number of copies has been made for distribution to the designated board members.
- Transmit and deliver the completed board packets to the seller's agent or the managing agent in proper form.
- Follow up with the seller's agent or the managing agent and re-solve any open matters or questions that need to be addressed for the completion of the board packet and interview process.

Important Things to Remember When Preparing a Board Packet

In assembling the board packet, it is essential to create an organized, clean presentation. Most brokers will use tab dividers or colored pages to separate sections. The following guidelines should be adhered to:

- Include a transmittal cover sheet.
- In most cases, particularly for "image" buildings, applications should be typed and submitted in folders. At the very least, ap-plications should be printed neatly.
- Liquid assets should be fully verified. The verifications should be presented in the order they appear on the balance sheet.
- All tax returns (including schedules) should be signed.
- Contracts should be fully executed.
- Reference letters should be typed and presented on business stationery if possible.

- If a guarantor is used, this person must present the same financial disclosure information as the primary applicants.
- If two or more people (other than a married couple) are buying the home, each must submit a separate, complete board package.
- Make sure you read over the directions carefully. The last impression you want to give is that you can't follow instructions.

Board Criteria and Documentation Requirements

In most instances, there are no written rules available about what will or won't be satisfactory to a board. Indeed, the criteria for one buyer might be somewhat different from those required of another. However, the following guidelines, gleaned from experience, may help brokers and buyers define typical issues in given types of buildings and the information that may be required to support the decision-making process.

Income

An **average building** will want applicants to use no more than 30% of their gross income for debt service and maintenance.

A **conservative building** would prefer that applicants use no more than 25% of their gross income for debt service and maintenance.

An **"image" building** would prefer that applicants use a much smaller portion of their income for debt and maintenance — 15% at most.

As a general rule, think of 30% as your guide. In fact, all debt should ideally be limited to 33% of gross income.

Other Important Income-Qualifying Considerations

In addition to the basic income requirements outlined above, there are frequently other considerations that must be addressed:

- Applicants who are paid substantially on commission and who don't have a track record in their field of at least two years are not likely to qualify for a mortgage. In evaluating commission-only applicants, banks and co-op boards will take the average of two or three years' earnings as their guide.

- Some buildings do not consider commissions or bonuses to be reliable income.
- If an applicant's income is below the requirement, he should consider obtaining a guarantor, a co-applicant or a smaller mortgage.

Assets

Liquidity

Liquidity consists of cash and assets that can be converted to cash within 90 days. These would include stocks, bonds, Treasury bills and notes, annuities, the cash value of life insurance and similar financial instruments. Retirement accounts, such as IRA accounts, KEOGH accounts and SEPs, are liquid accounts in some cooperatives and not in others, and the buyer should ascertain the building's policy.

A **lenient building** will normally require liquidity of at least one year's maintenance and debt service after the apartment is purchased.

An **average building** will expect two to three years' debt service and maintenance in liquidity.

A **conservative building** will look for liquidity equal to 50% of the price of the apartment.

An **"image" building** may require liquid assets of two to three times the cost of the apartment.

Asset Verification

The purchaser's obligations are confirmed by a credit report. However, the assets must be verified. You will need to provide the following:

Cash: Generally, copies of the two most recent bank statements for checking accounts, savings accounts, money market funds, etc.

Stocks and bonds: Copies of the broker's monthly statement or copies of the certificates themselves. These should display the balance net of any margin loans on the account.

Controlled corporations: A letter from the corporation's accountant stating the gross payment received by the purchaser for the prior year and the estimated payment to be made to the purchaser for the current year. You will also need a copy of the corporation's last tax return and the corporation's last financial statement, both prepared by a certified public accountant.

Accounts and notes receivable: For an account receivable, a copy of the bill sent to the customer describing the amount due and payment terms. For a note receivable, a copy of the note with the amount and terms of repayment.

Real estate: If there is a mortgage, the credit report will provide proof of ownership by detailing the mortgage encumbrance, but providing a copy of any statements or bills would be desirable. If there is no mortgage, a copy of the real estate tax bill will suffice. If the purchaser is under contract for the sale of any real estate, the contract and status of any existing contractual contingencies should be submitted. If property is leased, a copy of the lease should be provided. If the value of the real estate is crucial to meeting an asset test, then an appraisal of the property should be performed.

Art and collectibles: For art and collectibles of significant value, a current appraisal or a copy of an insurance policy in which these items are identified.

Life insurance (cash value): A copy of the statement from the insurance company showing the current value of the life insurance policy.

Retirement funds/IRA/KEOGH/profit-sharing plans: For each retirement program, a copy of the statement from the administrator of the plan showing the current balance.

Gifts: If all or a portion of the funds used for the down payment is derived from a gift, it is important to provide a gift letter from the donor affirming that the gift is unrestricted.

Liabilities

If you have any loans, you need to provide to the board documentation verifying the amount you owe and the terms for repayment.

Accounts Payable

If you have any bills outstanding that represent material obligations to vendors, you should identify the amount you owe. Normally, these are significant items that relate to services provided to you, such as major medical bills, dental bills and other professional obligations of a substantial amount. You should include the last statement provided by the vendor reflecting the balance due.

Credit Lines

Banks often provide to individuals credit lines that may or not be secured by certain assets. These credit lines offer a stated maximum balance that the borrower may use, and allow flexibility in borrowing and making payments as needed. You should provide the documentation relating to the credit line terms, and well as the last statement indicating the outstanding balance you currently owe.

Credit Cards

Credit cards are personal obligations that must be documented. You should include in your financial information the most recent balance on your last credit card statement, as well as the statement itself. If you have more than one credit card, provide documentation for each one.

Alimony and Child Support

If you are obligated to pay alimony or child support, you should show any court judgments or agreements that express your obligation, as well as proof that you are current in meeting this obligation. The amount of the obligation you should show is either the bulk payment amount stipulated on the alimony and child support agreement, or the monthly amount you owe for the current year separated from the amount you will owe in subsequent years.

Mortgages

Mortgage obligations relating to vacation properties and personally owned investment properties should be disclosed. You should include your last bill listing the principal amount, or your mortgage note. If there is income on the property, you should show the income net of the mortgage and monthly obligations.

Notes Payable

There are two types of notes that are important for a board packet: bank notes and personal notes. Bank notes are short- or long-term loans for a stated amount, and should be included in the board packet along with the latest monthly statement. For long-term notes (i.e., longer than one year), you should break out the monthly amount owed for the current year from the sum of the loan. Personal notes of a stated term longer than one year should also be included, with the regular payment amount clearly identified. If the personal loan has no regular payment amount or stated duration, it should be viewed as a current obligation due within the year.

Endorsements and Guarantees

If you have agreed to co-sign or guarantee a loan for another individual, you are potentially subject to a claim for the loan principal and unpaid interest if the primary borrower defaults. This is called a *contingent li-*

ability and must be identified in the board packet along with its terms. Further documentation may be necessary if the amount of the guarantee is large or the presented risk is high.

Other Loans

Certain loans are uncategorized, such as auto loans or leases, chattel agreements or boat loans. The terms of these loans must be identified and the last monthly loan statement provided.

Other Balance Sheet Considerations

If an individual has significant non-liquid assets, this may be a material factor in the board's consideration. Such assets would include a business, a trust fund that provides significant income but whose principal is not available for distribution, and/or assets that are held for investment purposes, such as real estate, art, collectibles or other valuables.

In an "image" building, the board will frequently expect the purchaser to have a net worth in the millions of dollars. If a purchaser's income exceeds the required amount, the board will normally weigh this against a lower-than-desired asset balance.

Cooperative Board Approval
Rights and Limitations

A co-op board has broad rights to reject a prospective applicant. In *Levandusky v. One Fifth Avenue Apartment Corp.* (75 N.Y.2d 530 (1990)), the New York State Court of Appeals overturned an earlier standard requiring a showing of reasonableness and held that the new standard by which a board's decisions will be reviewed is the *business judgment rule.* This rule states that the courts will respect decisions made by a board of directors as long as there is no evidence of bad faith or fraud. The rule also provides that the court need not establish whether the outcome was desirable — only that it was prudent at the time of the decision. The onus is on the plaintiff to prove that proper business judgment was not used.

However, there is one area in which the courts will vigorously protect the rights of prospective buyers and sellers: discrimination. An array of federal, state and local laws provide protection and redress to a broad range of protected classes. No board may discriminate on the basis of race, color, familial status, disability, national origin, religion, sex/gender/gender identity, age (over 18), marital status, military status, sexual orientation, citizenship/alienage, lawful occupation or partnership status.

Rights of Condominium Associations

A condominium is considered real estate, and under law the board is not permitted to impose *restraint of alienation* in the transfer of real estate. However, the condominium can be afforded the right of first refusal, which gives it the right to stand in the shoes of a purchaser and acquire property on the same terms and conditions offered in the contract to the buyer. In evaluating whether to exercise its right of first refusal, the condominium has the right to request information about the buyer in order to ascertain that the buyer meets the appropriate standards desired by the condominium. Normally the right-of-first-refusal requirement has a deadline by which the condominium must exercise or waive this right. This deadline is normally 30 days from the date that all information requested by the condominium board has been provided by the buyer in a satisfactory manner. If the information provided to the board is insufficient, the board can continue to refuse to issue the waiver until all requested information has been received.

On some occasions these information requests can become continuous, thereby creating a challenge for the parties seeking to complete the transaction. While there have been instances in which lawsuits have arisen, the economic costs of pursuing the lawsuit have made the alternative — merely selling the property to another buyer — the seller and buyer's preferred course. Generally a title company will not insure the title and a bank will not close on a loan to a prospective buyer unless a waiver of the right of first refusal has been issued.

CHAPTER 10

Federal and New York State Income Taxation

Regarding the Ownership and Sale of Residential Real Estate (for all tax legislation through 2012)

Disclaimer

The following explanation of federal tax rules regarding the ownership and sale of residential real estate is by no means authoritative. Laws in this field are constantly changing, and the intricacies can be adequately understood only by an expert. This information is intended to be no more than a guideline and should not be relied upon without the advice of a qualified tax professional.

Primary Residence: Treatment of Gain on Sale

Homeownership has always received special treatment in the Internal Revenue Code, and in most instances these benefits are conferred in New York State and City tax codes as well.

Exemption for up to $250,000 in Profit ($500,000 for Married Couples)

If a married couple sells their primary residence, they may exclude up to $500,000 in gain from tax. In the case of an individual, the exemption is $250,000. In order to be eligible, the taxpayer must have owned and occupied the home as a primary residence for at least two of the five years preceding the sale (IRC Sec. 121). However, if you live in the home for less than two years and you meet certain prescribed conditions, including change or cessation of employment, divorce or legal separation, death or multiple births from the same pregnancy, you can allocate the exemption by the fractional portion of time you are there to the two-year required period (Treas. Reg. Sec. 1.121-3).

Example of the Profit Exemption Program

John and Sara Thompson buy their first home for $100,000. Their neighbor is a movie star who wants to expand his apartment by buying theirs. They agree on a price of $600,000, and the deal closes two years after they purchase the home. Since they are married, the profit exemption ceiling is $500,000. All the gain is tax-free. If they decide to buy another home for $600,000 and sell that home after two years of use, all the gain will also be tax-free as long as the sale price is not more than $1,100,000 and they have owned the home for a minimum of two years. The computation of gain is determined based on each transaction. There is no limit to the number of times the exemption can be used.

Definition of Tax Basis in the Sale of a Primary Residence

A profit on the sale of a personal residence qualifies for *capital gains* treatment, though a loss does not qualify as a deductible loss, whether capital or ordinary (IRC Sec. 165). The tax basis is the cost of the property, plus the itemized costs defined as follows:

1. Any permanent improvement that extends or enhances the useful life of the property by more than one year is a capital improvement and can be added to the cost of the home for determining its tax basis (IRC Sec. 1016). This would include any assessment levied on the owner by the cooperative or condominium where the funds are used for a capital improvement to the building.

2. Any costs incurred in effectuating the purchase of the home, such as title insurance, legal expenses, appraisal fees, lead-testing fees, deed-recording costs, tax stamps and transfer fees are not currently deductible but must be added to the property basis (Treas. Reg. Sec. 1.263(a)-2, 1.1012-1(a)). Thus, they can be subtracted from the profit earned on the eventual sale of the

property, but not on the tax return for the year the expenditure was incurred. This does not include costs associated with obtaining a mortgage, which are discussed below.

Any other personal property is treated as a personal, living or family expense, and is not a capital asset entitled to capital-gains recognition (IRC Sec. 165(c), 165(f); Treas. Reg. Sec. 1.165-9(a), 1.262-1(b)(4)).

Example of Tax Basis Application in the Sale of a Personal Residence

Mary Gold is single. She purchases a home for $100,000. At that time she pays a lawyer $1,000 and incurs other transfer costs of $500. Five years later she makes significant improvements to the home, costing $75,000, and makes sure to maintain adequate records of the cost of these improvements. In addition, Ms. Gold purchases furnishings that cost her $50,000. She then sells her home for $250,000, and the purchaser buys her furnishings as well for $25,000. Therefore, she receives a total of $275,000.

The tax basis of Ms. Gold's home consists of the original cost of $100,000, the $1,500 in direct costs to effectuate that purchase, and the $75,000 in permanent improvements she made, for a total of $176,500. The furnishings are not permanent improvements, and are not part of the tax basis. Accordingly, the profit on the sale is $73,500. This gain is exempt from tax because the profit is less than $250,000 and Ms. Gold lived in the home for more than two years.

Tax law provides no cost basis for furnishings during the period of ownership, since furnishings are normally considered a personal, family or living expense (IRC Sec. 262). However, on the date the furnishings were sold, they became property converted to an asset held for the production of income. The Internal Revenue Code provides that in the event of a conversion from asset to income, the basis is either the cost or fair market value, whichever is lower. Since the property was sold for $25,000, it is reasonable to assume that this represents fair market value. Therefore, although the cost of the furnishings was

$50,000 to Ms. Gold, the basis (fair market value) and the amount received were each $25,000, resulting in no taxable gain or loss to Ms. Gold. This example can be summarized as follows:

Sale price of home	$	250,000
Original cost	plus $	100,000
Fees added to the basis	plus $	1,500
Improvements	plus $	75,000
Total	$	176,500
Realized profit	$	73,500
Profit exemption on home sale	$	250,000
Amount of home sale subject to tax	$	0
Taxable gain on furnishings	$	0

The Cost of Obtaining Financing

Points paid to a bank to obtain a mortgage for a primary residence or qualifying vacation home are deductible only if they are paid for by separate check at the closing, rather than being deducted from the amount given to the purchaser by the bank (Temp. Reg. Sec. 1.163-10T(j)(2)(i)). These fees are viewed as additional interest on the loan. However, the application, appraisal fees, mortgage recording costs and other costs involved in obtaining the loan are nondeductible personal expenses (IRC Sec. 262).

Example of Tax Treatment of the Costs Associated with Obtaining Financing

Frank Johnson gets a mortgage of $900,000 to purchase a home. He pays an application fee of $250 to the bank and an appraisal fee of $450 to the bank's appraiser. At the closing he pays legal fees of $600 for the bank's attorney and mortgage recording costs of $1,915.50. Mr. Johnson's total cost is thus $3,215.50. None of this is deductible, and none can be added to the tax basis of the property. However, Mr. Johnson also pays the bank $9,000, which represents one point of the loan amount. He pays this by a separate check at closing, rather than accepting a check for $891,000 from the bank (the $900,000 mortgage less the $9,000 in points). Mr. Johnson is permitted to deduct on his current-year tax return the $9,000 as additional interest on his mortgage.

Adjustments to Sale Price

U.S. tax law permits a seller to reduce the sale price of a personal residence for tax purposes by the following means:

1. All expenses involved in effectuating the transaction, including legal fees, broker's commissions and any costs incurred by the seller in transferring ownership are deductible. The gross selling price less these costs is the amount realized in the sale (Treas. Reg. Sec. 1.263(a)-2, 1.1012-1(a)).

2. Sellers may also deduct expenses incurred in fixing up the home for sale as long as the work was performed within 90 days preceding the consummation of the contract, and payment for the improvements was made within 30 days after the date of the sale. The amount realized less these costs is the adjusted selling price for tax purposes (IRC Sec. 1034(b)(1)-2).

Example of Adjustments to Sale Price

Martin Gross wants to sell his home. He paints the apartment, performs some kitchen cabinetry repair work for $2,000, and replaces all the windows for $10,000. He finds a buyer who signs a contract to purchase the apartment for $200,000 within 90 days of the work's completion.

At closing, Mr. Gross pays his attorney $1,000 in legal fees, the broker $12,000 in commission and closing costs of $2,000. The total costs of effecting the sale are $15,000, so the amount realized on the sale is $185,000. He pays the cabinetry expenses within 30 days after the closing, and is therefore entitled to deduct $2,000 in fixing-up expenses. The adjusted selling price for tax purposes is $183,000.

The $10,000 expended on the window replacement is not a fixing-up expense. It is a capital improvement that extended or enhanced the useful life of the property for more than one year, and was thus added to the tax basis of the home rather than applied against the selling price. The taxable profit on the home is reduced by the $10,000 spent for replacing the windows, without any time restrictions, since it added to the basis of the property. It is important for Mr. Gross to retain all documents verifying the cost and nature of the improvement, in order to justify the adjustment to his tax basis if called upon to do so.

Real Estate Taxes and Interest on a Primary Residence

Any real estate tax or interest expense associated with a mortgage secured by a primary residence or vacation home is a deductible item in determining taxable income. (There are certain conditions, which are noted on page 165.) The interest deduction is limited to interest on a mortgage with a maximum principal of $1,000,000. The deduction for mortgage interest is also available for an equity credit line on a home, but only up to $100,000 of principal (IRC Secs. 163, 164).

Example of Tax Treatment of Real Estate Tax and Mortgage Interest

One year ago, Gordon Honig purchased a cooperative apartment for $500,000. At that time, he obtained a mortgage for $300,000, which bears interest at 6% and requires a monthly payment of $1,800, or $21,600 per year. This consists of $18,000 in interest ($300,000 at 6%) and $3,600 in amortization (reduction of the principal). His maintenance is $800 per month, or $9,600 per year. An accountant's statement of the building's performance shows that 25% of the main-tenance fee, or $2,400, is used to pay interest on the building's mort-gage, and that an additional 25% is used to pay real estate taxes. The remaining 50% is used for operating expenses.

Mr. Honig is allowed to deduct $20,400 for interest (the $18,000 interest on his mortgage plus his $2,400 share of the interest on the building's underlying mortgage). Additionally, Mr. Honig is entitled to a deduction of $2,400 for his allocable share of the real estate taxes paid by the building. There is no deduction permitted for amortization of the mortgage or the cost of building operations.

Limitations on Deductions for Interest on Home Mortgages

Section 163 of the Internal Revenue Code permits taxpayers to take an annual deduction for the interest on their primary residence and a vacation home, though it limits the yearly deductible interest to the amount charged on a mortgage of $1,000,000 (IRC Sec. 163(h)(3) (B)(i)) as well as an equity credit line of $100,000 (IRC Sec. 163(h) (3)(C)(ii)). Thus, only the interest applicable to the first $1,100,000 is deductible and interest above this amount is not. In addition, the code defines "qualified residence interest" as interest incurred on a loan for the acquisition of a primary residence or vacation home, or on an equity credit line. The Internal Revenue Service defines an acquisition loan as a loan obtained at the time of the purchase of the property or 90 days thereafter. Therefore, if the taxpayer refinances a home the deduction is limited "to the extent the amount of the debt resulting from the refinancing does not exceed the amount of the refinanced debt." (IRC Sec. 163(h)(3)(B)).

An exception exists if the proceeds from the refinancing are used to perform a capital improvement to the residence. This will increase the qualifying debt invested in the property and will permit an increase in the amount of the loan that can qualify for interest deduction to the extent of the investment made. However, there is only a 90-day window to make the improvements from the date the loan is received. Alternatively, the taxpayer can place the money in a separate account, and can treat these funds as tax-deductible so long as he can prove that the money went to no other purpose than the capital improvements specifically identified (Temp. Reg. Sec. 1.163-8T).

Examples of Limitations on Deductions for Interest on Home Mortgages

John Jones buys a home for $500,000, and gets a mortgage for

$300,000 to complete the transaction. Over the years the home increases in value to $1,000,000 and the loan balance is reduced by his monthly payments to $225,000. He then decides to refinance based on the home's appreciated value, and seeks a new loan for $600,000. The only interest he can deduct is that portion relating to the $225,000 loan being replaced. He can also identify a portion of the loan as an equity credit line to increase his deduction by $100,000, but $325,000 is the maximum amount he is permitted to deduct.

Angela Katz decides to purchase a home with all-equity cash. She decides a year later to get a mortgage on her home. None of the interest on this mortgage is deductible, since it is not an original-acquisition mortgage and she did not obtain the loan within 90 days of her original acquisition.

Howard Smith is a senior citizen who has lived in his home for many years and has fully paid off the mortgage. Like most senior citizens, he views the equity in his home as his primary source of wealth, which he can exploit in retirement. He is having medical problems, and decides it is the time to get a new mortgage in order to pay his doctors' bills. However, because he paid off his original mortgage, he is entitled to no tax deduction on the new mortgage.

Non-Deductibility of Land Leases

Some cooperative corporations do not own the land on which their building sits, but merely lease it for an extended length of time. These *land leases* are considered rent for the use of land. A deduction is not normally permitted to the homeowner for any payments related to the land lease (IRC Sec. 262), although there are certain limited cases in which this rule does not apply. Lease payments can be deductible by the homeowner where the payments are equivalent to the tax that would have been paid, the payment was imposed by specific state statute and the payment is for a public purpose. This is the case even if the charge is designated as a lease payment (generally referred to as payments in lieu of taxes or PILOT) (Rev. Rul. 71-49). PILOT lease payments made by Battery Park City's condominium owners, for example, are fully deductible.

Non-Deductibility of Assessments

Assessments levied by the cooperative corporation on tenant-share-holders for building improvements are normally not deductible (IRC Sec. 262). However, capital assessments used for replacements or improvements in the building can be added to the unit owners' basis and adjusted against the eventual proceeds from the sale of the property (Rev. Rul. 81-152 1981-1 C.B. 433).

Costs Associated With Moving

Moving expenses are not normally deductible. However, an exception can be made if you are moving as a result of a new principal workplace that is located at least 50 miles away from your previous home, and you are employed for at least 39 weeks at that job. This rule also applies to self-employed individuals, but they must work in the vicinity of their new home for at least 39 weeks out of the first 12 months after they close and at least 78 weeks during the first 24 months (IRC Sec. 217).

Using Retirement Funds to Purchase a Home

The federal tax code generally permits the use of up to $10,000 in retirement funds from a qualified plan for the purchase of your first primary residence without incurring any penalty for withdrawal. However, you are still responsible for paying any deferred taxes applicable to that money (Treas. Reg. Sec. 1.408A-6). You are also entitled to borrow from a 401(k) up to 50% of the amount vested, or $50,000, whichever is less, which can be used for the purchase of a home or investment real estate.

Discharging a Mortgage Indebtedness on a Principal Residence

Congress has recognized that the recession has created undue hardship for many homeowners, precipitating foreclosures and short sales. In the past these often resulted in taxable gain through discharge of indebtedness, unless the taxpayer was bankrupt or insolvent. To address this consequence, Congress enacted the Mortgage Forgiveness Debt Relief Act of 2007, which, as amended by the 2008 Economic Stabilization Act, generally provides that any taxpayer whose mortgage indebtedness is discharged in whole or in part on a principal residence between the years 2007 and 2012 will not be subject to recognition of gain (IRC Sec. 108(a)(1)(E)). As of 2013, all mortgage forgiveness is subject to tax.

Special Withholding Rules for Foreign Owners of Real Estate

Foreign owners of United States real estate are subject to special tax withholding rules related to a United States real property interest. The law, the Foreign Investment in Real Property Tax Act (generally referred to as FIRPTA), requires that the purchaser withhold taxes equal to 10% of the total amount realized by the foreign entity or person (IRC Sec. 1445). In the event that the property is a personal residence and the amount realized does not exceed $300,000, there is an exemption to this rule (IRC Sec. 1445(b)(5)). The amount withheld can be reduced if the foreign taxpayer receives a withholding certificate from the IRS, assuming the amount of tax actually due is less than the 10% withholding amount or such other prescribed circumstances (Rev. Proc. 2000-35, 2000-2 C.B. 211).

New York State also requires the purchaser to withhold the estimated tax on the transaction for out-of-state residents selling New York State property.

Rules Relating to the Ownership
of Investment Property

All expenses associated with the operation of business or investment property are normally deductible. Any expenditure made to cover ordinary and necessary operating expenses of an investment property is fully deductible, as long as the property is being held with the intent of making a profit. If the payment relates to a service or improvement with a useful life of more than one year, it must be capitalized and deducted over that useful period as amortization or depreciation (IRC Secs. 162(a), 212, 167).

An owner of investment property is entitled to a depreciation deduction, which is a non-cash expense that reduces the tax basis of the property. *Depreciation* is the standard method for recognizing the expiration of the useful life of an asset. The depreciation deduction is based on the original cost of residential real estate and is spread out over a period of 27.5 years. Accordingly, 1/27.5th of the full tax basis of the depreciable property is deducted each year for 27.5 years (IRC Sec. 168(c)).

Example of Deductions on a Condominium

Martin Sanchez buys a condo at the beginning of the year for $500,000. He rents it out for $4,000 per month. His monthly common charges are $500 ($6,000 per year), and he has a monthly mortgage payment of $22,500 ($19,500 in interest and $3,000 in amortization for the year) and a yearly real estate tax bill of $5,000. In addition, Mr. Sanchez pays a real estate broker $6,000 to rent the apartment under a two-year lease and makes repairs to the apartment in the amount of $500. When Mr. Sanchez prepares his yearly tax return, this is how these items will be treated:

Income

Rent . . . .$ 48,000
$4,000 per month for 12 months, as defined in the lease

Expenses

Common charges. . . . .$ 6,000
Fully deductible as an ordinary and necessary expense

Real estate taxes . . . .$ 5,000
Fully deductible as an ordinary and necessary expense

Repairs ....$ 500
Fully deductible as an ordinary and necessary expense

Interest on mortgage ....$ 19,500
Fully deductible as investment interest expense

Principal amortization ....$ 0
Not deductible as a return of a loan

Broker's fee.. $ 3,000
*Since the fee covers a two-year lease, it must be
"amortized" over a two-year period: $3,000 in the current
year and $3,000 in the subsequent year. Depending on
market conditions, this fee may be paid by the tenant. In
that case, it would not be deductible by the owner.*

Depreciation...$ 18,182

Example of Depreciation of a Condominium

Since this is the purchase of an investment property, Mr. Sanchez is entitled to take a deduction for depreciation on his condominium unit of 1/27.5th of his original tax basis of $500,000. Therefore, his depreciation deduction is $18,182. Mr. Sanchez must also reduce his tax basis by a comparable amount, to $481,818. In the subsequent year, when he is again entitled to a depreciation deduction of $18,182, he must again apply this figure against his tax basis, reducing it to $463,636.

When Mr. Sanchez sells the apartment, his profit is the difference between the net selling price and the tax basis. Therefore, if he sells the property at the end of the second year for the same price he initially purchased it, $500,000, he will have to recognize gain in the amount of $36,364 ($18,182 × 2), which is the amount of accumulated depreciation during the two years of ownership. This *depreciation recapture* is taxed at a special rate of 25% (see page 175).

Depreciation and Tax Basis in a Cooperative

Depreciation is permitted for a cooperative apartment that is used for investment, trade or business. A full deduction is permitted for the maintenance payment as an ordinary and necessary business expense, except for that portion utilized to repay the underlying mortgage principal of the building. The tax basis of a cooperative apartment is the price paid for the shares plus the apartment's allocable portion of the building's mortgage (IRC Sec. 216).

Example of Deductions on a Cooperative Unit, Including Depreciation

Dean Morris owns a cooperative apartment in a building that permits owners to rent their units as long as they pay a sublet fee equal to 10% of the monthly maintenance charge. He has a tenant who pays rent of $4,000 per month. Mr. Morris purchased the property for $500,000 with $150,000 in cash and a $350,000 mortgage at 6% interest, payable at $2,100 per month. Therefore, in the first year his interest charge is $21,000, and his amortization of principal is $4,200 (the difference between the full payment and the interest portion). Mr. Morris pays $800 per month in maintenance ($9,600 per year). In addition, he needs to make repairs in the apartment to fix some faulty plumbing, which cost him $500.

The financial report he receives from the cooperative corporation shows that $2,000 is Mr. Morris's allocable portion of the building's yearly real estate taxes and $1,500 is his allocable portion of the building's yearly mortgage interest. In addition, he paid $500 for principal amortization on the building's underlying mortgage over the course of the year, which is factored into his maintenance charge. His allocable portion of the building's mortgage, based on his fractional ownership interest, is $30,000. If this were his primary residence, the real estate tax and mortgage interest would be the only items Mr. Morris would be allowed to deduct. However, since this is an investment, he is also entitled to deduct all other costs incurred in operating the building as an ordinary and necessary business expense. The only amount he is not able to deduct is his portion of the amortization of the building's mortgage, $500 for the year. His tax computation would be as follows:

Income

Rent. . . . . $ 48,000
$4,000 per month for 12 months, as defined in the lease

Expenses

Deductible maintenance charge . . . . $ 9,100
$9,600 in maintenance less $500 for the building's mortgage

Repairs . . . . $ 500

Sublet fee . . . . $ 960
10% of maintenance charge (varies by building)

Interest . . . . $ 21,000
$25,200 payment less the $4,200 associated with principal amortization ($350,000 at 6%)

Depreciation . . . . $ 19,272
$500,000 purchase price for the stock plus $30,000 underlying mortgage pickup provides a tax basis for depreciation purposes of $530,000. This amount is deducted over 27.5 years (1/27.5th per year)

Total expenses . . . . $ 50,832

Taxable loss . . . . $ 2,832

Depreciating Capital Improvements

If an improvement having a useful life of more than one year is made to a co-op or a condo after the initial purchase, the cost of the improvement is added to the tax basis of the property. This sum may also be depreciated, but its useful life must be separately determined (IRC Sec. 168).

Example of Depreciating Improvements on Investment Property

Dr. Emersen purchases a condominium for his dental practice for $500,000, and then makes improvements having a useful life of more than one year, including alterations of interior walls, built-ins, painting and carpeting. The alterations to the interior walls have a useful life of 10 years and cost him $50,000. The built-ins, painting and carpeting have a useful life of five years and cost him $30,000. The deductible depreciation expenses are as follows:

Original cost of condo...................................$ 18,182
$500,000 with 27.5-year useful life

Wall alterations ....$ 5,000
$50,000 with 10-year useful life

Built-ins, carpeting and painting........................$ 6,000
$30,000 with 5-year useful life

Total depreciation expense.............................$ 29,182

Limitations Regarding the Deductibility of Passive Losses

A loss on investment real estate is passive if real estate is not the investor's primary business. A *passive loss* on investment real estate may be offset only against active income (for example, salary and wages) up to $25,000, and only if the taxpayer's adjusted gross income is under $150,000. If the adjusted gross income exceeds this amount, then no loss can be applied against active income. However, the loss may be recognized in future years, either when the property shows a profit or at the time of sale as a deduction against any gain (IRC Sec. 469).

Example of Passive Loss Rules

John Byrnes, an advertising executive, owns a condominium apartment that he rents out for $2,000 per month. He has operating expenses, interest and depreciation that total $5,000 per month, giving him a total loss for the year of $36,000. Since real estate is not his active business, the loss is a passive loss. However, since he has an adjusted gross income for tax purposes of $120,000, below the limit of $150,000, he is entitled to deduct $25,000 against his alternative income.

Although the excess of $11,000 ($36,000 less $25,000) is not deductible in the current year, it becomes a passive-loss carryover. If, in the subsequent year, Mr. Byrnes sells the property and has a profit of $50,000, he is entitled to deduct $11,000 from his profit in reporting capital gains income from the sale.

Limitations Resulting from "At-Risk" Rules

In order to be entitled to a deduction on investment real estate, you must be *at risk* for any indebtedness on the property, or finance the property with institutional or bank financing. Any amounts that are not at risk may not be considered in determining a loss. These rules do not apply to a primary residence (IRC Sec. 465).

Example of "At-Risk" Rules

Mary Lou Richardson wants to purchase a condominium for investment. To improve the terms, the owner of the property agrees to provide $100,000 in *nonrecourse financing* at 10% if Richardson invests $50,000 in cash. Nonrecourse financing means that the seller can look only to the property to satisfy the debt, and cannot make a claim against the buyer's personal assets in the event of default. Since this financing would not be carried out in the usual way through a qualified institution providing mortgages to the public, the nonrecourse quality of the loan precludes it from being considered "at risk." The only money at risk in this case is the $50,000 invested by Ms. Richardson, and at-risk rule limitations specify that any net losses can be deducted only to the extent of the invested $50,000.

Rules Relating to the Sale of Investment Property

When investment property is sold, gains are normally subject to capital gains tax, and any loss is a capital loss. A capital gain or loss is the difference between the net sale price and the adjusted tax basis of the property. These are the current rules:

- For real estate held for less than one year (short-term), capital gains are taxed at ordinary rates (maximum 39.6% for federal tax through 2013) + 12.85% for state and local = 47.35% (after adjustment for deductibility of state and local taxes on federal returns, and assuming the inapplicability of the alternative minimum tax). A Medicare surcharge tax of 3.8% might also apply.

- For real estate held for at least one year, capital gains are taxed at 15% for federal tax purposes unless the taxpayer's income exceeds $400,000, in which case the tax rate is 20%. However, for real estate held in excess of five years, the capital gains rate is 18% in most cases. State and local taxes remain at ordinary rates. A Medicare surcharge tax of 3.8% might also apply (see page 176).
- For low-income taxpayers, the capital gains tax is reduced to special lower rates (IRC Sec. 1(h)).

Special Recapture Rules for Depreciation

Real estate that is used for the production of income (such as an apartment owned for investment) or in a trade or business (such as a condominium unit from which you run an office) is a depreciable asset. While your primary residence is not depreciable, the portion of your home used exclusively for business purposes may be depreciated if it qualifies under Section 280A of the Internal Revenue Code. Currently this can be done only by allocating a portion of the purchase price attributable to the trade or business and then depreciating this amount over 27.5 years. Improvements to the portion of the property allocated to the trade or business may also be depreciated (IRC Secs. 167, 168).

If a given property has been depreciated, the amount of the accumulated depreciation previously claimed is subject to a special tax rate of 25% when the property is sold.

Example of Capital Gains Rules Where Depreciation Was Taken

Brooke Lee buys a condo for investment for $100,000. She rents it out for two years and then sells it for $120,000. Because it was used for the production of income, the property qualifies for depreciation, and Ms. Lee claims $3,636 in depreciation each year as a deduction against her rental income. The accumulated depreciation for the two-year period is $7,272. When the unit is sold, this sum is taxed at

25% for a total recapture liability of $1,818. Since this property was held for more than 12 months, it is subject to a 15% capital gains tax applied to the $20,000 profit. Thus, Ms. Lee's tax liability is $3,000 on the profit and $1,818 on the accumulated depreciation, for a total of $4,818. Because it is below the profit threshold, the Medicare surcharge tax of 3.8% would not apply.

Medicare Surcharge Tax on Net Investment Income

The Patient Protection and Affordable Care Act, often referred to as Obamacare, creates a new Internal Revenue Code, Section 1411, which will impose a 3.8% Medicare surchage tax on rental income and property sales where the amount of profit exceeds a threshold on the taxpayer's return of (a) $250,000 in adjusted gross income for taxpayers filing jointly; (b) $200,000 in adjusted gross income for married taxpayers filing separately; or (c) $125,000 in adjusted gross income for all others. This would include income from rents as well as profits from the sale of capital assets, including home sales (although the profit exemption of $500,000 on a joint return or $250,000 on a single return still applies (IRC Sec. 121)).

Capital Losses

A capital loss may be used to offset a capital gain. However, if there is no capital gain, then only $3,000 of the loss can be deducted each year against ordinary income. Any balance must be carried forward to succeeding years (IRC Secs. 1211, 1212).

Example of Capital Loss Rules

Mortimer Stone owns investment property that he sells for a loss of $25,000. Since the property is a capital asset, the loss is a capital loss. Mr. Stone also sells some stock, giving him a $10,000 capital gain. In preparing his taxes, Mr. Stone can net his capital gain against the capital loss to arrive at a $15,000 net loss (a $10,000 capital gain less a $25,000 loss). However, he can apply only $3,000 of the capital loss against his ordinary income. The balance of the capital loss, $12,000, must be carried over to the next year and may offset future capital gains. He can also apply it against future ordinary income (up to $3,000 each year).

Installment Sales

An *installment sale* permits capital gains to be spread out over a number of years, and permits deferred recognition of profits as payments are received over the payment term. A sale of property on terms providing for payment over more than one year can be considered an installment sale. In this case, profits can be recognized in the year they are received. The principal received is divided by the percent of profit from the sale (i.e., the ratio of the selling price to the tax basis), and the resulting amount is taxed at capital gains rates (whereas interest received on the loan is taxed as ordinary income). However, if any portion of the installment indebtedness is converted to cash before the prescribed term, the gain must be recognized upon its receipt (IRC Sec. 453; Temp. Reg. Sec. 15a.453-1(b)(3)(i)).

Example of Installment Sales Treatment

Michael Strong seeks to sell his condominium apartment, but financial problems with the building have made it difficult to find a bank that would provide financing to prospective buyers. Therefore, he agrees to provide the necessary financing to his purchaser, Rita Long. The terms are $50,000 in cash and a private mortgage (referred to as a *purchase-money mortgage*) of $100,000 bearing interest at 8%, to be paid in equal installments of principal over the next 10 years. Only the profit paid with the principal is considered a capital gain in an installment sale — interest must be recognized in the year it is received as ordinary income. This loan is personally guaranteed by the purchaser, so it is not subject to at-risk limitations (see page 174).

Mr. Strong's tax basis for the property is $75,000, so his profit would be $75,000 (the total sale price of $150,000 less the tax basis), or 50% of the selling price. The sale closes at the beginning of the year, and at the end of the year Mr. Strong prepares the following analysis for his tax return:

Payment received at closing ....$ 50,000

First-year principal payment on mortgage[1]............$ 10,000

Total cash received on sale............................ $ 60,000

Profit percentage on sale................................. 50%

Total capital gain on installment sale (first year) .....$ 30,000

[1]In addition, Mr. Strong receives interest at 8% on the open mortgage balance, which is taxed at ordinary rates.

In the second year, Mr. Strong receives an additional $10,000 installment on the mortgage (plus 8% interest on the remaining open mortgage balance), which is also subject to the 50% profit ratio, so he recognizes a capital gain of $5,000. At the end of the second year, Mr. Strong goes to his bank and is able to obtain a loan of $50,000, secured solely by the purchase-money mortgage of the installment sale. The $50,000 is deemed a conversion to cash and is taxable in the year received.

Phantom Gain

A sale in which the property's tax basis has been depreciated below the amount of mortgage indebtedness can generate *phantom gain*, which is taxable in the year of sale. Phantom gain exists when there is profit but no correlating cash receipt (IRC Sec. 1001; Treas. Reg. Sec. 1.1001-2, *Crane v. Commissioner*, 331 U.S. 1 (1947); *Commissioner v. Tufts*, 461 U.S. 300 (1983)).

Example of Phantom Gain

Melvin Singer owns a condominium for investment purposes that he purchases for $300,000. He obtains a mortgage that is interest-only (no reduction of principal) in the amount of $250,000. After 10 years of ownership, Mr. Singer has depreciated his property down to an adjusted tax basis of $200,000. However, the interest-only mortgage still remains at its original amount of $250,000.

At the end of the 10 years, Mr. Singer sells the property for $275,000. Rather than recognizing a $25,000 loss (the sale price of $275,000 less the purchase price of $300,000), he has to show a gain of $75,000 (the difference between the net selling price of $275,000 and the adjusted basis of $200,000). It does not matter that $250,000 has to be repaid to the bank or that the bank loan exceeds the property's basis. Gain or loss on a transaction for tax purposes does not take into account that the amount borrowed has to be repaid upon the disposition of the asset. Thus phantom gain occurs: a significant profit has to be recognized for tax purposes although little or no cash is realized on the sale.

Using Retirement Funds to Purchase Investment Real Estate

Funds from a retirement account in a qualified plan can generally be used to purchase investment real estate, but there are certain limitations. The investment must be at fair market value, and must be prudent in light of the investment objectives and distribution requirements dictated by the plan. It may not be used for personal purposes or rented to a family member. Mortgages can be taken, but they must be guaranteed by the plan and not personally (IRC Sec. 4975; Treas. Reg. Sec. 1.408). In the event that a mortgage is taken, the property is subject to a special tax called the *Unrelated Business Taxable Income* (UBTI) tax for that allocable portion of the income that was financed (Treas. Reg. Sec. 1.513-1(b)). This rate graduates up to 35% for any income over $9,550. In addition, the ownership of the property must be maintained by a trustee or a custodian of the plan or account.

Example of Purchasing Real Estate Using Retirement Funds

David Jones has an IRA and wishes to invest a portion of the funds in this account in real estate. Thus, he does the following:

1. He advises his IRA plan trustee of his intention to buy real estate, and appoints a custodian to take control of the property on behalf of the plan at such time as he makes an acquisition. The trustee agrees to disburse $500,000 to the custodian for this purpose as a prudent investment under the terms of the IRA plan.

2. He identifies a condominium property and enters into a contract to purchase the property on behalf of the IRA plan. Thereafter, the custodian controls title to the property.

3. He identifies a managing agent to manage the affairs of the property and submits any profits generated by the property to the custodian on behalf of his retirement plan.

After holding the property for one year, Mr. Jones sells it for $600,000. Because the property was held for investment, it is subject to capital gains tax. However, this tax is deferred until the proceeds are distributed to Mr. Jones from the plan after his retirement.

Recent Changes in the Tax Law and How They Affect Buyers, Sellers and Owners of Real Estate

Congress has passed a number of laws — notably the American Taxpayer Relief Act of 2012 and the Health Care and Education Reconciliation Act of 2010 — that contain changes to taxes associated with real estate. This overview addresses material elements of these tax law changes as they affect buyers, sellers and owners of residential property.

The American Taxpayer Relief Act of 2012

Rise in Top Rate

The new tax law institutes an additional tax bracket for high-income earners. If a taxpayer's taxable income exceeds $400,000 as a single filer or $450,000 as a married couple, the tax on any additional income above this threshold will be 39.6%. Since the top-income thresholds are so high, it's unlikely that a typical buyer will be subject to the provisions of this change, particularly given that the thresholds take any allowable itemized deductions into account. Accordingly, many brokers will likely continue to cite 35% as the applicable federal tax rate for most prospective buyers. However, taxpayers who earn more than $500,000 should be sensitive to the law change, and may wish to compute their tax deductions for homeownership using the 39.6% rate.

Example of the New Tax Rate

John and Susan Smith have both had successful years and will report a combined income on their 2013 tax return of $2,000,000. As homeowners, they can deduct the interest they pay on their mortgage as well as their state taxes, which together add up to $300,000. They also made a tax-deductible contribution to charity in 2012 of $400,000. Thus, when eliminating their itemized deductions, they show a taxable income of $1,300,000. Since this amount exceeds $450,000, they must pay 39.6% on $850,000, which is the amount of their taxable income exceeding $450,000. This is in addition to the tax they must pay on the first $450,000 of income.

Change in Capital Gains Rate for High Earners

For taxpayers in the top income bracket under the 2013 tax law, capital gains will be taxed at 20% (versus 15% in prior years). An exception exists for certain property sales occurring as of January 1, 2013: if a taxpayer purchased a property during or after 2001 and has owned it for more than five years, his profit from the sale of the property will be taxed at 18%, not 20%.

Example of the Capital Gains Rate for High Earners

Harry Johnson is a single homeowner with an annual income of $250,000. His itemized deductions for the interest paid on his mortgage and for state taxes total $70,000, making his total taxable income $180,000. In 2013 he decides to sell a piece of property that he has held as an investment since 2011, and makes $100,000 in capital gains from this sale. Because his taxable income is less than the threshold of $400,000, his profit from the sale is taxed at 15%. If his income were $450,000, his capital gains rate would have been 20%; if he had bought the property in 2003, it would have been 18%.

Phaseout of Itemized Deductions for High Earners

Taxpayers whose adjusted gross income — their income before itemized deductions — exceeds $300,000 for a married couple or $250,000 for a single individual are no longer permitted to reduce their taxable income by the full amount of the itemized deductions they have incurred. In these cases, the total amount of allowable deductions is reduced by 3% of the amount by which the taxpayer's income exceeds the relevant threshold. Itemized deductions cannot be reduced by more than 80%, however.

Example of Phaseout of Itemized Deductions for High Earners

Maxine and Robert Stein are homeowners with an adjusted gross income of $1,000,000. Their itemized deductions for 2013 total $500,000, consisting of mortgage interest payments of $200,000, charitable contributions of $100,000 and other qualifying expenditures of $200,000. Since this total exceeds their itemized deduction threshold of $300,000, their allowable deductions are reduced by 3% of the excess, or $6,000. Therefore they are entitled to an itemized deduction of $494,000 instead of $500,000.

Forgiveness of Debt on an Acquisition Loan for a Primary Residence

The American Taxpayer Relief Act of 2012 extends a provision of the Mortgage Forgiveness Debt Relief Act of 2007, which grants a tax exemption on any income associated with debt cancellation on a primary residence. The current law, which allows exceptions for up to $2,000,000 in debt forgiveness, is designed to protect taxpayers from excessive tax burdens associated with mortgage restructuring or fore-closure. However, as of 2013, the provision has expired and tax is now due on forgiven debt relating to a home sale.

Example of Forgiveness of Debt on an Acquisition Loan for a Primary Residence

Sam and Bonnie Siegel were having economic difficulties and persuad-ed their bank to undertake a short sale of their primary residence at a price of $1,000,000, though the debt outstanding was $1,300,000. The bank agreed to forgive the excess mortgage obligation under the terms of the short sale.

As the beneficiaries of a forgiven debt, the Siegels would normally have been subject to gain recognition — but given that the property was their primary residence and the loan in question was granted for the purchase of the home, they were able to exclude the gain from their taxable income. If the Siegels had refinanced their home and the loan was therefore not their original-acquisition loan, they would not have been permitted to exempt the gain from tax recognition. If this transaction occurs in 2013 or thereafter, they would have to recognize a capital gain of $300,000 even though they received no money and sold due to economic distress.

Health Care and Education Reconciliation Act of 2010

3.8% Medicare Surcharge Tax on Net Investment Income

Though the Health Care and Education Reconciliation Act was signed into law in March 2010, its Medicare surcharge tax provision has only become effective in 2013. All taxpayers with net investment income — legally defined as passive income from interest, royalties, dividends, annuities and rents as well as capital gains — exceeding $200,000 for individuals or $250,000 for married couples will now be subject to a special surcharge tax of 3.8%, which will apply to all net invest-ment income over the applicable threshold. As the name implies, the revenue collected by this tax will be used to fund Medicare benefits. A second Medicare surcharge tax of 0.9% will also apply to all wages and self-employment income exceeding the same thresholds.

Example of 3.8% Medicare Surcharge Tax on Net Investment Income

Martin Stone is married, and he and his wife earn an annual income of $350,000. Martin also has a net investment income of $900,000, consisting of capital gains of $500,000, interest income of $100,000 and rental income of $300,000. Since this total exceeds the Medicare surcharge tax threshold of $250,000 for married couples, he is subject to a 3.8% tax on the excess amount, which comes to $650,000 × 3.8% = $24,750. This is an additional tax above and beyond the capital gains tax, which for Martin would apply at a rate of 15%.

Increase in Taxation of Excess Profit

The law continues to permit a *profit exemption* on the sale of a primary residence equal to $500,000 for married taxpayers and $250,000 for individuals. When a taxpayer sells his home for a profit exceeding the applicable threshold, only the excess is considered taxable, and is taxed at ordinary rates for income and capital gains. Accordingly, for a single taxpayer, the first $400,000 in excess of the threshold (equal to $650,000 in total profit) is taxed at a capital gains rate of 15%, and all gains beyond that amount are taxed at 20%, assuming he purchased the property before 2001 or owned it for less than five years. Anything above $250,000 in excess of the profit exemption threshold, or over $500,000 in total profit for married taxpayers, would also be subject to a 3.8% Medicare surcharge tax.

Most buyers and sellers will not experience significant increases in their tax obligations as a result of these legal changes. For high-earning taxpayers, the changes in the law described above only marginally impact the advantages of owning versus renting. While the new law increases the federal tax rate, which would normally make ownership a better alternative given the opportunity for itemized deductions, it also places restraints on recognizable deductions for wealthy taxpayers. The low interest rates that currently prevail in the marketplace might also seem like a good incentive to buy now, but given that the tax code currently permits interest deductions on only the first $1,000,000 of an acquisition mortgage, these low rates are not particularly meaningful. Ultimately, most high-earning taxpayers are motivated by lifestyle and long-term investment strategies, so it is unlikely that the new law will change existing levels of supply and demand for high-priced properties. Most mainstream properties, meanwhile, are largely unaffected by the new tax law.

Tax Rules for New York State

New York State and New York City impose a real estate transfer tax and a mortgage-recording tax. The transfer tax is 1.4% for transfers under $500,000, and 1.825% for transfers above this amount. The mortgage recording tax is 1.8% of the loan amount for sales under $500,000 and 1.925% for sales above this amount. New York State also levies a *mansion tax* on sales over $1,000,000. This tax is 1% of the sale price plus the amount of any transfer taxes paid by the buyer.

New York conforms to federal tax laws in exempting profit for a primary residence: up to $250,000 per individual or $500,000 per couple. It also permits the deduction of interest on a primary residence, as well as *like-kind exchanges* for investment properties (IRC Sec. 1031). However, New York does not have a capital gains tax, so all taxes on gains are levied at ordinary rates.

New York State Tax Recognition of Part-Time Residence/Vacation Homes

In New York State, full-time residents are responsible for reporting all income from all sources and paying tax on that income to the state. However, if the taxpayer qualifies as a part-time resident, only the income derived from business generated within New York State is subject to tax. If the property is in New York City, city taxes would apply if state taxes are due (N.Y. Tax Law Sec. 605(b)(1)(B); N.Y.C. Admin Code Sec. 11-705(b)(1)).

In the past, the guidelines offered by New York State provided that if you were a domiciliary or resided in the state for more than 183 days (any portion of a day is counted as a full day), you would be considered a full-time resident. However, a decision by the New York State Tax Appeals Tribunal concerning a couple named John and Laura Barker has created a degree of uncertainty. John Barker worked in New York as an investment manager and commuted from his home in Connecticut. The Barkers purchased a home on Long Island as a vacation residence, which they used from time to time. The court held that the state statute defines a temporary residence as "a cottage or vacation home where temporary occupancy is inherent" in the nature of the abode. In the case of the Barker home, it was capable of being utilized as a full-time residence since it was suitable for year-round use. In addition, Barker worked in New York State for more than 183 days. Thus, even though the Barkers insisted that they were Connecticut residents, the court held that the Barkers were New York State residents under New York State law. While New York State tax authorities affirm that they do not consider this case reflective of a policy change concerning part-time residency, it has still created a cautionary environment.

Tax authorities use five primary factors in evaluating whether a location is the taxpayer's domicile:

1. The size and value of the home, as well as whether it is capable of being used year-round.
2. The time spent at the location.
3. "Near and dear" qualities, such as valuables and personal effects, that are normally kept in a primary residence.
4. Whether the taxpayer has an active involvement in a New York business.
5. The location of the taxpayer's family (to be used only if the first four factors do not clarify the taxpayer's status).

Attorneys generally recommend that their clients maintain a diary of their daily whereabouts as well as any supporting documents, including credit card receipts, telephone bills, E-ZPass records, expense account records, travel itineraries, ATM receipts, utility bills, taxi and car service receipts and similar evidence.

Special Tax-Planning Techniques

Technique 1: Private Financing Installment Sales

Sometimes the only way to sell a property at a good price is to give the buyer special terms. An installment sale permits you to gear the repayment schedule to the needs of the buyer, spreading out payments over a series of years rather than requiring a lump sum at the time of closing. The seller's gain is recognized only to the extent of the profit on each payment received. The profit is determined by applying the percentage of profit on the sale as a whole to each payment. In addition to spreading out the recognition of gain over a number of years, an installment sale can be used as a device to convert cash payments from interest income to capital gains (IRC Sec. 453) as long as the rate of payment meets minimum imputed interest rates specified by the IRS from time to time (IRC Sec. 1274).

Example of Private Financing Installment Sales

Robert Baker would like to sell his condominium unit, which he holds for investment, for $500,000. His tax basis is $300,000. A prospective purchaser, Adam Roth, has offered him $400,000 and would like to purchase the property as an investment. Mr. Roth has $100,000 in cash and plans to obtain a mortgage for $300,000 at 10% interest, so his monthly payment will be $2,635 ($300,000 × the monthly factor on page 137 of 0.878). Mr. Baker offers Mr. Roth a deal — a purchase price of $500,000 with $100,000 down and the same monthly payment he would make to the bank, $2,635 per month. Mr. Baker is able to maintain this monthly amount by reducing the interest rate he charges on the remaining $400,000 to 7.9%, which is above the minimum imputed interest rate required by the IRS.

The advantage of this transaction to Mr. Baker is that it is an installment sale, so only a portion of the $100,000 he is to receive at closing will be taxed at the capital gains rate. The remaining balance will be received over a number of years under installment rules. Since the loan is structured so that it has a high proportion of principal (taxed at the capital gains rate) to interest (taxed as ordinary income), Mr. Baker makes more after taxes than if he had sold his condominium for a lower price at a higher rate of interest.

The transaction is also appealing to Mr. Roth. He is paying the same cash down and incurring the same monthly cost, but because the purchase price is higher, he will be entitled to greater depreciation, since the property is being held as an investment.

Technique 2: Contract Vendee Sales

There are times when transferring the title to a property on a given date would have adverse consequences, and yet the buyer and seller are eager to perform the deal and transfer tax ownership within that time period. A *contract vendee sale* (also known as a *land contract sale* or an *escrow agreement transfer*) can resolve this problem. The parties enter into an unconditional agreement to sell the property at a specific price and terms. However, rather than closing within a few months, the contract calls for a closing date further in the future. During this interim period, possession of the property is given to the purchaser, who accepts the burdens and benefits of ownership. For tax purposes, the date of recognized ownership will be the date of contract and possession, rather than the date of title transfer (*White v. Commissioner*, T.C. Memo. 1974-69; *Kindschi v. Commissioner*, T.C. Memo. 1979-489; *Estate of Franklin v. Commissioner*, 544 F.2d 1045 (9th Cir. 1976)).

Example of Contract Vendee Sales

Alice Adams owns a condo apartment for investment purposes that she purchased for $300,000. She is having trouble selling the apartment because the sponsor owns a significant number of units in the building, and banks are resistant to providing financing to buildings with a limited number of owner-occupants. Her own mortgage becomes due upon the sale of the property, so if the sale is privately financed she will immediately owe her bank $200,000 upon closing. She proposes a contract vendee sale to Ken Stevens with the following terms:

- A purchase price of $400,000, with a nonrefundable $40,000 cash down payment going to the seller, who shall hold these funds as trustee.
- $360,000 will be paid to the seller at the date of closing, which shall be in five years.
- Mr. Stevens will take possession 30 days after the contract is signed, and at that time will accept all the burdens and benefits of ownership, including paying maintenance, insurance, real estate taxes and general upkeep.
- Mr. Stevens and Ms. Adams agree that for tax purposes the date of transfer is the date of possession, and that each will record the transfer of ownership as having occurred on that date.
- Mr. Stevens agrees to make payments of $3,600 per month to Ms. Adams as interest on an interim loan, as defined in an escrow agreement and secured by the contract.
- The contract is to be recorded against the property.

For tax recognition purposes, ownership in the property transfers from Ms. Adams to Mr. Stevens, but under New York real estate law it does not, since a transfer of title did not yet occur. Thus the mortgage has not been violated. Attorneys for both parties must verify that this transaction does not violate any other conditions expressed in the existing mortgage on the condo.

Technique 3: Renting to Relatives and Gifting Ownership
Parents who buy an apartment for the purpose of renting it to a child

are entitled to all the tax advantages of investment ownership, provided that the rental arrangement has the same terms and conditions as it would if the property were rented to an unrelated third party. Therefore, a lease should be signed and monthly rental payments should be made at fair market value.

Parents can, if they so desire, gift the apartment to their child by transferring partial value of the property to him or her each year in an amount not to exceed $14,000 per individual ($28,000 if both parents elect to make the gift). This amount is the maximum yearly gift permitted that can be given by any one individual to another without being subject to gift tax. While this is most commonly done with relations, there is no requirement that the gift be to a family member, and an apartment can be rented and gifted to an unrelated party with the same effect. It is important that this gift not be in the form of a rent reduction, which can subject the transaction to alternative rules (*Estate of Kelly v. Commissioner*, 63 T.C. 321 (1974); *Estate of Barlow v. Commissioner*, 55 T.C. 666 (1971)).

Example of Renting to Relatives

George Grossman decides to purchase a condominium apartment and rent it to his daughter Jane, who has just started a job in New York City. He buys an apartment for $170,000 with $70,000 in cash and a mortgage of $100,000. Jane and her father enter into a lease at $1,800 per month, the fair market rent. Mr. Grossman holds the apartment as an investment, recognizing rental income and taking deductions for all ordinary and necessary expenses, including depreciation.

At the beginning of the ownership, Mr. Grossman gives his daughter $14,000 in equity value in the condominium. This gift is the maximum he can make without being subject to the gift tax. Since this represents one-fifth of the equity in the apartment, Jane can recognize a one-fifth ownership interest in the property and is entitled to a deduction for that portion of the interest and real estate taxes associated with this partial interest as her primary residence on her tax return.

In the second year, Jane's father gives her another $14,000, and so on, until finally, after the fifth year, Jane has been given an accumulated total of $70,000 in gifts, which equals the full equity value of the property. She transfers title to her own name and obtains a new mortgage, then pays off the old mortgage, which was in her father's name. She now has total ownership. Since her father did not exceed the $14,000-per-year gift tax limitation, no gift tax has been incurred. Additionally, since the rental income was consistent with fair market value, all tax deductions associated with the investment ownership of the property, including depreciation, are valid as they may relate to any ownership interest held by Mr. Grossman. Jane's basis for the property is the donor's basis after the reduction for depreciation taken by her father. However, since this is her primary residence, Jane is entitled to a $250,000 profit exemption when she sells the property.

Technique 4: Renting with an Option to Purchase
Selling an apartment is sometimes difficult because of a buyer's inability to arrange financing or as a result of economic uncertainty. Renting to a prospective purchaser with an option to buy can be an effective means of maximizing profit while giving flexibility to one or both parties. Options can be in the form of a "put," which compels the buyer to purchase, or a "call," which compels the seller to sell. Both can be used in the same transaction (IRC Sec. 1234).

Example of Renting with an Option to Purchase
Steven and Susan Burton sell their primary residence for $250,000 with a $100,000 profit, and want to purchase a larger apartment to accommodate their growing family. However, in looking at homes for sale, they realize that they cannot find anything they like for less than $500,000, which is $100,000 more than they can afford. To purchase an apartment at this higher price, they would have to save an additional $25,000 and increase their salaries by at least 10%.

Ronald Silverman has an apartment the Burtons like that he is willing to rent for $4,500 per month for two years. Agreeing to the rent, the Burtons negotiate an option to purchase the apartment for $550,000 at any time within the two years, giving them time to accumulate the necessary funds and increase their income. This also allows them to get out of the deal if economic circumstances prove unfavorable. Meanwhile, the cash received from the sale of their previous home could be earning interest, helping them accumulate the down payment for the eventual purchase.

Mr. Silverman is equally pleased, since he has a two-year lease at a favorable rent and the potential to sell his apartment at a good price. He is entitled to all the tax benefits of ownership until the option might be exercised. This is a call option, since it gives the purchaser the right to force the owner to sell. If Mr. Silverman could have compelled the Burtons to purchase the apartment for $450,000 at the end of the lease, it would have been a put.

Technique 5: Like-Kind Exchanges

The tax code permits the transfer of like-kind property without tax effect if the property is held for business or the production of income (i.e., not a primary residence, secondary residence or other personal-use property). The meaning of "like-kind" has been broadly construed, and can include a condominium, a cooperative apartment, a single-family house, an apartment building or conceivably any form of real estate.

While this arrangement is most easily understood when it is a simple property transfer between two participants (for which the tax code specifically states that there is no tax effect, unlike for most barter arrangements), a particularly advantageous and more complicated arrangement is a *three-way triangular exchange*. Under this procedure, a buyer purchases a property based on specifications defined by the seller. The purchaser then exchanges this property with the seller in a like-kind exchange. The trade need not be simultaneous, as long as the overall intent is to perform a like-kind exchange and a qualified intermediary maintains control over the funds. Special consideration must be made for mortgages and any transfer of cash along with the property transfer. This is called *boot*, and may result in some tax liability for the receiving party.

If the exchange in not simultaneous, certain basic time requirements must be met in order to qualify for a successful like-kind exchange:

- The seller has only 45 days after the sale of the property to identify a replacement property.
- The seller must close the transaction within 180 days after the prior property has been sold and closed.
- The funds received from the sale cannot be released and must be held by an escrow agent until the subsequent purchase transaction takes place (IRC Sec. 1031; Treas. Reg. Sec. 1.1031(a)-1(b); Rev. Rul. 57-244, 1957-1 C.B. 247; *W.D. Haden Company v. Commissioner*, 165 F.2d 588 (5th Cir. 1948); *Biggs v. Commissioner*, 632 F.2d 1171 (5th Cir. 1980); Rev. Rul. 90-34, 1990-1 C.B. 154).

Example of a Like-Kind Exchange Transaction

Alan Berman has owned a condominium apartment in Manhattan as an investment for 20 years. There is no mortgage on the property, and he has deducted a significant amount of depreciation. He would have a substantial gain if it were sold. Mitchell Dunn would like to buy the apartment. Because of the tax consequences, Mr. Berman proposes a like-kind exchange for an apartment building he has been eyeing in New Jersey.

Mr. Berman works out an all-cash purchase of the apartment building at a price acceptable to Mr. Dunn. Thereafter, Mr. Dunn buys the apartment building and exchanges it for the New York condo. The arrangement works favorably for both parties: Mr. Berman is able to use the wealth he accumulated by owning the condominium without being obligated to pay a large capital gains tax, and Mr. Dunn is able to obtain a favorable price for the apartment as consideration for entering into the like-kind transaction. Mr. Berman's adjusted basis is the same as for that of the condominium. Mr. Dunn's basis is the same as it was for the apartment building. If cash or mortgages were involved, however, certain special precautions would have to be considered because of the existence of boot.

Technique 6: Investing Pension Funds in a Limited-Liability Company

Normally, retirement accounts are permitted to buy real estate. However, if a mortgage is taken to purchase the property, there is an adverse tax consequence because the property becomes subject to the Unrelated Business Taxable Income (UBTI) tax. In addition, you may not personally guarantee a mortgage taken by a qualified retirement plan. However, you can purchase property jointly with a retirement plan so that the plan owns a portion of the real estate and you individually own the remaining portion. In this case, you can arrange for the mortgage to be applicable to your portion of the ownership, which would eliminate UBTI-qualifying income. The use of a *limited-liability company* (LLC) is an acceptable means of facilitating this arrangement, and special allocations of profits, losses and capital may be permissible depending on the circumstances. This strategy could be used to purchase a condominium, but would not in all likelihood be permissible in a co-op.

Example of Investing Pension Funds in a Limited-Liability Company

Michael Green has an IRA plan. He decides that he wants to use a portion of these funds to invest in a condominium. He identifies a studio apartment he can buy for $250,000. He calls his bank and relays his intentions, and the bank agrees to act as custodian for the purchase. Mr. Green then calls the trustee of his IRA plan and advises him about the purchase as well. The trustee approves the purchase as prudent and agrees to remit the necessary funds to the bank, which will act as custodian until the funds are required.

Mr. Green then arranges with his attorney to form a limited-liability company. The company has two members: Mr. Green as an individual and Mr. Green's IRA. Each member receives 50% ownership. A corporate agreement is prepared by Mr. Green's attorney that calls for the IRA to contribute $125,000 in cash for its ownership interest. Mr. Green contributes his personal guarantee to a $125,000 mortgage obtained by the LLC. Thereafter, the LLC buys the property with cash contributed to it by the IRA and the mortgage obtained by the LLC.

At year end, Mr. Green's tax return allocates 50% of the profits and losses to the IRA and 50% to Mr. Green personally. There is no UBTI tax because the IRA used only cash to purchase its interest.

Technique 7: Increasing Depreciation Deductions

One of the great advantages of owning real estate is depreciation, which is a noncash expense associated with the "using up" of the property over time. Depreciation permits cash flow generated from the property to be sheltered from tax. Under current law, an owner of a residential condominium or cooperative that is held for business purposes or for investment is entitled to depreciate this property over 27.5 years. However, in the case of *Hospital Corporation of America v. Commissioner* (109 T.C. 21 (1997)), the tax court held that depreciable tangible property installed in a building that is not a structural component may be separately depreciated over a much shorter time period, normally five or seven years. In addition, an accelerated depreciation method, *double-declining balance depreciation*, may be used. This method permits twice the deduction offered over the conventional straight-line method in earlier years but requires an annual adjustment to the tax basis of the property, thereby reducing the level of depreciation in later years (IRC Sec. 168(b)(1)). Examples of this kind of property would include cabinetry, appliances, air conditioners and furnishings. Additionally, in the year that tangible personal property is purchased, you may take only a half-year depreciation (IRC Sec. 168). In subsequent years, a full-year depreciation is generally permitted with some technical exceptions.

Example of Increasing Depreciation Deductions

Arnold Jacobs purchases a condominium for $300,000 at the beginning of the year for investment purposes. In the contract, tangible personal property is segregated and identified in the amount of $50,000, which is equal to its fair market value; the remaining real estate therefore has a tax value of $250,000. Mr. Jacobs decides to rent the apartment furnished, so he purchases additional tangible personal property in the form of furnishings for $25,000. He segregates all tangible personal property from the remaining real estate on his books. The property is rented, and after common charges, real estate taxes and other costs of operation, it generates an annual positive cash flow of $35,000. Mr. Jacobs computes his depreciation deduction by dividing the real estate value of $250,000 by 27.5 years for a balance of $9,090. He then takes the tangible personal property of $75,000 (identified in the contract at $50,000 plus his additional furnishings of $25,000) and divides it by seven years to get $10,714. He uses the double-declining method, so he now must double this amount to $21,428. However, in the first year, he can take only one-half of this amount, $10,714. The computation is as follows:

Net income from operations before depreciation.... $ 35,000

Real estate depreciation .... $ 9,090
  $250,000 ÷ 27.5 years

Tangible personal property............................ $ 10,714
  first-year allowance ($75,000 ÷ 7 years × 2) ÷ 2

Total allowable depreciation .... $ 19,804

Recognized income for tax purposes.................. $ 15,196
  in year one

In the first year of ownership, if Mr. Jacobs treated the entire property as real estate using conventional methods, he would divide the entire cost of $325,000 by 27.5 years, which would result in a depreciation deduction of only $11,818. Therefore, in the first year, he shelters an additional $7,986.

In the second year of ownership, assuming all income and expenses are the same, his depreciation deduction for the real estate will remain at $9,090. However, his depreciation deduction for tangible personal property will now be based on a full-year double-declining balance amount less prior depreciation taken. This would be computed as follows:

Projected income . . . . $ 35,000
in year two

Real estate depreciation . . . . $ 9,090

Tangible personal property

Original cost . . . . $ 75,000

Accumulated depreciation . . . . *minus* $ 10,714

Adjusted value . . . . *equals* $ 64,286

Divided by asset life . . . . $ 9,184
7 years

Double-declining balance depreciation . . . . $ 18,368
× 2

Full depreciation deduction . . . . $ 27,458
in year two

Recognized income for tax purposes . . . . $ 7,542
in year two

In the second year, because Mr. Jacobs can use a full year of double-declining balance depreciation and cost segregation, he can shelter an additional $15,640 of income.

Technique 8: Expanding Interest Deductions on a Primary Residence

U.S. tax law provides that an owner of a primary residence shall be entitled to an interest deduction on their original acquisition loan up to a principal balance of $1,000,000. In addition, the homeowner shall also be entitled to a deduction on the interest on a home equity credit line up to a principal balance of $100,000 (IRC 163(h)(3)(B)(i)–(ii)). The code also permits an interest deduction for business and investment loans, with limited conditions. For an investment loan, an interest deduction can be taken to the extent of generated income, with any excess applied to subsequent years (IRC 163(d)(1)). In the case of a business loan, interest may be deducted as long as it is an ordinary and necessary expense (IRC 163 (h)(1)(A)). Any form of collateral can be used for the loan, including a taxpayer's primary residence.

Example of Investment Interest on a Primary Residence

John Samuelson wants to purchase property for investment. He needs $3 million in equity for the purchase, and seeks a return on investment of 7%. His bank agrees to grant him a loan secured by his primary residence, which is worth $6 million and has no existing mortgage. Since John's investment income exceeds the interest expense he incurs, the interest on his home loan is totally deductible. Because it is investment interest, it does not matter that it exceeds the tax threshold of $1 million.

Tax Requirements for Cooperative Corporations and Condominium Associations

Requirements for a Cooperative Corporation

Besides issuing shares of stock and leases for the apartments owned by the corporation, the corporation must, according to the Internal Revenue Code (IRC Sec. 216) and New York State law (N.Y. GBL Secs. 352-eee, 352-eeee), meet other criteria to qualify for the special tax benefits that allow its tenant-shareholders to pass along real estate taxes and interest deductions on their personal tax returns. These requirements are as follows:

1. The corporation must have only one class of stock outstanding. While different apartments may be assigned different numbers of shares, all shares must have equal rights. If a cooperative corporation provides unique privileges to some stockholders and not to others, it creates a second class of stock, and the corporation does not qualify.

For example, if the cooperative corporation designates certain stock as preferred stock requiring additional payment and offering a dividend, this is a second class of stock and disqualifies the corporation. It doesn't matter that the corporation may have couched the payment as debt. If certain stockholders have privileges distinguishable from others, the right of the corporation to pass through tax deductions to the tenant-shareholders will be placed in jeopardy.

2. Each stockholder of the corporation must be entitled, solely by reason of ownership of stock in the corporation, to occupy for dwelling purposes a house or an apartment in a building owned or leased by the corporation.

The right to dwell in the apartment does not mean that the tenant-shareholder actually has to live there. It is sufficient that the tenant-shareholder has a right to dwell that is superior to that of the cooperative corporation. If apartments in the building are occupied by rent-controlled or rent-stabilized tenants who have legal rights to continued occupancy because of local ordinances, the corporation still qualifies as a cooperative corporation. The tenant-shareholder of an occupied rent-controlled unit has a dwellable right superior to that of the cooperative corporation. Additionally, a doctor who uses an apartment for his or her business is not disqualified, provided the apartment is dwellable, even though the doctor does not choose to dwell in it.

3. No stockholder of the corporation may be entitled, either conditionally or unconditionally, to receive any distribution from the corporation not out of earnings and profits of the corporation except upon a complete or partial liquidation of the corporation.

In the event that a cooperative corporation accumulates excess funds, these funds may be disbursed to tenant-shareholders directly if they are derived from earnings and profits of the corporation. However, no distribution may be made or disbursed from any other source unless the corporation intends to partly or completely liquidate itself. According to the Internal Revenue Service, one exception exists: if there is an *overassessment*, the excess may be returned to tenant-shareholders in the year of the assessment without violating this provision (Rev. Rul. 56-225, 1956-1 C.B. 58).

One interpretation of this provision centers on the word "entitled." Since it is rare for any shareholder to be entitled to a dividend, almost every kind of distribution would appear acceptable, since the board would be resolving to do it rather than being compelled to do it under an entitlement arrangement.

4. A percentage requirement must be met with respect to (a) the source of the corporation's gross income; (b) the square footage of the corporation's property used for tenant-shareholders for residential purposes; or (c) the corporation's expenditures for the acquisition, construction, management, maintenance or care of the corporation's property for the benefit of tenant-shareholders.

The cooperative corporation must meet one or more of the following requirements in order to qualify as such for tax purposes:

1. Eighty percent or more of its income must be derived from tenant-shareholders.

2. At all times during the year, 80 percent of the square footage of the corporation's property must be used or available for use by the tenant-shareholders.

3. Ninety percent or more of the expenditures of the corporation must be paid or incurred for the acquisition, construction, management, maintenance or care of the corporation's property for the benefit of the tenant-shareholders (IRC Sec. 216(b)(1)(D)).

Requirements for Condo Tax-Exempt Status

Condominiums may be treated as tax-exempt homeowner associations as long as particular criteria are met. These requirements are described in Section 528 of the Internal Revenue Code and are as follows:

1. The condominium must be organized and operated to provide for the management, maintenance and care of association property for the common benefit of all members, and must be organized to

enhance the beneficial enjoyment of the private residences by their owners (Treas. Reg. Sec. 1.528-3(a)).

2. Sixty percent or more of the condominium's gross income for the taxable year must come from membership dues, fees or assessments received from residential condominium unit owners.

3. Ninety percent or more of the condominium's expenditures for the taxable year must be for the acquisition, construction, management, maintenance and care of the condominium property.

4. No one unit owner may benefit over others through the distribution of the net earnings of the condominium, other than by acquiring, constructing or providing management, maintenance and care of association property, and other than by rebate of excess membership dues, fees or assessments.

5. The condominium must elect exempt status for the taxable year.

In contrast to the rules that must be met for cooperatives to qualify for deductibility of real estate tax and interest at the homeowner level, electing tax-exempt status as a housing association is not critical to deductibility. Rather, electing the exemption permits the condominium to accumulate funds and profits without fear that such funds will be subject to tax. In a cooperative, this is less of a concern, since depreciation of the corporation's building affords a tax shelter for additional cash flow beyond operating expenses.

Format for a Personal Tax Return

The following is a generic form showing the structure used for personal income tax returns. It is useful for understanding the underlying framework behind tax terminology and its application. It is not to be construed as a complete and accurate form for tax-filing purposes.

Total cash received for the year $_____

Less changes in assets, liabilities and other non-income items:

Loans received	minus	$_____
Return of loans provided	minus	$_____
Insurance proceeds received on losses for which you suffered damages	minus	$_____
Gifts received *may be subject to separate gift tax filings*	minus	$_____

= GROSS INCOME $_____

Less tax-exempt income:

Tax-exempt income received *(e.g. tax-exempt interest or dividends)*	minus	$_____
Deferred-income programs *such as IRAs or 401(k)s*	minus	$_____

= GROSS INCOME SUBJECT TO TAX $_____

Less deductions for adjusted gross income (AGI)

Business-related expenses	minus	$_____
Investment-related expenses	minus	$_____

= ADJUSTED GROSS INCOME (AGI) $_____

Less itemized deductions of personal expenses:

Interest deductions relating to primary and vacation homes as permitted	minus	$_____
Real estate tax deductions on primary and vacation homes as permitted	minus	$_____
Personal deductions *e.g. charitable contributions, medical expense allowances*	minus	$_____

State income tax liability   *minus* $_____

Personal exemptions for dependents   *minus* $_____

                        = TAXABLE INCOME $_____

Multiplied by applicable tax rate   _____%

                = TAX BEFORE TAX CREDITS $_____

Less tax credits $_____

                    = FEDERAL TAX LIABILITY $_____

Tax Rates

Federal Income Tax Brackets for 2013

Bracket	Single ends at	Married, Joint Filers ends at	Head of Household ends at
10%	$8,925	$17,850	$12,750
15%	$36,250	$72,500	$48,600
25%	$87,850	$146,400	$125,450
28%	$183,250	$223,050	$203,150
33%	$398,350	$398,350	$398,350
35%	$400,000	$450,000	$425,000
39.6%	$400,000+	$450,000+	$425,000+

The capital gains rate is 15% unless the taxpayer's taxable income exceeds $400,000, in which case the rate is 20% if the holding period is less than five years, and 18% if it exceeds five years. (There are exceptions to this rule; e.g., for low-income taxpayers in the 15% bracket, the rate is 10% based on a holding period of one year.)

For depreciable property, the amount of recaptured depreciation on a sale is taxed at 25%.

The Medicare surcharge tax would apply for passive income exceeding $200,000 for individuals and $250,000 for married couples. This is an additional tax of 3.8% on the excess amount.

New York State and New York City Tax Rates

These tax charts display the tax brackets applicable to earnings within the stated threshholds. In computing the tax effect of home owner-ship, you should subtract from your income the amount of deduction you would be entitled to as an owner (real estate tax + interest on your home). For example, if you are single with an income of $300,000, and you have ownership deductions for real estate taxes and mortgage interests of $50,000, your income for tax purposes would be reduced to $250,000. For New York State, the first $200,000 of your income would be taxed at 6.85% and the remaining $50,000 would go into the next bracket and be taxed at 7.85%. For New York City, the first $50,000 of your income would be taxed at 3.591% and the remaining $200,000 would go into the next tax bracket at 3.648%.

New York State Tax Rates for 2013

Tax Rate	Single ends at	Married, Filing Jointly ends at
6.85%	$200,000	$300,000
7.85%	$500,000	$500,000
8.97%	$500,000+	$500,000+

New York City Tax Rates for 2013

Tax Rate	Single ends at	Married, Filing Jointly ends at
3.591%	$50,000	$ 90,000
3.648%	$500,000	$500,000
3.876%	$500,000+	$500,000+

The rate for any city resident is the sum of the two tax rates. For example, if a taxpayer earns $200,000 and is married, the New York

State tax is 6.85% and the New York City tax is 3.591% for a combined tax of 10.441%. State and local taxes are generally deductible on the federal tax return. Therefore, the tax rate must be adjusted by taking the applicable rate figure (10.441%) and multiplying it by one minus the applicable federal tax rate. A married taxpayer with a reported income of $200,000 filing jointly would have an incremental federal rate of 28%. Thus, the state and local tax would be $0.10441 \times (1 - 0.28) = 7.517\%$.

CHAPTER 11

Investing in Cooperative and Condominium Apartments

While most cooperatives and condominiums are owner-occupied, a significant number of people acquire New York City properties for investment. The reasons for doing so include:

Participation cost: Few investors can afford to buy an entire building in New York City, but purchasing an individual apartment can be an affordable way to invest in the market and can offer similar returns on a percentage basis.

Management: Managing a building can be extremely time-consuming and complex. By purchasing an apartment, the investor gets to take advantage of the professional management hired by the condominium association or cooperative corporation to handle the affairs of the property. The cost is included in the monthly common charges or maintenance.

Diversification: Buying individual apartments rather than a whole building permits an investor to diversify his or her holdings. For example, an investor could purchase an apartment on the East Side and one in Greenwich Village, or buy a studio as well as a two-bedroom apartment. Diversification permits the owner to take advantage of the unique features offered by each segment of the market in order to maximize returns. Diversification also permits partial liquidation through the sale of a single apartment, whereas a building is normally sold in its entirety.

Appreciation: The New York City market has experienced dramatic appreciation, which has been most pronounced in cooperatives and condominiums. Investors can enjoy significant rental income while they watch their assets appreciate over time.

Tax advantages: Real estate held for investment offers significant tax advantages when compared with alternative investments. It is an appreciating asset that can generate a long-term capital gain, and yet it is a depreciable asset that permits the sheltering of yearly income. Indeed, in certain instances, the asset can even provide tax shelter benefits for alternative income.

While the maintenance charge to a homeowner is only partly deductible for tax purposes (real estate taxes and mortgage interest), an investor who rents the same apartment can deduct the entire maintenance charge as a business or investment expense (except for the usually small portion that relates to amortization of the underlying mortgage principal). When the property is sold, the gain is taxed at favorable capital gains rates, except for the portion relating to accumulated depreciation. That amount, which has been deducted in prior periods, is subject to a special tax rate of 25%.

Types of Investments

The various ways to invest in the New York City apartment market are as follows:

Straight Purchase: Condominium

Very little is controversial about the straight purchase of a condominium, as long as the unit deed presents no limitations on the right to rent or sell. Generally, mortgages are readily available to qualified applicants for 75% or more of the purchase price, at a rate that is approximately 0.25% to 0.50% above the standard homeownership interest rate.

Straight Purchase: Cooperative

Purchasing a cooperative apartment for investment can be a challenge, as most properties have limitations on the right to rent or sell. In addition, there are frequently limitations on the length of time an owner may sublet a co-op, and prospective tenants must generally go through an application process as extensive as that required of a buyer. The deductions available through co-op ownership are the same as for a condominium, including the right to take depreciation.

One unique feature of cooperative investment is the determination of the cost of the property for tax purposes. The price of the cooperative shares and that portion of the underlying building mortgage related to the apartment are added together to create the tax basis. For buildings where there is no board approval requirement (which brokers refer to as *condops*), the economic advantages are the same as for a condominium.

Unsold Shares

An important element in understanding unsold shares is that certain rent laws currently in force in New York City — namely rent control and rent stabilization — afford tenants in occupancy the right to occupy their apartments for as long as they wish with certain restrictions, and limit rent increases to governmentally prescribed levels. The sponsor of a conversion who owns unsold shares is subject to the tenancies in force and the related legal protections. Since possession is unavailable and the flow of income is restricted, the value of these apartments is substantially less than it would be if they could be rented or sold at market levels. Accordingly, sponsors will generally sell these properties at a substantial discount. Buyers look for returns on their investment through subsequent increases in rent as permitted under law, and by future vacancies in units, which can then be rerented or sold at market rates.

In the course of converting a building to cooperative ownership, many sponsors reserve for themselves special rights on units they hold as unsubscribed shares, permitting them to rent and sell these apartments without board approval. In many instances, these unsold share rights are transferable to third-party investors, and an investor acquiring these apartments receives the same right to rent and sell them without board approval. Financing is generally available at 50% of the purchase price as long as the rental income, less the monthly carrying costs, equals or exceeds approximately 125% of the monthly debt payment.

It is strongly recommended that anyone purchasing unsold shareholder rights consult an attorney regarding the requirements to qualify as a designee of the sponsor, and to confirm that any special rights will truly be transferable to the purchaser.

Occupied Apartments

Apartments that do not have unsold-share status and are occupied by a legally protected tenant present a situation similar to that just described, except that there are no special rights to rerent the apartment or to sell the property without board approval. Profit is derived from government-controlled rent increases and the potential gain on the sale of the apartment when it becomes vacant.

Insider Rights

During a conversion to cooperative or condominium ownership, the sponsor will normally offer the tenants a discount on the purchase price to encourage them to subscribe to purchase their own apartments. This tenant discount has value, and knowledgeable investors can purchase the right to buy the apartment from the tenant in occupancy. Normally, this right is transferred via an assignment agreement, whereby the tenant transfers to the investor his legal position in the apartment, including the right to buy at the discounted price. After the conversion, the investor can resell the apartment at its full market price (referred to as a *flip*).

Insider rights are a special situation and are rather speculative. The investor must be well acquainted with the conversion process and retail property values in order to avoid the pitfalls of owning the right to buy an apartment in a building that never converts, or whose plan is amended in a way that could be detrimental to the apartment's value.

Methods of Valuation

There are two methods of defining the value of an apartment for investment: the income approach and the market approach.

Income Approach to Valuation

This approach calls for the investor to determine the property's rate of return by taking the rent currently collected, or the perceived market rent in the case of a vacant apartment (as long as it is not subject to rent stabilization controls), and subtracting the common charges and real estate taxes (for condominiums) or maintenance charges (for cooperatives) to arrive at the *operating profit*. This is the asset's cash return on investment. The investor should then compare this rate of return with alternative opportunities to select the best investment. The investor can also translate the operating profit into a fair-value figure by dividing the profit by the investor's accepted rate of return on a real estate asset. This is often referred to as the capitalization rate.

Example of the Income Approach

John Santiago is considering the purchase of a one-bedroom condo. The asking price is $500,000. It is currently vacant. Mr. Santiago estimates the rental value to be $2,500 per month. The monthly carrying charge is $750, and the monthly real estate tax is $250. Therefore, the monthly operating cost is $1,000, and the operating profit is $1,500. Mr. Santiago multiplies this by 12 to get a yearly profit figure of $18,000, which he then divides by the asking price of $500,000, yielding a cash return on his investment of 3.6%. In considering his alternatives, Mr. Santiago sees this apartment as offering the best rate of return and decides to make an offer. He does not consider the cost of a mortgage because the interest rate will be the same for whatever condo he may buy. If he decided that he wanted a return of 4%, he would divide the $18,000 by 0.04 to get $450,000, and this would be the offer he would make.

Market Approach to Valuation

In the market approach, the investor analyzes the aesthetic qualities of the unit, as represented by the five primary motivators of location, building, air, light and space, along with the economic criteria of price and monthly carrying cost (see Chapter 4). By doing this analysis and analyses of similar properties, the investor can ascertain fair value.

Example of the Market Approach and Income Approach Used Together

Mary Lerner is thinking about buying a studio condominium for $350,000. It is in Midtown, which she evaluates in terms of location as a 6 on a scale of 1 to 10. The building has a doorman and is in good condition, and she considers it a 7. The apartment layout is conventional, and there are no special amenities. It is on the fifth floor, facing south toward the street, so Ms. Lerner gives it a view rating of 5. The space in the main room is 32' x 12', which she considers large. The monthly carrying charges are $350, and the real estate tax is $150. The rental value on the unit is $1,300 per month. In light of other properties she has seen, the asking price of $350,000 is a little high in terms of market value, and she decides it is worth only $325,000.

Ms. Lerner then evaluates the property using the income approach. By deducting the monthly common charges of $350 and real estate taxes of $150 from a projected rent of $1,300, she gets an operating cash flow of $800 per month. She multiplies this by 12 and gets a yearly figure of $9,600, which she divides by the $350,000 asking price, which yields a rate of return of 2.7%. This is lower than the 3% rate of return she would like. So she divides the operating cash flow by 0.03 and gets $320,000. Ms. Lerner decides to use this figure for her offer. Had the market value been lower, she might have used that as her guideline.

Evaluating Economic Return and Risk

When an investor considers making a purchase, he engages in a process of evaluation that focuses on economic return as well as risk.

Economic return is a function of the income stream generated by an asset from regular operation, plus appreciation return from the increased value of the asset over time. Appreciation consists of two components. The first of these is macroeconomic appreciation, and refers to the general health of the national and local economy. The second component of appreciation is referred to as *unique risk*, and refers to the special attributes associated with the asset being purchased and the chance that those qualities will stimulate an additional return beyond those generated by macroeconomic conditions. In the case of real estate, unique risk would focus on qualities of the asset's location and features specific to the building.

In dealing with location factors, smart real state investors focus on two primary attributes:

Bridging: Where there are two vibrant areas separated by an area of economic malaise, investors are often attracted to the area of malaise as an investment opportunity. This is called *bridging*, in that the underperforming area forms a "bridge" between two vibrant ones. Investors perceive that there are strong forces seeking to merge the vibrant areas with the underperforming area, so the likelihood of future opportunity is very strong.

Expanding the coast: This situation occurs when investors seek to purchase assets on the edge of a vibrant area, under the expectation that the area will naturally expand and that they will enjoy the benefits of that expansion.

Additional Risks

An investor should evaluate potential micro risk to minimize the possibility of surprises. Some things to consider are outlined below.

Unusual Increase in Maintenance or Building Assessment
Review the financial statement (including the notes) of the cooperative or condominium carefully. Is the mortgage coming due? Is there an ad-

equate reserve fund? How are the funds being spent? Try to evaluate the risk of an assessment or maintenance increase reducing your rate of return. If you identify problems, you need not abandon the transaction. Instead, add a discount factor to your computations, and then voice your concerns in negotiating the price with the seller.

Balloon Mortgage

It is common for a mortgage on investment property, including loans secured by co-op and condominium apartments held for that purpose, to have a term of five to ten years and to mature before the loan principal has been fully amortized. The final payment is a large one, including repayment of the remaining principal. This is called a *balloon mortgage*.

Normally, when these mortgages mature, they are renegotiated at the rates prevailing at the time of renewal. However, the bank has the right to not reissue the loan, or to reissue it with less favorable terms. Investors should look for financing that coincides with the length of time they expect to hold the property. A long-term mortgage on investment property can usually be obtained, but it will cost more. In most cases, the bank will ask for personal guarantees on the loan.

Rental Tenancy Risk

The income flow from an apartment held for investment is dependent on the financial capability of the tenant. If the tenant cannot pay the rent, the investor must hire a lawyer to enforce his or her rights, which can be frustrating, unpleasant and costly. Most investors use a broker to assist them in setting standards that minimize their risk and help them find a qualified tenant. A credit check should be performed and references called. A good rule of thumb is that the tenant should have a yearly income that is at least 40 times the monthly rent. Currently the brokerage fee for New York City apartment rentals is paid by the prospective tenant; however, when the demand weakens, sometimes the landlord pays the broker (called an *owner-paid* commission or *OP*).

Small vs. Large Apartments

Buying several small apartments permits diversification and the flexibility to partly liquidate your investment portfolio by selling one apartment while retaining others. Renters of small apartments, however, have a greater tendency to default, since they generally have less money.

Many investors avoid large apartments because they represent a much larger initial cash outlay and do not allow for as much diversification or flexibility. However, since there is currently a significant shortage of them, the prices and rents on these apartments have risen dramatically. Additionally, larger apartments attract wealthier renters who pose less of a default risk.

Unsold Shares and Occupied Apartments

When you purchase an occupied apartment or unsold shares, it is usually because you are hoping that the tenant will move out and you will be able to sell or rerent the apartment at the market rate. My recommendation is that you focus on small apartments such as one-bedrooms and studios, which have a higher turnover rate than larger apartments.

Purchasing Insider Rights

When negotiating the purchase of insider rights, make sure that you verify the offering plan's estimate of the market value of the apartment. Many offering plans exaggerate this figure. The money should also be held in escrow by an attorney until the closing and transfer of title take place and the tenant leaves the apartment.

Lead

In 2004, New York City enacted legislation entitled the New York City Childhood Lead Poisoning Prevention Act (also known as Local Law 1 of 2004), which placed substantial burdens on landlords to remedy lead contamination in apartments built prior to 1960 where a child under seven years old resides. The law requires that the landlord send a yearly notice to tenants seeking to determine if a child under seven is living there, and if so, a lead test must be performed, with a copy of the report given to the New York City Department of Housing, Preservation and Development (HPD).

If lead is present, the landlord must make the apartment lead-safe by performing prescribed remediation procedures, including removal or encapsulation of any lead contamination. Even more onerous is the law's presumption that the landlord is responsible for any lead contamination to the child, which implies considerable liability exposure.

You should check for lead before you buy, and if there are any young children in an apartment you rent, make sure you get the apartment tested right away. The estimated cost for remedying lead contamination in an apartment is $10,000 to $15,000. You can find more information at the website for the New York City Coalition to End Lead Poisoning, www.nmic.org/nyccelp.htm, or on HPD's website at www.nyc.gov/html/hpd/html/for-owners/lead-paint-treatment.html.

Bedbugs

Bedbug infestation is a serious issue in New York City. While the law does not seem to apply to cooperatives and condominiums, it does apply to any rented apartment, including apartments rented in cooperatives and condominiums. Section 27-2018.1 of the administrative code of New York City requires that there be notice of any bedbug infestation for any newly leased apartment following a vacancy. In addition, the owner is responsible for any remediation.

Renting a Furnished Apartment

Furnished apartments often have transient tenancies, with occupancies running as short as one night and as long as one year. The wear and tear may be considerable and the cost of management significant. Additionally, a condominium association may legitimately restrict the level of rental activity if it views the transient occupancy as inconsistent with the residential nature of the building. Co-ops are generally very stringent about short-term rentals, though a long-term rental of a furnished apartment creates no special issues as long as other board requirements are met. The income premium can be substantial, and the tax treatment of furnished rentals is favorable. Current regulations permit depreciating personal property in a residential unit over a term of five years from the date it is placed in service. This can greatly enhance the tax shelter of the income flow.

Managing an Apartment

When an investor purchases an apartment, the legal obligations that normally exist between a landlord and a tenant now vest in the apartment owner. Tasks such as painting and keeping the fixtures and appliances in good repair can be a significant undertaking, particularly if the building is old and the apartment is in marginal condition. Many investors seek professional management to deal with day-to-day responsibilities. The cost of unit management normally runs between $100 and $250 per month. If you don't have the time, hiring a professional is well worth the money.

CHAPTER 12

Analyzing a Building's Financial Statement

The task of analyzing the financial performance of a building is one of the greatest sources of confusion for many buyers. They frequently fear that something about the building's affairs may be amiss, and rightly believe that the financial statements of the building can provide essential clues to its performance. The key to analyzing a financial statement is not to find out if the building is running at a loss (which many buildings do) or has a large underlying mortgage (which is also common), but to identify the risk of a future increase in maintenance charges beyond ordinary adjustments for inflation.

A useful tool for guidance on evaluating the financial affairs of a building is the website of the accounting firm Kleiman and Weinshank LLP, kwnycpa.com, where users can access a database of financial reports for cooperatives and condominiums through the tab *Internet Links > Financial*. The database contains the yearly profit and loss statements for a wide array of cooperatives and condominiums of various sizes.

An inquisitive buyer can use this information to evaluate the financial performance of a property against other properties of similar size, in order to determine if there are material differences in costs that may have relevance to his or her purchasing decision. A word of caution: Kleiman and Weinshank acts as the accountant for many properties with very different levels of service and financial philosophies. You should use the database to gain an impression of various costs, but should not automatically assume that a given building has a problem just because its financial figures may diverge from those of other properties in the database.

Critical Components of a Financial Report

In analyzing a financial statement, you should focus on four critical parts: the *accountant's opinion letter*, the *statement of financial position* (balance sheet), the *income statement* (statement of operations), and the *notes to the financial statement*.

Accountant's Opinion Letter

The accountant's opinion letter is a document addressed to the board of directors of the condominium association or cooperative corporation that is found in the front of the financial statement. It should contain the phrase "presents fairly," and there should be no restrictive language, such as "subject to" or "except for." Where restrictive language exists, you should read it carefully — it may be important.

If the opinion letter refers to a "compilation" or "review," then building's affairs have not been audited, and should be viewed with suspicion. If a statement is audited, it means that an independent certified public accountant has followed certain independent confirmation procedures to verify that the information is correct. In the case of a "compilation" or "review" financial statement, these verification procedures have not been performed or were performed to a lesser degree. As a general rule, particularly for larger buildings (those with more than 40 apartments), you should presume that a compilation or review opinion means that there is a problem. Additional investigation, such as reading the minutes of the board meetings, should be performed to ensure that no unforeseen issues exist.

According to standard guidelines, accountants are supposed to add a paragraph to their opinion letters regarding the remaining useful life of the building's components. This requires that the building engage an engineer or comparable building expert to perform a review of the building's physical plant. In practice this is rarely done because most boards refuse to incur the cost of the survey, and because many believe that the results are deceptive, frequently implying that the building is substantially obsolete. Such evaluations are likely, for example, to consider an elevator obsolete in 15 to 20 years, when in truth elevators are rarely replaced but rather upgraded over time. The reports are also frequently misunderstood, because they give the impression that enormous sums must be spent to replace obsolete assets, when in fact this is not the case. Managing agents regularly complain that an engineer's interpretation of a building component's useful life does not conform to their actual experience. Therefore, they often discourage co-ops and condos from undertaking this study, and boards readily agree, particularly in light of the adverse implications for resales. Nevertheless, accountants include that paragraph in a supplemental section of the opinion to minimize their professional legal exposure for not having identified material risks associated with the cooperative or condominium.

As a result of the new Fannie Mae requirements that buildings allocate 10% of their revenues to reserve replenishment, there has been a renewed interest in evaluating obsolescence. This is because Fannie Mae will provide a waiver of the 10% requirement if a building can provide evidence that its existing reserves are adequate for its operational needs. An obsolescence evaluation can prove helpful in getting this waiver.

Statement of Financial Position (Balance Sheet)

A *balance sheet* is a financial snapshot by the cooperative corporation or condominium association of what it owns (assets), owes (liabilities), and is worth (net worth, stockholder capital or equity — assets minus liabilities) at a specific point in time, usually as of December 31 of each year. The important components are as follows:

Cash, Cash Equivalents and Reserve Funds
A building should have enough financial resources to be able to han-

dle contingencies. For a building in reasonable condition, $5,000 per apartment in reserve funds is adequate, although some accounting firms recommend three months' building expenses.

Some buildings maintain large cash balances in operating accounts, while others maintain minimal balances in investment or money market funds. To equalize these variations, your evaluation should include all cash and cash equivalents, both from bank accounts and investment accounts.

Some buildings have an item in their financial reports entitled "due from managing agent." Normally this is cash held by the managing agent for the purpose of making current disbursements to vendors by the building, and can be counted as cash.

Accounts Receivable or Tenant Arrears

Generally, the only receivables a cooperative or condominium will identify are payments due from tenant-shareholders or commercial tenants. Arrears should not exceed 5% of the total yearly operating revenue.

Accounts Payable

An excessive amount owed to vendors can indicate that the building is having financial trouble. If the accounts payable figure is more than 10% of the yearly maintenance revenue, this should be investigated.

Mortgages

The mortgage balance is normally found in two parts of the balance sheet. One is the current portion, which is due within one year, and the other is the long-term portion. By combining the two figures, you can determine the full amount of the mortgage outstanding as of the date of the financial statement. The portion of the building's mortgage allocated to each apartment (determined by the percent of the building's shares allocated to that apartment), assuming that the building is average and the apartment is average for its category, should be in approximately the following range:

Studio .... $30,000 to $50,000

One-bedroom .... $40,000 to $80,000

Two-bedroom .... $50,000 to $150,000

Three-bedroom .... $75,000 to $250,000

There are many reasons for variations from these guidelines, and many excellent apartments exceed these criteria. However, in general, a higher mortgage will mean a higher-than-average maintenance charge.

Since a condominium does not have an underlying mortgage, capital improvements cannot be funded by refinancing. Condominium capital improvements are normally made by spending the accumulated reserve or by special assessment.

Income Statement (Statement of Operations)

The income statement shows the flow of activity during a given period, usually one year. It tells what has been earned, what has been spent and what is left over. In many cooperative buildings, the net income is negative. There is nothing wrong with this. If collected income approximates disbursements, then depreciation (a non-cash expense) will normally result in a negative income figure. If depreciation is added back to net income, you will get an approximation of the positive cash flow received by the building for the year after operating costs. This is the amount added to the building reserve fund. The building's aim is not to generate a profit — which will be subject to tax — but merely to cover operating costs and build adequate reserves. The following is a general guideline for evaluating the expenses of a building as a percentage of yearly maintenance collections:

Mortgage payments 25–40%

Real estate taxes 35–40%

Payroll, payroll taxes and benefits 20–30%

Other operating expenses 20–30%

In many excellent buildings the figures may vary from these guidelines. Frequently these variations are due to a higher-than-average mortgage balance. A more detailed method for analyzing an income statement is presented later on in this chapter.

As a result of changes in the terms required by Fannie Mae in offering loans on apartments, buildings are now obligated to budget 10% of their yearly homeowner collection to replenishing their reserve accounts. This will likely create income statements showing profits, and those that have losses might be at higher risk of not qualifying for Fannie Mae loans.

Notes to the Financial Statement

The notes at the end of the financial statement detail and clarify the information presented. Though all notes are important, some deserve special attention.

It is recommended that careful examination be made of the note concerning mortgages. This note will give the maturity date, the amount of the monthly payment and any special terms. A near-term mortgage maturity is not necessarily bad. Often when a building refinances, the monthly payment is significantly reduced because of a lower interest rate or reduced principal payment (amortization).

If the building is on a land lease, it is important to review the note relating to the terms of the lease. Pay careful attention to the maturity date, extensions and renewal options that may exist.

Careful examination should be made of the note relating to the reserve fund. Be sure to establish that these funds are in appropriate financial instruments, and that there are no lending arrangements through which the cooperative or condominium is borrowing money from the reserve fund. If you see a line item identified as "funds due to/from," it effectively means that the cooperative or condominium is dipping into the reserve to support operations without actually reducing the stated balance in the reserve fund account. You should check whether there is a note pertaining to any restricted balances, which are funds that are not readily accessible to the building when a need arises. These funds should not be included in determining the available reserves of the building.

It is also recommended that a careful review be made of any note related to contingent liabilities and/or legal matters. This note would describe any pending lawsuits. Most of the time, lawsuits — even ones that seem onerous — are covered by the building's insurance policy, as long as the claim is made against the cooperative or condominium. If, on the other hand, the co-op or the condo has initiated the action, then all legal costs must be borne by the building. This can be an expensive, drawn-out undertaking, and you should be fully aware of its implications.

Another note to pay attention to is "subsequent events." The accountant is required to report any material change in the building's affairs until the date that he or she signs the accountant's opinion letter, even if it is after the date noted on the financial statement. If there is a subsequent event, it should be carefully reviewed.

Most footnotes contain a statement saying that the cooperative corporation or condominium association has not included a chart outlining the remaining useful life of the building's components, as recommended by the American Institute of Certified Public Accountants. This footnote is included because attorneys and other advisers for most boards recommend that the board not include such a chart, as it could be misleading and result in litigation.

Analyzing the Income Statement

This overview should not be construed as a professional evaluation, which should be performed only by an appropriate expert with knowledge of the specific property.

It is useful to compare the expenses of a specific property against a benchmark, in order to establish a level of acceptable (or unacceptable) performance. To offer a standard for comparison in light of the variation in property size across a universe of apartments, this standard can be expressed as a percentage of revenue. This way, though the actual dollar amounts of the expenditures may vary between large and small buildings, the relationship of a particular expense to income remains comparable. A negative variance is an expenditure that is greater than the standard percentage (i.e., the building spent more than the standard amount for that expense category). A positive variance means the building spent less than the standard percentage for that expense. What this variance implies about the building and its finances is important. There are three ways that a variance can be interpreted:

Negative element: The variance signals a possible assessment, increase in monthly charge or diminishment in the level of service in the building if the problem remains uncorrected.

Neutral element: The variation is probably meaningless to the future cost of ownership and should not result in a future assessment or increase in monthly charge above inflation.

Positive element: The variation signals a possible lowering of the monthly cost of ownership below any increase due to inflation, or a favorable change in the level of service offered by the building.

Consider a series of standard buildings — including a small 10-unit property, a 50-unit property, a 100-unit property and a 200-unit property — that are intended to represent a typical building's operations given its size. For this example, it is assumed that each standard building is run effectively and has no material adverse conditions. Let us also assume that all standard buildings are constructed of brick. If your building is modern with large windows, the level of heat used would be greater than in the standard building. This is a negative variance, but a neutral element, because it does not signal a future increase in the cost of ownership beyond inflation.

A variance of more than 10% exists if an item that should be 25% of revenues is less than 22.5% or greater than 27.5% of revenues. It is 10% of the standard expense that is measured, not 10% of the total revenues.

Before evaluating the income statement of a specific building, you should personally inspect the property to formulate a general sense of its physical condition. As you analyze the building's financial information, this inspection should confirm the figures that you are seeing.

Procedure for Performing an Income Statement Evaluation

Step 1. Write down all the income and expense figures on a sheet of paper, and attempt to combine the line items to conform to the expense categories delineated in the standard presentation. The numbers you need can often be found in an addendum to the financial report or in the notes to the financial statement.

Step 2. In order to determine a percentage allocation for each expense to total revenue, you must create a denominator by adding maintenance revenue and other sources of long-term income, such as lease income and laundry income. Do not use extraordinary income or items such as sublease fees and transfer fees, since these are nonrecurring items.

Step 3. In the notes to the financial statement, identify the actual monthly debt payment (as distinguished from the interest portion of the debt payment). Replace the figure for mortgage interest with the full amount paid for the year in debt service.

Step 4. Add depreciation to the net loss or net income figure expressed at the bottom of the income statement in order to determine the approximate amount of operating cash flow contributed to the reserve fund. Remember, depreciation is an expense item for which the building expends no cash. If this figure is negative, it means that the reserve fund is being depleted to support operating expenses.

Step 5. Normalize the denominator as required. Each line item constitutes part of the whole of all expenses. To the extent that one component of the whole varies significantly from the standard, each other component's percentage is materially affected. In this case, an adjustment must be made to normalize any major expense category so that the variation from the standard can have meaning for the other expense items. Normalization creates a rough means of adjusting the denominator to remove the skewing effect of any significant variation in a single expense category.

There are only three expense items significant enough to require the normalization computation: (1) debt payment, (2) real estate taxes and (3) payroll. Divide each of these items by the denominator to determine the percentage variation from the standard. If the variance is greater than 10% in one or more categories, it can have a ripple effect on the subsequent analysis, and the following steps should be taken:

- If the figure is above the standard, determine the difference in the percentage between the actual figure and the standard. Subtract this amount from 100% and multiply the result by the denominator. This should be used as the new denominator for all subsequent computations.
- If the figure is below the standard, figure out what percentage of revenue the actual expense item represents. Determine the difference between that number and the standard percentage and add 100% to the difference. Multiply this amount by the existing denominator to get the new denominator, which should be used for all subsequent computations.

Example of Normalization

A building has gross revenue, after adjusting for nonrecurring income, of $1,000,000 — the denominator. The debt payment on the property (numerator) is 40% of the adjusted gross revenue (denominator). The standard percentage for debt payment is 25%. This is a variation from the standard of well over 10% and is significant. The difference is an overage of 15 percentage points. Accordingly, the denominator must be adjusted downward using the following procedure:

Standard debt payment...................................... 25%

Reported debt payment...................................... 40%

Difference.. 15%

Adjustment factor............................ 100% − 15% = 85%

New denominator .... $1,000,000 × 85% = $850,000

Therefore, $850,000 should be used as the denominator for subsequent calculations.

The same analysis is used to determine the variation for payroll, using the new denominator of $850,000. It is determined that payroll is at 21% of $850,000, while the standard is 26%. This is a significant variation of more than 10% from the standard. Therefore, normalization for this second expense item must be performed as follows:

Standard payroll 26%

Reported payroll 21%

Difference.. 5%

Adjustment factor............................ 100% + 5% = 105%

New denominator.............. $850,000 × 105% = $892,500

Using $892,500 as the new denominator, it is determined that the variation between standard real estate taxes and this property's real estate taxes is only 1%. Therefore, no normalization adjustment is required. Accordingly, the denominator used for all other line-item expenditures is $892,500.

Step 6. After normalizing the denominator to adjust for variations in the three major expense items, you can use this new adjusted denominator to compute the percentage of each other expense item to ascertain the variance from standard.

Step 7. When any expense is a material variance from the standard, ask your broker to inquire about its cause to determine if it will impact the operating performance of the property. It might foretell a higher risk of assessment or a maintenance increase above inflation.

Standard Operating Expenses for Various Condominium and Cooperative Properties in New York City

(in thousands)

	10 units	50 units	100 units	200 units
Real estate tax	$125	$625	$1,200	$1,800
Debt payment	30	225	400	700
Payroll	18[1]	500[2]	650[3]	780[4]
Payroll tax	2	52	65	78
Pension and welfare	180	215	260	312
Workers comp	2	8	12	15
Gas	10	45	50	70
Heating	35	65	150	200
Water and sewer	8	35	70	90
Building supplies	6	18	33	50
Repairs & maintenance	24	80	140	200
Elevator maintenance	10	21	40	40
Insurance	15	45	54	100
Management	10	45	55	80
Legal	5	5	10	24
Accounting	6	9	13	14
Other professional	2	6	6	6
Corporation tax	15	15	15	15
Office administration	8	10	14	30
Total expenses	$511	$2,024	$3,237	$4,604

[1]No doorman

[2]Full-time doorman, one super

[3]Full-time doorman, one super, one porter

[4]Full-time doorman, one super, one handyman, two porters

Understanding the Meaning of Variances to Standard Debt Payment (Including Land-Lease Payments)

The following sections of this chapter will help you understand the significant components of a building's financial statement and the meaning of some of the material differences that may occur between the amount shown on your building's income statement and the standard performance of a similar building.

Debt Payment

Definition

Debt payment is the cooperative corporation's yearly cost to carry the long-term financial obligations of the building, including mortgage interest, amortization and any long-term land rent.

High interest rate: If there is a high interest rate, the loan probably hasn't been refinanced because of a restriction on doing so or a high prepayment penalty. You can determine when the mortgage comes due from the notes in the financial statement. It may be that upon refinancing, the building will be able to gain additional reserve cash or lower maintenance. Either would be a positive element.

Low interest rate: If there is a low interest rate, the new mortgage may have a higher payment upon refinancing unless the old mortgage was amortizing — that is, if part of the original principal was repaid each month along with interest, which would lead to a lower initial principal balance for the new loan. Banks frequently offer 15- or 30-year amortization schedules with maturities of 10 years. The monthly payments will pay off the principal balance fully in 15 or 30 years, but whatever balance remains at the loan's 10-year maturity date must be paid in full to the bank. Usually, the lowered principal on refinancing is adequate to compensate for any rise in interest rates with no increase in debt payment, so this is generally a neutral or even a positive element. However, if the original interest rate is low and there is limited or no amortization, the full principal balance will have to be refinanced at a higher rate of interest. This would be a negative element.

High principal balance: A high principal balance is unimportant unless refinancing at the same interest rate will be difficult. This is particularly true if the loan is a standing (non-amortizing) mortgage. If the loan is amortizing, this is a neutral element. If the loan is standing, this could be a negative element.

Low principal balance: A low principal balance means that the building is equity-rich. As a mortgage amortizes, the principal portion of each debt payment goes up, while the interest portion goes down. As a result, the tax deduction for interest on the mortgage lowers with each payment. However, on refinancing, the building can increase its cash reserves without having to increase maintenance, and homeowners will get a higher tax deduction as a result of an increased portion of the new payment being for interest. This could be a positive element.

Land rent: A land lease means that the landowner has the option to eventually sell the land to the co-op corporation, adjust the rent when the lease has terminated, or take possession of the land and the building at the end of the lease. A land lease adds an element of risk that should be carefully considered in determining an apartment's value.

The lease, as a long-term obligation, is included under debt payment as a component of cost. Since buyers usually become aware of the existence of a land lease before negotiating a final price, the lease itself is a neutral element, as it was already taken into account. However, if the lease term is less than 50 years, it has increasing importance in determining the property's value and future costs. The uncertainty of negotiations with the landowner for extending the lease term or purchasing the land is a negative element until it is resolved.

Real Estate Taxes

Definition

Real estate taxes on a building are the yearly payment required by New

York City based on a percentage of the assessed value of the property.

Real estate taxes above standard: In new buildings, the assessed value is based on a percentage of the cost of construction. These properties commonly have higher taxes than older properties, whose valuation is determined by comparison to other existing properties. Since the real estate tax is known to the buyer at the time the purchase price is negotiated, this variation has already been considered, and it is a neutral element when reviewing yearly operating costs.

Real estate taxes below standard: It could be that the property has a low assessed value or that it is covered by one of the city's tax incentive programs, particularly J-51 or Section 421a. These programs offer developers temporary real estate tax reductions to encourage new construction or substantial rehabilitation. Look at the notes to the financial statement to ascertain if the building is covered by one of these programs. If so, determine the phase-in period for full real estate taxation. If the property is a participant in one of these programs, then real estate taxes will increase at some point in the future, as will the apartment owner's monthly cost. This could be a negative element.

Payroll

Definition

Payroll is direct and indirect compensation given to building employees. It includes salary, employer tax obligations, health and welfare payments, employer insurance, union dues and other costs incurred by the building to retain the services of the employees.

Payroll above standard: If a building has fewer than 80 units and full-time doormen, it will have above-standard payroll costs because each unit will bear a larger responsibility for covering the same cost as units in a standard building would. A 160-unit building can support twice the staff and not vary from the standard. This variation is further minimized in even larger buildings, since the cost of having more lobby persons, porters and handymen is covered by a larger population of owners.

However, the ratio of staff to occupants is not always the real issue of a payroll variance — it could also be significant overtime. Buildings often use existing employees to cover labor holes, and end up paying more in overtime than if the building had hired additional personnel. Sometimes the problem is that building personnel are working in private apartments, and are able to handle their building responsibilities only by working additional hours. In certain buildings there are substantial capital improvements that need to be performed, and the building regularly uses employees rather than outside contractors to address these problems. This limits the employees' available time for customarily assigned duties. The net effect of these scenarios is that the building is underserving the homeowners and overpaying at the same time. High payroll can therefore be a neutral or negative element.

Payroll below standard: One might think that the economies of scale in large buildings would cause the cost of personnel per apartment to decline. It rarely does. The technical proficiency of the staff in big buildings is frequently higher, necessitating higher salaries for the superintendent and handymen. Also, there are larger areas to clean and more activity in the lobby to support. Accordingly, even in a large building, a below-standard payroll may indicate that the property is underserving its homeowners by being understaffed or by not having adequately trained personnel in place. A below-standard variance could be a neutral or a negative element.

Utilities (Gas and Electric)

Definition

Utilities are electrical and gas charges incurred by the building to support common elements and services.

Utilities above standard: Utilities will be high if the building provides central air-conditioning as a common service. (Most buildings, including the standard building, have wall- or window-unit air conditioners that are bought by homeowners.) Utilities will also be high if the building air-conditions a large lobby that has high ceilings and long hallways. The building will also spend more if there is substantial external lighting and/or fountains. However, usually in these cases a building's electrical use is constant year to year, and thus the expense is generally a neutral element.

Utilities below standard: Utilities could be below standard if the building is penny-pinching by keeping the hallways and stairwells dim, or if the elevator or some other building system has been out of operation for a period of time. On the other hand, low electrical cost may be a result of using lower-cost fluorescent lighting. Therefore, low utility costs could be either a negative or neutral element.

Building Maintenance and Repair

Definition

Maintenance and repair charges are the cost of keeping the building clean and operating in a manner consistent with homeowner expectations. It includes all contract labor except for elevator maintenance, which is separately accounted for.

Maintenance and repair above standard: High maintenance and repair expenditures might mean that the building is being vigorously maintained. However, there is another possibility: if building systems are obsolete and not replaced at the end of their useful lives, the building will incur high maintenance and repair costs to keep the equipment operational. This would imply that a future assessment and/or a maintenance increase might be needed to replace a system that becomes too costly to maintain. This is particularly true if the building has limited reserves. If the building looked unkempt when you performed your physical inspection, and the maintenance and repair charges are high on the statement, it is reasonable to reach this conclusion. Therefore, maintenance and repair costs above standard could be either a neutral or a negative element.

Maintenance and repair below standard: If the building has new systems that are covered under warranty, the level of maintenance and repair may be low. Conversely, the building might be mismanaged and under-cleaned, or items requiring repair might not be properly tended to. If maintenance and repair charges are below standard, it could be a neutral or negative element.

Elevator Maintenance and Repair

Definition

Elevator maintenance and repair includes the cost of the elevator service contract as well as additional labor and materials to maintain the elevators in good working order.

Maintenance and repair above standard: If the elevator is new or recently renovated, elevator companies often provide a warranty period and the likelihood of costly breakdowns is reduced. Thus, expenditures for elevator repair would be lower, which could be a positive element.

Maintenance and repair below standard: If the elevator is in need of an upgrade, it is common to see a considerable increase in service visits to deal with ongoing problems. This would result in higher-than-normal costs, which would be a negative element.

Supplies

Definition

Supplies refer to the cost of cleaning chemicals, hardware and related purchases used to ensure the clean and orderly operation of the building. It does not include significant equipment purchases or materials used for capital improvements, which are treated as assets and can be found on the balance sheet of the cooperative corporation or condominium association.

Supplies above standard: It is not uncommon for supplies to be confused with maintenance and repair items. However, in most financial statements, supplies are itemized separately and usually refer to charges from hardware stores. If the amount is above standard, it may indicate that the building is not careful in purchasing or utilizing its supplies and that there is significant waste. High supply costs could also mean that the building is using employees to maintain obsolete systems, which would require an excessive level of hardware purchases. Generally, high supply costs are a neutral or a negative element.

Supplies below standard: The building may be purchasing supplies in bulk to lower the cost. It could also be that the building is under-cleaned. This could therefore be a neutral or negative element.

Heating Expenses

Definition:

Heating expenses are the cost of the fuel — oil, gas or steam — used to heat the building throughout the year. Oil costs can vary as much as 10% based on the grade of oil used. Gas prices are currently less than those of oil, but the relationship between the two has varied considerably over time. The price of gas is generally 80% that of oil. Steam is the most expensive form of heating, and costs about twice as much as gas or oil.

Heating above standard: Heating costs can be above standard if steam heat is used or if there are inefficiencies in the heating system. But the reason could also be more subtle. The standard building is of brick construction and is well protected from the elements. A building that has greater exposure to wind or is closer to water will cost more to heat, as will a building with large windows and open terraces. Another factor is the weather: colder winters are more expensive than warm ones. In large measure, however, the heating system is unchangeable, so higher-than-standard heating costs are a neutral element.

Heating below standard: Lower heating costs may be due to an efficient heating system, the type of building construction or a warm winter. It could also be that the heating system is inoperable at times, or that the temperature in the building is maintained at a low level. Therefore, a lower-than-standard heating cost is a neutral or negative element.

Administrative and Other Expenses

Definition

Administrative expenses include the cost of cell phones for employees, stationery, supplies, photocopies, postage and other office costs incurred by the cooperative or condominium that are not covered by the management company. Other expenses include professional and consulting fees and taxes (including franchise taxes).

Administrative and other expenses above standard: These costs will be above standard if the management agreement specifies that the co-op or condo shall be responsible for expenses normally borne by the management company, or if the building provides nonstandard services. For example, some buildings have on-site management personnel. In most cases, the cost of the on-site office and employees will be borne by the co-op or condo as an additional administrative expense. Some buildings may also provide a newsletter and actively communicate with residents. More often than not, expenses above standard are due to higher levels of service, and are a neutral element.

Administrative and other expenses below standard: If the bills are not mailed, but are placed under each owner's door, or if the management agreement provides that the management company pick up certain expenses not normally included, such as photocopying or postage costs, administrative expenses could be below standard. On the other hand, if the management company is responsible for administrative costs normally borne by the building, the building will normally pay more for this added feature. This will cause administrative expenses to be lower, but management fees will be higher. Accordingly, administrative expenses below standard are a neutral or negative element.

Management Fees

Definition

Management fees are the cost of professional services to oversee the af-

fairs of the building, including personnel and operational systems. These fees also cover the cost of bookkeeping, including all services associated with receipts, disbursements, reporting and maintenance of files and corporate records.

Management fees above standard: There are three reasons management fees may be above standard. First, they may be levied by the sponsor of the cooperative or condominium, who also controls the building's funds. This occurs when the sponsor has significant influence through a large ownership position in the cooperative corporation or condominium. The New York State attorney general's office has sought to minimize such abuses by limiting the right of sponsors to vote their shares to five years after the date of conversion.

Second, the management company may have performed services beyond those normally provided. For example, management companies often oversee major capital improvement projects for a significant additional charge.

Third, the building may have selected a company with a higher fee in the hopes of receiving better service.

In each case, the higher fee is usually immaterial or limited in duration. Thus, this is a neutral element.

Management fees below standard: Sometimes a sponsor managing a converted building charges a very low management fee in order to reduce the maintenance charge so that he can sell apartments more effectively. Once the sponsor abandons this position, the building will have to pay a new manager a much larger fee.

If the managing agent is not the sponsor, the fee may be low because some charges are recognized in other sections of the statement (including administrative and other expenses and payroll expense). This would be the case if a portion of the employment cost normally paid by the managing agent were paid by the cooperative or condominium directly. Some co-ops and condos hire the managing agent to perform only the accounting function, and thus the fee charged is lower. This may create problems if the building is underserved in essential areas. A management fee below standard could be a neutral or a negative element.

Definition

Insurance is the cost of protecting the cooperative corporation or condominium association against calamities affecting the physical plant, liability, employee or fiduciary misconduct and other identified risks. It does not include employee insurance, which is a fringe benefit associated with payroll.

Insurance expense above standard: The amount of insurance needed is a subjective decision. Some boards want extensive coverage for every conceivable risk with minimal deductibles, while others opt for self-insurance, in which the first level of financial risk is borne by the cooperative or condominium. Therefore, a variation from the standard does not imply any kind of material problem. Additionally, pricing on insurance can be volatile due to factors having nothing to do with the operation of the building. Insurance above standard is generally a neutral element.

Insurance expense below standard: Boards are supposed to evaluate insurance on a regular basis, but many do not. Rather, they renew the existing coverage without considering that replacement costs increase over time. If insurance is not revised periodically, the premium will remain low, but the coverage will become inadequate.

The insurance expense may also be low because the building is over-reliant on self-insurance. In almost all policies, the first level of risk, the deductible, is borne by the insured. If the deductible is extremely high, the cost of insurance can be lowered. However, if any calamity affects the building, the cost may be passed on to homeowners in the form of an assessment.

A third reason could be that the building participates in a bulk insurance program, which some management companies provide to their clients. Bulk programs bundle many buildings together as one risk to lower overall costs. This is usually an excellent cost benefit. Therefore, an insurance expense below standard could be a negative, neutral or positive element.

Water and Sewer Charges

Definition

Water and sewer charges are the cost of water service to the property.

Water and sewer charges above standard: New York City requires in most instances that residential properties use water meters. Therefore, the cost of this service is a function of water use. A building could have high water and sewer costs if the number of water fixtures in the building is above average. This would be likely if the building has a higher number of large apartments than the standard building. This is a neutral element.

Water and sewer charges below standard: Normally, low water and sewer expenses are due to fewer water fixtures than in a standard building. This would imply an apartment mix weighed toward smaller apartments. This is a neutral element.

Contribution to the Reserve Fund

Definition

Under new Fannie Mae guidelines, buildings are now required to allocate 10% of the funds collected by tenant-shareholders (or unit owners in a condominium) to replenish the building's reserve fund. If there is a sufficiently funded reserve already in place, a waiver of this requirement can be obtained. However, if the fund is not sufficient and the replenishment allocation is not made, banks may refuse to lend funds to a prospective buyer interested in purchasing an apartment in the building. The purpose of the reserve fund is to enhance, extend or replace an existing asset in the building that no longer adequately serves the homeowners or has become obsolete or dysfunctional. The reserve fund should also be utilized to handle unexpected events or contingencies. It is common for a building to set up a special fund specifically allocated for some designated purpose or improvement. Reserve funds should not be used as a supplemental means to cover ongoing operating expenses.

Contribution to the reserve fund above standard: It is appropriate, if not essential, that a building make a greater-than-standard contribution to the reserve fund if there is a proposed capital project, an uninsured contingent liability or a high level of deferred maintenance. However, it may be unnecessary to make a high reserve fund contribution if the building already has a substantial balance and the board is augmenting reserves for no specific purpose. In any case, a high reserve fund contribution is normally a positive element.

Contribution to the reserve fund below standard: It would be appropriate for a building to make a lower-than-standard reserve fund contribution only if the building already has excess reserve savings and there is no reason to further augment them. In all other cases, a deficient contribution means that the building is not creating an adequate base of funds to handle unexpected contingencies or capital upgrades. A less-than-standard reserve fund contribution could be a negative element.

Sizing up a Building's Financial Position

After evaluating the operating costs for a specific building against the standard, you should be able to draw an overall conclusion. Normally, one or two glaring issues, or a number of interrelated variances, can reveal critical information about the building's overall financial health. For example, if a building is in weak economic condition, you may see negative variances in materials, supplies and maintenance expenses coupled with an overage in payroll costs. This may mean that the building is charging too little for monthly maintenance and will have to put significant pressure on homeowners to raise additional revenue.

When a co-op building is over-mortgaged, it will often seek to keep monthly maintenance costs at market levels by reducing services or deferring normal improvements. This is not a good long-term solution, and eventually necessitates substantial assessments to cure building ailments that were previously ignored.

I propose that you keep your eye on the big picture rather than focusing on any specific variation. Explore what a variation may mean in terms of future dollar outlays or potential reductions in service. In most instances, the risk you identify is already factored into your price. For example, you're going to pay less for an apartment in a building that looks old and tired than in one that looks new and pristine. If you see evidence of what you already know in the financial statement, don't be surprised.

CHAPTER 13

Strategies for Selling an Apartment

Deciding to Sell Your Home

Selling a home is rarely just an investment decision; it is also a lifestyle decision. You are leaving your old world and entering a new one. This new world may be very different from your former one. It may include a change in your marital status or the formation of a family. Whatever the case, deciding to sell a home is not merely about money. It is also about addressing your new needs.

A number of factors will determine how much you can spend on a new home: equity capital (non-borrowed invested cash), your reported income (expressed on your tax return as your adjusted gross income) and your creditworthiness.

Your other big consideration is why you need to sell. Clearly identify the issue motivating you and translate it into a specific type of apartment that meets your new needs. Determine the number of bedrooms, location, type of building and services, layout, elements of light and view and amount of space that you require. Then use the various websites and periodicals available to you to research the cost of this type of property. Try to identify at least three or four apartments that might meet your needs. As you evaluate what is available, you will become aware of price and quality trade-offs in the marketplace. This is the starting point when you are thinking about selling: not defining how much you are planning on selling your property for, but figuring out where you will go after you sell it and how much your new home will cost.

In evaluating your choices, you should focus on something real estate brokers refer to as the "leap." This is the amount of money you will have to pay to move from your existing home to the new one you intend to acquire. Often in a declining market, the amount of cash necessary for a leap declines. While you may sell your home at a lower price than you would hope for, you might buy your next home at a low price as well. Focus on the size of the leap rather than the selling or buying price.

An important consideration is whether to sell first and then purchase, or to purchase first and then sell. In the vast majority of cases, selling first is the better choice. Most real estate salespeople can tell you stories of enthusiastic buyers who decided to put down a deposit on a new home based on the belief that they could sell the old one in short order and gain the money necessary to close from a quick sale. These situations often turn out to be nightmares in which the home can't be sold, or the timing between the sale and the purchase becomes problematic.

A more secure choice is to sell your home, then take your time finding the best alternative, knowing that you have the money to spend without uncertainty. This can best be accomplished by moving into a rental apartment for a short term. Many landlords will permit tenants to sign a one-year lease with the option of moving after six months, as long as the tenant gives the landlord three months' notice of his or her intent to move out. Another alternative is to enter into a short-term apartment rental on a month-to-month basis. These can be very expensive since they compete with the tourism industry, but they might still be cheaper than committing to a longer-term lease. It is also easy to store any unneeded furniture in a secure storage facility until you need it.

Some sellers become confident that they can commit to purchasing another home after they have entered into a contract for the sale of their property. However, in many cases, the contract has been signed and challenges have still emerged. Cooperative board rejections have become more common, condominiums have refused to issue right-of-first-refusal waivers, and banks have rejected loans even when everything appears to be satisfactory — sometimes even after issuing a commitment letter. Real estate brokers have become extremely cautious, and often continue to show apartments after contracts have been signed because so much can potentially go wrong with even the best of deals. The solution to this quandary for the seller is as follows:

- Informally, attempt to find out from the president of the cooperative board what parameters the board uses at the current time in the approval process. Any guidelines you might receive, both financial and non-financial, are important to know.

- Make sure that when you receive a bid, you also receive information about the buyer's reported income and cash down payment. You should request a preapproval letter from a bank to confirm that the buyer is capable of getting a mortgage. You also want to get information about the buyer's employment and overall financial health. Typically your broker will request an official offer that sets forth the proposed terms of the deal along with a brief statement about the buyer's financial condition.

- Even if the buyer is qualified to purchase the co-op or condo and meets the standards necessary for board approval, you should direct your real estate broker to continue to show the apartment. Don't assume everything will work out. Keep actively looking for another buyer to serve as a backup.

Determining the Value of Your Apartment

Your apartment will sell when it is competitively priced against other choices a buyer might consider. While it does have relevance, the price that other apartments have sold for in your building is not necessarily indicative of the present value of your home. Rather, you have to evaluate the apartment as if you are a buyer making a decision today. Compare your property to other possible alternatives, and evaluate your property honestly against the competition using the procedure proposed in Chapter 4. Rate your apartment based on the elements of location, building, air, light and space. Compare your maintenance or

common charges to the average monthly cost for comparable properties, and adjust the price upward or downward for a low or high monthly
cost, respectively. A good procedure is to take the difference, multiply
it by 12 months and divide it by the current mortgage rate — this represents the lost or gained borrowing power of the difference amount.
Ask yourself honestly: if I were a buyer, would I want to see my property
compared to other choices in the market? For a frame of reference, you
can go to Bellmarc.com and investigate the inventory for your category.
If there is an abundance of choices available for sale in your area,
type of property and/or price range, then you should assume there is
excess supply relative to demand, which will create downward price
pressure. However, if there is a limited inventory, then the reverse is
true and your pricing should be firm.

Creating a Strategy for Selling

When you have decided to sell, you should call several real estate brokers to get their estimates of your apartment's value, and learn how
they would serve your interests if they represented you in the sale. Real
estate brokers can provide a number of invaluable services, including:

Confirming your valuation: While you should develop your own sense
of the market, it is important to get a broker's confirmation — or a
response to the contrary. Either way, he or she should not merely estimate your apartment's value, but also provide substantive support for
that valuation based on his or her knowledge of the market. A word
of caution about the value offered by a real estate broker: it is not a
promise. It is an evaluation by a person who is anxious to build a relationship with you and is basing what he or she says on what you want
to hear. This does not mean that the real estate broker is disingenuous
— rather, it is an honest estimate by an optimist.

Defining the state of the market: A real estate broker can give you an
up-to-date impression of buyer activity that goes beyond reports and
newspaper articles. Most of those published reports concern trans-

actions that took place three months ago or more. In an active real estate market, three months can mean a completely different state of the world.

Developing a marketing strategy: Selling your apartment requires that the real estate agent promote the property to other brokers as well as to consumers. Thus, the broker will prepare a listing information sheet that properly displays the important information about your property. This information will be immediately disseminated to other brokers using the Real Estate Board of New York Residential Listing System. In addition, the broker will be able to place the listing onto the major websites serving the New York City market, particularly NYTimes.com and StreetEasy.com. Make sure the broker informs you of which websites he or she has used to list the property. You should make sure that you check these sites to verify that the information is accurate and presents your property in a satisfactory manner. Be particularly careful about ensuring that room dimensions are correct and that all financial information is complete and accurate. You should also make sure that photographs are taken of the apartment and that they are appealing. For a large home, a professional photographer is essential. It is also important that the apartment listing include a floor plan.

Implementing an effective selling strategy: A broker should be able to explain the entire selling process and tell you how he or she will actively participate. The plan should include finding qualified buyers, negotiating a deal on terms acceptable to you, ensuring the buyer is able to obtain a mortgage, ensuring that any board application materials are properly compiled in a timely fashion, and generally monitoring the transaction as it moves toward completion. One important tactic often used by brokers is to host an open house, which requires that the sales agent promote a specific date and time when he or she will be present at the property and invite any person to visit it for a viewing. Prospective buyers like open houses because they can merely walk in without making special arrangements. Generally fliers will be prepared to hand to visitors, and questions about the property can be readily answered. In some cases, particularly with high-priced properties, an agent will conduct a broker open house. This event is hosted for the real estate brokerage community in order to promote interest in the property among various brokerage firms. While open houses are a helpful mechanism for promoting a property, many buildings frown on them because of security risks and the number of unescorted people coming into the building. It is therefore important to make sure that your building permits open houses before any are arranged.

Selecting a Broker

First and foremost, a good broker should be someone you like and believe in. He or she should be knowledgeable about the market and acquainted with the kinds of issues you have. The ideal broker has good verbal skills and is persuasive. You also want someone who respects how important this transaction is to you, and is accommodating and flexible.

When you invite brokers to your home, listen carefully. At the first meeting, what they say to you is more important than what you say to them. You are interviewing them to find the person who will most effectively represent your interests. The person you select is your agent; you are his or her principal. Be careful not to automatically choose the most successful broker — many times these professionals are handling a large number of properties, and their ability to personally serve you might be limited. You want a broker who you know will spend his or her time working to sell your property.

New York State Agency Disclosure Rules

New York State requires that all residential real estate brokers provide to prospective buyers, sellers, renters and landlords a *disclosure form* as a condition to doing business. These disclosure forms clarify the role of the broker in performing his or her service and identify who the broker represents during the course of any professional engagement. The state requirements mandate that the salesperson identify whether he or she is a *seller's broker* or a *buyer's broker* to each party he or she is engaged with. The agency disclosure form ensures that everyone involved in the transaction is fully informed of each broker's primary interest in serving one party or the other. The disclosure form must be presented to the seller before the real estate broker enters into a listing agreement with the seller, or at the time of the first substantive contact with the buyer. Normally one form is given to the buyer or seller, and another is signed, returned to the sales agent and maintained in the agent's records.

The requirement that brokers provide disclosure forms to buyers and sellers has created a degree of confusion for real estate sales-people, because many times it is possible to represent the interests of both the buyer and seller. For example, a salesperson may have a client who is interested in an apartment for which the salesperson's brokerage company may have an exclusive. Thus, while the buyer has a relationship with the agent, the agent has a conflict of interest in that his or her firm has a relationship with the seller. The state form requires that both buyer and seller give consent to this *dual agency*. Because there are so many opportunities for potential conflicts of interest, the state disclosure form has a standard provision permitting the buyer and seller to agree to "advanced informed consent to a dual agency" by the salesperson. Requesting that the buyer and seller sign this provision has become common practice for many real estate brokerage firms in order to provide the greatest level of flexibility.

There may be occasions in which a buyer or seller does not wish to sign the disclosure form. The state acknowledges this possibility, and affords the broker an alternative procedure referred to as an *affirmation*, which is a written statement by the salesperson indicating that he attempted to present the disclosure form and the buyer or seller refused to sign it, along with an explanation for the refusal. This must be witnessed by two parties and maintained by the brokerage company.

Entering Into an Exclusive Agreement to Sell Your Home

Normally, a broker will want you to sign an exclusive agreement giving him or her the sole right to sell your apartment. This agreement comes in two forms: an exclusive right to sell, and an exclusive agency. The *exclusive-right-to-sell agreement* provides that when your home is sold, a commission is owed to the broker regardless of who sells it. The *exclusive-agency agreement* provides that the broker is your sole representative, and will be entitled to a commission unless the sale is made directly by you without the participation of any broker or agent.

Obviously, brokers prefer the broader protection of the right-to-sell agreement, since it eliminates potential misunderstandings and provides greater assurance that their efforts to sell the property will eventually be rewarded. However, the exclusive-agency agreement is appropriate if you intend to try to make a sale yourself. If so, you will want to have your efforts acknowledged and confirmed up front as distinct from the broker's arrangements for selling the property.

Attributes of a Good Real Estate Brokerage Company

Specialization

A good real estate brokerage company will be a specialist in your market. Brokers who handle many different kinds of properties usually have less expertise than those who serve specific niches. Your broker should be well acquainted with the neighborhood your apartment is in, which is often evidenced by the brokerage company's having an office in that area. You should also gain a sense of how active the broker is. You want someone who is prepared to make a full commitment to selling your property.

Trained Sales Force

Training is fundamental for providing the highest-quality service, and a brokerage company that emphasizes training will have a more effective sales force. At the very least, each salesperson should be well versed in the standard-form contract, preparing a board packet, selling techniques and negotiating strategies.

The Internet and Computers

Every firm now uses a computer system to serve its customers. While some computer systems have more features than others, most are capable of filtering listings and providing essential information. It is critical that the company have an effective website: it should provide an easy means for users to access listings and review property information. It should look professional and link to major listing services like NYTimes.com and StreetEasy.com. In addition, the company should be directly accessible by email, and the salesperson should be able to send you listings of new opportunities regularly.

CHAPTER 14

The Challenges of Selling an Apartment

Common Issues Encountered by Sellers

You Are Selling an Apartment with a High Maintenance Cost

While a seller will want the highest possible price for his or her apartment, a buyer will attempt to buy at the lowest cost. The terms "price" and "cost" are not synonymous. The price-conscious seller cares about the amount of money to be received at closing, while the cost-conscious buyer cares about the amount of cash that must be invested and how much it will cost to carry the apartment from month to month.

A high monthly maintenance in a cooperative or high common charges and real estate taxes in a condominium augments the cost of carrying an apartment. Therefore, a buyer will seek to reduce the purchase price to bring the cost in line with that of other properties. The appropriate price reduction is theoretically calculated by treating the excess over normal monthly cost as equivalent to monthly debt service on additional borrowing. This excess amount should then be used to compute the necessary debt principal that would be required to generate an interest payment equivalent to the maintenance overage. Thereafter, the price of the apartment should be reduced by removing that additional borrowing from the purchase price.

For example, consider an apartment with a price of $500,000, which would be its fair market value assuming it has an average maintenance charge. However, the apartment has a maintenance charge of $2,000 per month, which is deemed to be $500 per month, or $6,000 per year, higher than the average maintenance charge for comparable apartments. The long-term cost of borrowing money is 5%. Therefore, the computed borrowing value of this excess is $120,000, determined by dividing the excess cost per year by the long-term interest rate. According to this theoretical model, the purchase price should thus be adjusted downward to $380,000 to reflect the excess maintenance.

While this theoretical model appears logical, it occasionally results in a price significantly below what the seller is willing to accept. In this case, market forces predominate to create the appropriate price adjustment. The following strategies can be used to find a compromise:

- The seller can provide a supplemental fund to support the maintenance for a limited time, such as five years.
- The seller can pay for a *buydown* of the buyer's mortgage rate. Most banks have buydown programs that permit, for a defined charge, a reduced interest rate and reduced monthly payment on the buyer's mortgage.

You Are Selling an Apartment in a Building With an Inadequate Reserve Fund

Buyers are often cautious about purchasing an apartment in a building that has an inadequate reserve fund. An acceptable reserve fund is defined by many brokers as $5,000 per apartment as long as there are no material adverse conditions in the building. Some accounting firms use the alternative standard of three months' operating expenses. Unfortunately, many buildings with inadequate reserve funds also tend to have substantial deferred-maintenance issues and are resistant to levying assessments against tenant-shareholders that are sufficient to improve conditions, except in dire circumstances. The risk of an assessment or increase in maintenance is accordingly difficult to determine.

One selling strategy is to look at the financial statements of three comparable buildings in the area and figure out the average allocated reserve fund for an apartment similar to the one you are selling. You can also get an impression of similar properties by going to kwnycpa.com, the website for the firm Kleiman & Weinshank, LLP, and evaluating the reserve funds for comparably sized buildings. You can propose giving the prospective buyer a separate supplemental payment equal to the difference between this amount and the percentage of the reserve fund allocated to the apartment in compensation for a projected future assessment. Your broker should assist you in obtaining these figures and computing these costs.

Another option is to advise the buyer that the price of the apartment if the building were in pristine condition would be greater than the current asking price, and that this lower price reflects a discount for the condition of the building and the uncertainty about future assessments.

Recently an underfunded reserve has become a more pressing issue for buildings, due to a change in the mortgage requirements stipulated by banks as a condition to offering financing to apartment buyers. Current rules now require that the cooperative or condominium provide in its yearly budget a contingency reserve allocation equal to 10% of the collected revenue from homeowners. This has created considerable controversy in a number of buildings due to the significant change in their budget guidelines. However, the banks are insistent on this contingency, and in some buildings significant increases will occur in yearly maintenance or common charges in order to meet this requirement. Buyers are therefore inclined to review the financial report in order to ascertain whether the reserve fund is adequate and whether a reserve fund replenishment allocation is in place. If it is not, buyers will assume that a significant maintenance increase is a real possibility. Sellers should address this issue by stating to the buyer that all buildings will be making this adjustment and there is no unique risk affecting this building when compared to others.

You Are Selling a Small Apartment

No apartment is small except by comparison to other properties in the marketplace. All apartments are evaluated on the basis of their comparable attributes, and a smaller property may have positive features that ameliorate that one negative aspect. The following strategies can be useful to sell a comparably small apartment:

- Paint the apartment white.
- Explain "how the apartment works," suggesting the use of built-ins, sofa beds and leaf tables.
- Emphasize that it is bigger than a hotel room and much less expensive.
- Explain that there is an economic cost to greater footage.
- Compare the cost of ownership on an after-tax basis with the rent alternative on page 47.
- Emphasize the apartment's positive attributes, such as the quality of the location, the building's services, the amount of light or the attractive view.

You Are Selling a Dark Apartment

To sell a dark apartment, you must remove any sense of dreariness. An effective window treatment can distract the eye from the lack of light, and artificial lighting around the window can add a dimension of comfort. You should also point out the significant price benefit over a similar apartment with light, and emphasize the apartment's favorable attributes, such as its desirable location, building services or size.

You Find the Right Apartment and
You Haven't Sold Your Home

When you find the apartment you want to buy and have not yet sold the apartment you own, you risk owning two apartments at the same time and having more expenses than you can handle. One way of dealing with this is to determine how much excess cost you would have to carry over a year because of the additional apartment and reduce the asking price for your current apartment by this amount. This should generate a number of bids by highly qualified, committed buyers. Since you are selling at a discount, you can demand a closing date that correlates in a timely manner with the closing date for your purchase.

Another alternative is to arrange for a bridge loan from a bank in order to close on your purchase and carry both properties. The bridge loan proceeds will support your added expenses for a while, but you will probably have to pay points as well as a higher-than-normal interest rate for the loan.

A third choice is to forget about your purchase and recognize that you can always find an apartment you like. Buying later may cost a little more, but the reduction in risk may be worth the money. The number of instances when buyers have bought what they thought was a great opportunity only to suffer the burden of carrying two homes for an extended length of time is substantial. My general recommendation is to sell your home before you buy another.

You Have to Sell Your Apartment at a Loss

If you sell your home at a loss, this loss is not tax-deductible. Many people falsely believe they can create tax recognition for a loss if they convert the property to investment property by renting it and then selling it later. They believe that since it was investment property when sold, the loss can be designated as an investment loss rather than a loss on the sale of a primary residence. This is not how the tax law works. At the time of conversion to an investment, you must reduce the valuation of the asset to its fair market value. Therefore, the loss you have already incurred is not converted to an investment loss and remains unrecognizable.

However, conversion to investment use is still a good idea in certain circumstances — particularly if the home's value has declined to an amount below the remaining mortgage. Selling in this case would be problematic, since the owner would have to pay the bank more than he or she would receive from the buyer at closing. In this case, it pays to consider converting the property to an investment by renting it at fair market value. The rental income should cover the carrying cost of the home and possibly even offer the owner a profit. Depreciation may be taken on investment property, so any profits will probably be tax-free. Owners have often converted primary residences to investment properties and found the profits to be so substantial that even when prices rose again they had little interest in selling. It is also important to note that the additional income generated by the property, when added to your other earnings, may improve your creditworthiness and help you get a mortgage on a subsequent home.

The Buyer Wants a Concession After
the Contract Is Signed

Once a contract is signed, both the seller and buyer have the right to compel performance under the terms of the contract. Indeed, the standard contract clearly states that the seller has the right to take possession of the 10% contract deposit as liquidated damages if the buyer fails to perform under his or her specified obligations.

However, there are times when the buyer will assert a breach of terms by the seller and will seek concessions based on those violations. In this case, it is not clear whether the buyer's deposit can be kept as liquidated damages, and the buyer may have a legitimate right to insist either that a problem be rectified or that there be a price concession commensurate with the damage caused. An unresolved dispute could hurt both parties because it could lead to expensive litigation. The seller should consider making concessions if he or she has misrepresented the amount of maintenance, if there has been an assessment not identified in the contract, or if there has been damage to the property. Some ways a seller can handle such problems are as follows:

- **For an error in the reported maintenance:** Calculate the difference between the old and new maintenance charges, multiply by 12, and offer to pay this sum. The rationale you can use is that buildings frequently make annual adjustments for maintenance and you are willing to pay the increased cost until the next adjustment period.

- **For an unexpected assessment:** If the assessment is for a capital improvement, take the position that the assessment improves the value of the property and therefore warrants no adjustment. If the buyer disputes this position, negotiate to share the assessment equally.

- **For damage to the apartment:** Bring in a contractor and get a bid for the repair. Tell the buyer that you will make a concession to the extent of the cost of the repair, based on the contractor's estimate.

- **For an unforeseen change in the circumstances of the buyer:** If the buyer wants a concession because he or she cannot get the money required to close the deal, you can consider either issuing a one-year personal note for the open balance at a high rate of interest or putting the apartment back on the market, keeping the buyer's deposit as liquidated damages.

- **For when market prices have declined and the buyer wants a concession in light of the apartment's lowered value:** Consider what you could conservatively sell the apartment for if the buyer abandoned the deal, and add to that the 10% contract deposit you could keep as damages. If that figure is less than the buyer is willing to pay, you should lower your price as a concession.

You Get an Offer Immediately After
You Place the Apartment on the Market

It is very common for a seller to receive substantial interest in his or her apartment soon after the property is listed for sale. All the salespeople who are informed about the new offering will search their existing buyer inventories to see if there are any viable candidates, and if there are, will quickly arrange appointments. Many of these buyers have already had considerable experience in the market and are ready to enter a bid after a single viewing. Some sellers misconstrue this initial flurry of activity as indicative of general market interest, so they tend to resist early offers. However, when the dust settles and these initial offers fade away, the seller must deal with the next round of buyers, many of whom have less experience and are reluctant to make offers without carefully exploring all the possible alternatives. The level of activity decreases, and offers become sparse.

It is my recommendation that you value your apartment carefully before you put it on the market. Then, when a good offer appears, take it and be happy. If you have reservations about an early offer and you're not sure it's worth taking, direct your broker to call other brokerage firms to tell them that you are about to accept an offer. If they have any prospective buyers who may be interested in beating the existing bid, they will tell your broker. An actual offer is usually better than a possible opportunity.

You Change Your Mind After You've Agreed to Sell Your Apartment

If you have not signed a contract, there is little negative consequence to breaking off with a specific buyer. New York State law requires that for real estate sales, including those of a cooperative or condominium apartment, the agreement must be in writing and signed by both parties in order to be enforceable. However, the real estate broker may have a right to assert a claim for his service if you enter into an agreement and then change your mind. The best way to handle this issue is to enter into a written exclusive agreement with a broker stipulating that a commission is due only if a contract is signed and the deal subsequently closes. This will effectively protect you from any broker claims.

If a contract has been signed and you have changed your mind, you can ask the buyer to relinquish his or her position and offer to make a payment to cover his or her costs. Depending on the settlement offered, you may get the buyer to accommodate you.

If you enter into one agreement to sell your home and another one to buy a new home, only to have the buy agreement fail, you remain obligated to sell your home. In this case, you should quickly look for another purchase, obtain a short-term rental, or renegotiate the price and terms to resurrect the purchase that fell through.

From time to time, there have been sellers who have demanded that their deal be conditioned upon the successful closing of the apartment they are on contract to buy. A responsible attorney will always recommend that a buyer not proceed with a deal structured this way.

There Is a Mortgage Contingency Provision in the Contract and the Buyer Fails to Obtain a Loan

If the buyer is in compliance with all the terms of the contract but his or her application for a mortgage has been rejected, the first step the seller should take is to ensure that the buyer complied with the provisions of the contract by submitting all required documents to the bank and putting in a bona fide application. Sometimes a rejection is due to the applicant's failure to properly comply with the bank's document requests. If so, the buyer may be in default of the contract, and the seller can keep the 10% contract deposit as damages if the buyer is unwilling to correct the problem.

If no bad faith was involved, the seller should get the name of the bank that rejected the prospective buyer and ask his or her broker to call the bank or mortgage broker to determine if the buyer would qualify for a smaller loan, or if there is any way to obtain the full sum. If the bank would be willing to lend a smaller amount, the seller should consider short-term private financing to fill in the gap (although this may need to be disclosed to the bank and the board of directors of the building). The seller should also consult a mortgage broker to find out if another financial institution might make the loan. Different banks have different lending policies; a rejection by one bank does not necessarily mean that another will not make the loan.

If the buyer refuses to try to find a loan through another bank or makes no other efforts to overcome this condition, it is best to give the deposit money back and find another buyer as quickly as possible. Before doing so, however, the seller should carefully read the contingency provision of the contract to determine whether the buyer has strictly complied with the specified dates and forms of notice called for in this provision. If not, the buyer may be in breach of the contract and must proceed with the purchase of the property — even in the absence of a mortgage commitment — or lose the 10% down payment.

The Board Won't Approve Your Buyer
Because the Price Is Too Low

Reticent boards anxious to protect the value of their apartments have become a serious problem for many sellers who desperately need to sell their homes. The issue arises because cooperative and condominium boards believe that the value of the apartments in their building is a function of the sale price of other apartments that have sold. Thus, if an apartment sells at a depressed price, it lowers the benchmark value of other homes in the building. Sellers have resorted to an assortment of adjustments to the purchase price as a means of avoiding this pitfall. The most common is a *construction concession*, whereby the stated price on the contract is adjusted downward by a separate agreement to compensate the buyer for certain necessary improvements. Banks are willing to accommodate construction concessions as long as the amount does not exceed 3% of the selling price.

An alternative strategy is to provide additional compensation to the real estate broker, who uses the extra funds as a payment to the buyer in order to induce him to enter into the agreement. Obviously the broker must obtain the consent of the buyer and seller to undertake this arrangement. Many brokers and attorneys are very upset by these arrangements and view them as inappropriate. They particularly note that it creates a deceptive appearance of the value of apartments in a building, which can mislead appraisers. Others recognize the seriousness of the challenge to the seller. If he can't sell the apartment because the value is less than the board will permit, what should he do?

The Board of Directors Rejects Your Buyer

In a cooperative apartment sale, one standard contingency is approval by the board of directors. If the board rejects your buyer, the first thing to do is to call the president of the board or the head of the admissions committee and ask if anything can be done to persuade the board to reconsider.

Sometimes the answer will be yes. Maybe the rejection was due to financial concerns, and a co-signer or a security deposit for the first year's maintenance payments will overcome the board's reservations. Maybe some financial information was missing that, if presented, would change the outcome. All of these possibilities and more should be explored. Another possibility is that the buyer acted in bad faith. If the buyer failed to responsibly prepare his or her board packet, or acted antagonistically in the interview, he or she may have caused the board rejection. If the buyer has acted in bad faith he has defaulted on the contract, and the 10% deposit can be held as damages.

You should also be prepared for no response. Most boards are reluctant to tell you their reasons for denial because it merely opens up a Pandora's box, and they are under no legal obligation to do so.

Should I Feel Secure If the Buyer Has a Mortgage Commitment?

It used to be that a mortgage commitment provided a degree of assurance to both the buyer and seller that the transaction would be successfully completed. A commitment letter was perceived as a legal promise by the bank to provide the necessary funds to the buyer to complete the purchase.

However, from time to time banks will now renege on these promises. This is because the commitment letter contains conditional language allowing the bank to alter its position if the lending policies and procedures of the bank change or there is a material change in the borrower's financial condition. Some banks will investigate the credentials of the building after the commitment letter has been issued, and if they determine that the building doesn't meet required standards, they will withdraw their commitment, asserting one of the conditions of the commitment has not been met.

While not a common event, the risk that the bank will renege if the borrower's financial condition has changed has added a degree of uncertainty. It can also create a serious problem for a buyer, because while the commitment letter contingency prescribed in the contract may have been met within the specified timeframe, if there is a subsequent withdrawal of the commitment after that date, the buyer's contract deposit can be lost unless the buyer can come up with the necessary funds to close.

To address this risk, attorneys for buyers often add a provision to the contract conditioning the transaction upon the funding of the bank loan, not merely the commitment letter, so that if the bank reneges on its promise the buyer can get his deposit back.

CHAPTER 15

The Challenges of Buying an Apartment

How Should I Look for Apartments?

The Internet

There are many websites currently available to help prospective buyers find listings, but some are more valuable than others. Most sites generally have a local focus and accept downloads from various brokerage companies of their listings on a regular basis, although some require brokers to subscribe in order to list their properties. At present, most national real estate sites are not able to provide current information on specific market listings as well as local websites can. The same goes for search engines such as Yahoo and Google, which are not really effective as real estate services. Some sites require the buyer to enter his or her name and email address as a condition to entering the site.

The following sites offer the best level of information and are active participants in the New York City market.

Brokerage Company Sites

All major brokerage companies serving New York City, including Bellmarc, have websites. These sites are primary sources used by brokers and buyers for the most up-to-date information. Most also have useful information about the local real estate market and buying a home.

NYTimes.com

NYTimes.com is *The New York Times'* website, and is often used by buyers and brokers. The site offers a wide array of information about listings for sale and statistical information about comparable apartment sales, as well as relevant neighborhood information and street views of properties. Open houses are also regularly listed. In addition, the site allows the user to see sales activity by neighborhood or address going back as far as January 2003. Finally, the system has an advanced search feature that permits the user to filter properties by specific amenities and keywords. NYTimes.com accepts feeds from all major firms, but it is a subscription service where brokers are charged to place listings on the site. Thus many listings, particularly those of smaller firms, may not appear.

StreetEasy

StreetEasy.com is probably the most popular of all major real estate sites, containing an abundance of listed properties and extensive information, including property histories. Open house information is regularly listed. Property searches can be performed by type of property, number of bedrooms, price range and neighborhood. An advanced search feature permits the user to use keywords, price per foot, boundary details, school districts and other parameters to identify apartments. StreetEasy.com receives listing feeds from all the major firms, and smaller firms actively participate in placing their properties on the site.

In addition to listings, the site also contains general information. The Manhattan Condo Market Index tracks relative market health over months and years. The StreetEasy Market Report provides information on price changes, activity levels and inventory for the entire real estate market as well as various neighborhoods throughout the city. Street Facts describes the average size, price per foot and total price for the current properties from transactions over the last 60 days. There is also a discussion board and a blog entitled Bubble Wrap.

OLR (Online Residential)

OLR.com is popular among real estate brokers because it receives direct feeds from the Real Estate Board of New York's listing distribution system, while other sites do not. Many brokers subscribe to OLR and use it as their primary listing system in serving buyers and sellers. It also is a popular site for obtaining building information.

Trulia

Trulia.com has a simple property search for both sales and rentals by type and price. It also permits refined searches by specific amenities. In addition, the site has a considerable amount of information about sales and rental activity, including a scoring system reflecting customer preferences for different neighborhoods. Trulia.com receives feeds from major brokerage companies. There is an advice section where buyers can ask questions and brokers will respond.

Zillow

Zillow.com offers maps and data about sales history, including its "Zestimate," a computerized valuation system that is generally viewed as unreliable by real estate brokers. Zillow receives feeds from major real estate companies in New York, but its site is not heavily populated with properties and can be somewhat difficult to navigate.

Craigslist

Craigslist.com is a difficult site to use for apartment research, since its selection parameters are less refined than those of other sites. However, it is often used by sellers seeking to sell their properties on their own, and the price to list properties is inexpensive. Many buyers complain that the site lacks a degree of credibility, since the company does nothing to control the quality of the data and apartment information is often limited. Nevertheless, for low-priced rentals or studio properties for sale, it still gets considerable attention.

Informational Sites

There are numerous websites for brokers, professionals, buyers and sellers to gather real estate information. The following are some of the most useful.

Property Shark: PropertyShark.com is a subscription service that provides information about specific properties and buildings, including histories of sales activity, comparable properties for sale and building information. You can also subscribe to foreclosure information and mailing lists of occupants in a given building.

TitleVest: TitleVest.com is a title company that has accumulated offering plans for most of the buildings in New York. These can be viewed for no charge online. The system is a little awkward to use and requires that you call TitleVest after you place your order. However, the offering plan for any building on file can be viewed free of charge. If a hard copy of the plan is desired, there is usually a fee of approximately $180.

Google: Google.com is useful for recent updates about the real estate community — the search string "New York City residential real estate" will normally yield a good representative sample of news about real estate in the five boroughs. In addition, the basic search engine can help you pinpoint addresses and useful building information: by Googling the address of a given building, you will often find that it has a website with details you need to know.

The Real Deal: TheRealDeal.com is a popular site for articles about real estate, which are also featured in a monthly magazine published and distributed throughout New York City. The magazine also covers both events in the residential real estate brokerage business and real estate in New York City generally.

Blogs

Numerous brokerage companies, search engines and others have created blogs about residential real estate in New York City. Some of these blogs contain useful information and insights into market activity, but in most cases they seem be vehicles for individuals to express opinions or judgments, and may have little or no value to someone seeking credible information. They can be consulted but should not be relied on.

Community Reviews

Certain sites attempt to review brokerage companies and grade brokers. I view these reviews very suspiciously. In most cases, a salesperson's poor grade is based on one or two comments from angry buyers who found themselves disappointed because they were outbid or made unreasonable demands that the salesperson could not realistically meet. In addition, I have repeatedly seen firms "game" these sites by arranging to have positive reviews placed by friends or others in order to boost their ratings. Every firm has good and bad brokers, and every firm seeks to do the very best it can for its customers and clients. Broker reviews distort the truth, and do a disservice to many good agents who are branded with negative comments that are totally outrageous and cannot be removed by the offended party.

Periodicals

In addition to the Internet, there are a number of newspapers that regularly promote properties. First and foremost is *The New York Times'* Sunday Real Estate section. In addition, *The Wall Street Journal* and *The New York Post* actively serve this market. Newspaper advertising has become a smaller component of total promotional efforts by real estate brokers since it offers less flexibility in presenting properties and is more expensive. Nevertheless, it is a viable resource that should be reviewed by any buyer.

Common Issues Encountered by Buyers

I'm New to New York.
What Should I Know Before I Buy an Apartment?

If you're new to the city, try to visit each neighborhood, and attempt to evaluate its personality and what it would be like to live there. Go during the day and at night. Brokerage companies' websites also have useful information about various neighborhoods that is worth reading.

After researching different areas, visit some of the websites identified beginning on page 263 to get an idea of the prices for each area. You may find that the more expensive neighborhoods are not where you expected they would be.

How Should I Evaluate the
Real Estate Market in New York City?

While newspapers can give you an overall impression of the marketplace, they often create an inaccurate picture. First, the reports generally provide information on sales activity based on closed transactions. Normally the time between an accepted offer and the closing of the deal is 90 days or more. Thus, for a buyer or seller looking to understand the current level of activity, the report is stale the day it comes out. The following are a number of more useful indicators that can help a buyer or seller gain a sense of the current market:

Inventory for sale: Go to Bellmarc.com and look at the listing inventory. Changes in inventory — whether up or down — give you an impression of the relative supply and demand. If the supply is low (under 9,000, while over 11,000 is high) it implies a tightening in the market and upward price pressure. It is important to look at the specific price category you are seeking, because certain categories in the market may be in limited supply while others are not.

StreetEasy.com: StreetEasy has a Manhattan Condo Index Report that is expressed as a single figure, and gives a good indication of the level of activity in the market. The report also portrays trends in major Manhattan neighborhoods, and gives information on the level of sales on a month-by-month basis.

New car sales: There is a surprisingly high correlation between improving new car sales and improving real estate sales, with a lag of about 30 to 60 days. A rise in new car sales implies that consumers are ready to make high-priced discretionary purchases.

Interest rates: The trend in interest rates creates short-term variations in demand. Where a buyer perceives that rates might go up, he or she is more likely to take action, thereby stimulating transaction activity. Conversely, transaction activity might slow down when the consumer perceives that waiting may be beneficial.

The stock market: Stock market indices have become an important barometer of business activity, including real estate sales. If the stock market goes down, real estate will suffer, while if the market appears to be surging, people will have more confidence about making a major purchase like a home.

What Is a Buyer's Broker?

When a seller employs the services of a real estate broker under an exclusive agreement, that broker is the *listing broker,* also referred to as the seller's broker. The seller's broker is a fiduciary of the seller and his or her goal is to achieve the best terms and highest possible price for the seller. Frequently there is a second broker, called the buyer's broker, who is a fiduciary of the buyer. His or her goal to achieve the best terms and the lowest possible price for the purchaser. When two or more brokers are involved it is called a *co-brokered* transaction. Normally, the entire commission is paid by the seller and shared by both brokers. The portion of the commission paid to the buyer's broker is given as consideration for presenting the property to the buyer. Since it is given for presenting the buyer and not for the transaction, New York State does not consider a buyer's broker to be in breach of his or her fiduciary duty if he or she accepts a commission payment from the seller.

When one broker is handling the entire transaction, it is referred to as a *direct deal.* The broker is effectively acting as a mediator serving the interests of both parties, and must therefore have the consent of both parties for this dual agency. This consent must be expressly granted on a New York State disclosure form outlining the broker's responsibility to the buyer and/or the seller in performing the transaction.

Occasionally, a broker will be given an assignment by a buyer to act as an advisor and find a property according to certain prescribed requirements. In these cases, it is not unusual for the buyer's broker to receive compensation from the buyer. However, it is illegal for a buyer's broker to receive compensation from the buyer and the seller for the same transaction without full disclosure and consent from both parties.

Should I Buy a Home With All-Equity Cash or Get a Mortgage?

Buying a home without a mortgage obviously reduces its monthly cost, since no debt payment must be made. However, given current tax law, an unforeseen wrinkle might discourage some buyers from taking this route. The law permits a tax deduction for *original-acquisition financing*, which is defined as a loan to acquire your residence that is taken no later than 90 days after closing. If a mortgage is obtained at a later time, it is deemed a replacement mortgage, and interest is deductible only to the extent of the mortgage being replaced (plus $100,000 of additional financing through an equity credit line). If there was no original mortgage, nothing is being replaced, so the total principal entitled to tax-deductible interest is limited to $100,000.

What Should I Do If I Have Insufficient Funds and Need a Guarantor?

Many potential buyers, particularly young professionals and students, will require additional support from a parent, relative or close friend in order to qualify for purchasing an apartment. Some co-ops and condos will permit this provided that the guarantor submits an application, tax returns and all supporting documentation as though he or she were the primary purchaser. Some buildings may also require an escrow deposit of at least six months' maintenance or common charges as additional insurance.

There are many other buildings, however, where guarantees are not permitted. In these cases the supporting party should consider becoming a joint owner. As such, he or she will be directly responsible for the obligations of the unit owner and shall be named on the stock and lease. Many boards are willing to accommodate this approach even though only one of the two owners will actually be occupying the apartment.

What Is an Escrow as a Condition to a Sale?

When a cooperative board has reservations about the financial qualifications of a prospective buyer, a common alternative to rejection is to require the buyer to deposit a sum to be held by the co-op for additional protection. The amount is normally a minimum of six months' maintenance, but can be as large as one or even two years' maintenance. Normally, after the stated duration has expired, the deposit agreement allows the buyer to request a return of the funds. However, the board can refuse to grant the request if it has continuing concerns.

Escrow deposits are also common in condominiums. The condominium board may refuse to sign a waiver of its right of first refusal unless there is an escrow deposit agreement.

Currently there is lively debate among real estate attorneys about whether escrow deposits are legal. From a practical point of view, however, for the prospective buyer about to close on a sale, paying the escrow deposit is a better choice than not moving forward.

Should I Make Multiple Applications for a Mortgage?

Applying to multiple banks causes more inquiries into your credit score, which can cause your score to go down. Furthermore, only an appraiser selected by the bank can be used to value the property. If you apply to another bank, you will have to pay for a second appraiser — the bank will not use the previous appraisal for its evaluation.

My suggestion is to consider using a mortgage broker or a bank that has a correspondent lending relationship with other financial institutions. Generally these parties will know the pitfalls associated with the current market, and will be able to guide you more effectively than you might be able to do on your own. In addition, they are better acquainted with the products offered by different banks and can advise you which one to choose. Some banks, however, do have aggressive programs that include excellent rates and provide assurances to prospective borrowers that if the bank's products are not appropriate choices for the borrowers given their financial requirement, that they will use other lender's offerings under a correspondent lending program.

Should I Get a Better Deal Because I'm Paying All Cash?

To a seller, almost every deal is "all cash." The cash comes from the buyer's deposit or the mortgage proceeds. Either way, the seller leaves the closing with a check equal to his or her selling price, less closing adjustments and the amount used to pay off his or her own mortgage. The issue that is important to a seller is closing risk. Your purchase is more attractive to the seller if it is not conditioned on obtaining a mortgage.

If you don't get a mortgage, you are paying all-equity cash. An all-equity-cash purchase would appear to be a wise course of action if the rate of economic return you are receiving from your investments is less than the interest cost you would incur on your home mortgage. For example, Mr. Jones has an investment in a mutual fund that provides a yearly rate of return of 3%. He is buying a home, and the mortgage interest rate available to him is 6%. Rather than take a mortgage, it would be more economically advantageous to liquidate some of his investment funds, thereby eliminating a 3% economic benefit but reducing a 6% economic cost.

There are a number of caveats that are important to consider in an all-equity-cash purchase. First, if you obtain a loan at a later time, you are limited in the amount of interest deduction you can take on your tax return. The tax law permits an interest deduction only for the original-acquisition loan. Second, obtaining money through a mortgage at a later time is a lengthy process involving an application, appraisal and approval. Normally this takes longer than 90 days.

Unless you have substantial capital, I recommend getting a mortgage, since it ensures that the tax deduction enhances liquidity and its interest rate is generally lower than that of other sources of funds. Play it safe and get a loan before any issue presents itself.

The Underlying Mortgage for the Cooperative Corporation Is Coming Due

A maturing mortgage is often a great opportunity, not a problem. Look at the notes to the financial statement in the building's financial report to find the total monthly payment for principal and interest. Then take the balance of the mortgage (which appears in two sections of the balance sheet: the current portion and the long-term portion) and divide the monthly payment by the principal. Multiply this figure by 12 to obtain the current yearly percentage of payout to principal. This figure will frequently be very high, since a maturing mortgage has a large amount of amortization with every payment. When the building refinances the mortgage, the payment may go down, as the principal of the loan has declined. This will cause the related payout percentage to be lower, conforming to a new payout schedule (15 or 30 years) on the lesser sum. In addition, while the principal amortization included with each payment will decline, the interest portion of the payment will increase. This means that upon refinancing, your maintenance will go down and your tax deduction will go up.

In recent years, more buildings have opted to take interest-only mortgages, which are merely renewed within five- or 10-year periods. There are few loans a bank would rather give than an underlying co-op loan on an established cooperative building. The risk associated with the renewal of an underlying mortgage should therefore not be considered a material problem.

How Should I Evaluate a Building on a Land Lease?

A number of buildings in New York City are land-lease cooperatives. These are properties where the cooperative corporation rents the land for a term of years as opposed to owning it. However, at the end of the lease, the right of possession reverts back to the landowner, and the ownership interest of the tenant-shareholders is extinguished. The yearly rental payments made by the cooperative are not tax-deductible.

The effect on the price of the apartment in a land-lease building can be considerable, depending on the length of time remaining on the lease. The following is a rough guideline for adjusting pricing for a land-lease cooperative when compared with a fully owned building of similar quality:

Remaining lease term	Price adjustment
In excess of 70 years	10% to 20%
50 to 70 years	20% to 25%
40 to 50 years	25% to 30%
30 to 40 years	30% to 35%
25 to 30 years	35% to 40%

If the length of the lease is less than 25 years, the value of the apartment begins to revert to a prepayment against the monthly cost when compared with the apartment's perceived rental value. For example, assume that 10 years remain on a land lease. Further assume that the maintenance on a cooperative apartment is $2,000 and that the perceived rental value is $5,000 per month; the difference of $3,000 per month multiplied by 120 months remaining on the lease results in a value of $360,000. It is common that this figure will be adjusted to reflect the *time value of money* and other risks.

In many instances, the land lease has options for extension beyond the identified lease term. The prospective buyer should interpret the future value based on the exercise of the options and evaluate the impact on future maintenance charges. I suggest you be very careful when reading about these options, because sometimes the change in rent payments after the exercise of the option can create an enormous increase in the monthly maintenance charge. You can find out about the land lease in the prospectus and the financial statement of the building.

Condominiums do not have land leases in New York. An exception is Battery Park City, where the land is owned by a government authority.

I Only Want a Condominium

Many buyers prefer a condominium to a cooperative because they believe they will not have to go to a board interview and reveal their personal finances to their prospective neighbors. However, many established condos in New York have a review process concerning their right of first refusal on any purchase, which can be cumbersome. Buyers have complained about this, but the condominium board is within its rights to make a reasonable request for information about the buyer and his or her financial condition in order to ascertain whether it wants to exercise its right of first refusal. Fortunately, the number of occasions when the condo has exercised this right is low.

I would suggest a condominium under the following circumstances:

- You absolutely refuse to reveal any financial information. Some condominiums will permit this, particularly in new construction.
- You are buying the apartment as an investment. Condos generally have more liberal rules regarding renting than co-ops do.
- You have limited down payment cash. You can normally purchase a condominium with a 10% down payment.

Generally condominiums apartments are more expensive to buy than cooperatives. This is due in part to the additional underlying mortgage on the cooperative building, which does not exist in a condominium and often results in a higher monthly charge. However, there is also a supply/demand premium for condominiums, since they constitute only about 30% of the total population of owned apartments and have a broader market that includes investors and foreigners. Generally the premium for a condo is between 20% and 30% over a comparable cooperative.

What Is a Condop?

The term *condop* has been applied confusingly to New York City real estate to describe the hybrid nature of a building's ownership form, and effectively has two meanings. The first is used among real estate brokers to designate a cooperative building in which there is no board approval requirement for the sale or rental of an apartment. The second meaning, however, is the legal definition: a building in which there is mixed residential and commercial use of the property, and in which the space for each use receives a separate unit deed, thereby qualifying the building as a condominium. The unit deed dedicated to residential use is owned by a cooperative corporation, which issues shares of stock and proprietary leases to specific apartments. Each year, homeowners receive two financial reports: the first covers the entire building as a condominium association, and the second covers the residential section of the building owned by the cooperative corporation. Therefore, the shares of the cooperative have underlying ownership of the condominium unit deed for the residential segment of the building, rather than a deed for the entire property.

Should I Buy an Apartment in a New Building?

Apartments in new buildings tend to sell for 25% more than resales. In the event that the building is "branded," meaning that it has been able to promote itself as a high-prestige property, this premium is substantially more. Many people feel it's worth the premium, because they are not buying the headaches associated with someone else's used wares. But the situation is often more complex than it seems. Some of the biggest headaches known to humankind are experienced by owners living in newly constructed buildings during the first two years of operation, when management is still trying to work out the kinks. This is particularly true if the building is unusually tall or architecturally dramatic, because this technology is always evolving. On the other hand, most people who buy these properties are happy they did. They enjoy the efficiencies of modern systems, the larger windows and the general feeling of newness and cleanliness. An important note: many new construction projects charge the sponsor's cost of transfer to the buyer. Make sure you clearly understand all the costs of transfer in order to properly evaluate your decision. You have seven days after you sign a contract on a new construction project to change your mind before it becomes fully binding on you.

Should I Look for an Apartment With a High Tax Deduction?

A high tax deduction in the maintenance charge is normally due to a high interest expense related to the underlying mortgage on the building, or to high real estate taxes. I often tell buyers that a high tax deduction is equivalent to switching the loan from being on your unit to being on the building. It's still a loan with interest, just applied in a different form. When making a decision, buyers can generally ignore the tax-deductible portion of maintenance and focus on the cash down payment amount and the monthly carrying cost.

I Only Want to Buy a Steal

I respect buyers who say they want a "steal." Who wouldn't? If an apartment is selling at an extraordinary discount, common sense will tell you there is probably a good reason. If you think you've found a steal, look closely at who is getting the better end of the deal. Usually, it's not you.

However, there are legitimate reasons that the seller might be motivated to sell at a discount — economic distress, a change in family status, estate issues or indifference. You should feel comfortable with the underlying reason motivating the discount. If you are looking for a steal, you should:

- Make sure you have cash readily available so you can deliver your down payment quickly after making an offer.
- Get information on buildings in which you think there might be good opportunities. Review the prospectuses and the most recent financial statements. If you know the property, you will be better prepared to sign a contract immediately when an opportunity arises. Speed is important.
- Make sure you have an attorney who can move quickly in reviewing a contract. You may even wish to have your attorney generate the contract in advance in order to stimulate the quickest possible response from the seller.
- Get preapproval on your mortgage financing in writing. You are not going to succeed in securing a steal if your offer has a mortgage contingency.
- Be prepared to move quickly. Don't get caught up in details — take risks with the belief that you will be rewarded. If you are not prepared to do this, pay a little more and consider it the cost of an insurance policy to reduce your risk exposure.

Everything Is Overpriced: There Is Nothing Worth Buying

In an environment where prices are depressed or declining, a buyer has a legitimate reason to hold off on buying. However, no one knows when the market might turn and values might start rising again, and usually those that hold off find themselves missing the trough and chasing a surging market. A better strategy is to try to understand the state of the market and the current competitive pricing environment, which can be done by investigating the active listing inventories on sites like Bellmarc.com. If the number of apartments of any given size and price is large, the abundant supply is putting downward pressure on prices. If the number is small, the seller of such an apartment will be in a relatively strong position. Once you have a clear perspective of supply and demand, you can start making bids. I suggest that you make an offer on any property that meets your buying formula. Some sellers will likely reject your bids, but you only need one to respond favorably in order to make a good deal. I tell salespeople all the time that good deals are made, not found.

The low interest rates currently available are an important reason to buy in the current environment. These rates effectively afford a buyer a dramatic reduction in the cost of ownership compared to the higher rates offered only a few years ago. Due to these lower prices and interest rates, the cost of ownership is now a better deal than it has been for some time.

I have found that the vast majority of people who own homes believe that their home is one of the best investments they ever made. My advice is to not wait for a better market, but to buy the best apartment you can afford today and begin your journey toward developing wealth. There are many hills and valleys, but the only way to get there is to get on the path and begin the journey.

I Want an Apartment With a Minimum Gross Footage

The gross footage of an apartment can be very misleading, because the computation is not necessarily done in a way you might expect. The Real Estate Board of New York uses a footage measurement that extends from the exterior face of the building to the center of the hall, a method that often yields results that do not describe the living space within the apartment. A more helpful figure would be the "net" interior footage, which is calculated by taking measurements from the interior common walls of the apartment, without consideration for interior room partitions. However, since there is no single way to determine square footage, much confusion and sometimes deception can arise about the size of a prospective new home. There have been a number of lawsuits in which buyers have complained that the gross footage they thought they were getting wasn't even close to the actual footage in the apartment.

Brokers therefore often look at square footage as more indicative of a class of apartments within a certain size range. It has become common for brokers to add a disclaimer to their promotional materials, advising the buyer that square footage is approximate and that the information is subject to errors. Brokers generally evaluate square-foot classifications as follows:

350 sq. ft. .... Straight-line studio

400 to 500 sq. ft .... Large studio or alcove studio

500 to 650 sq. ft. .... One-bedroom

650 to 1,000 sq. ft. .... One-bedroom with an L-shaped living room, generally referred to as a convertible two-bedroom

800 to 1,200 sq. ft. .... Two-bedroom

1,200 to 1,400 sq. ft. .... Two-bedroom or convertible three-bedroom

1,450 to 1,650 sq. ft. .... "Classic six" two-bedroom (includes formal dining room and maid's room) or three-bedroom

1,500 to 2,300 sq. ft. ..... Three-bedroom

1,750 to 2,700 sq. ft. ...... "Classic seven" three-bedroom (includes formal dining room and maid's room), large three-bedroom or four-bedroom

You should evaluate square footage by looking at where the footage is, rather than just how much there is. Focus on the "value" rooms:

the living room, dining room and master bedroom. If these rooms are not big enough to accommodate your lifestyle, then it doesn't matter how many square feet are in the apartment. Unless you are willing to embark on a substantial renovation, it's not big enough.

A notable dispute regarding square footage recently took place at 110 Livingston Street, a condo in Brooklyn. The sponsor's condominium plan presented a two-bedroom apartment as containing 743 square feet. A contract for the purchase of the residence was signed by the buyers, who subsequently measured the apartment and found it contained 634 feet. The buyer initiated a lawsuit, which was settled with a substantial sum being paid to the buyer. While the case does not set an official precedent because no determination was made by the court, it has created considerable controversy. Buyers should make sure to take their own measurements and should not depend on gross footage representations.

What Should I Do If the Apartment's Appraisal Is Below the Contract Price?

In an uncertain market, an appraiser valuing a home for a bank loan may be unusually conservative in his or her estimate. This might occur because the appraiser is less than fully acquainted with prices in a certain neighborhood, perhaps because he or she doesn't actively work in that market. In recent years banks have normally assigned appraisals based on a bidding system in which the winning candidate might be the cheapest, but might also be unfamiliar with local conditions. I have known salespeople to complain, for example, that the appraiser on their deal actively worked in Rockland County and had just decided to expand his or her business to Manhattan. It is therefore important that the real estate broker provide the appraiser with comparable sales that justify the price at the earliest possible time. The more the broker can acquaint the appraiser with comparable sales, the more the appraiser can make a well-informed decision on a justified value.

Can I Get a Discount if the Apartment Needs Work?

There are a lot of people who prefer "fixer-upper" or "sweat-equity" apartments because they plan to change any space they buy and don't want to pay a premium for finishings they intend to remove. The advantage of an "ugly duckling" is that the seller will give you a discount on the price to reflect the cost involved in improving the property, and then you can make the changes that suit your needs exactly.

Years ago, real estate developers sought to market apartments as "raw space." They believed that buyers would respond favorably to the discounted price and that these apartments would sell quickly. They were wrong: many buyers were incapable of envisioning the potential of raw space. However, some got great deals and turned the raw space into beautiful homes. When a buyer is hesitant about buying raw space, he or she should get an architect and contractor to evaluate the space and the cost of construction. In this evaluation, the total price of the apartment is the base cost — the listing price — plus the projected improvement cost. The buyer should give these plans, as well as their contractor's estimates, to the bank as part of his or her mortgage application. As long as the total estimate is less than the appraised value of the improved property, banks will be willing to finance the cost of improvements along with the original purchase price.

Sometimes in a tight market, old and tired apartments sell for as much as apartments in good condition. Since many buyers are already prepared to make substantial improvements to any apartment they buy, the fact that the apartment needs an upgrade is immaterial to their budget. When there is a lack of product, these buyers are willing to bid up the price because its condition is irrelevant to their decision.

Can I Combine Two or More Apartments Into One?

Given the scarcity of large apartments in New York City, it has become very common for buyers to purchase two or more apartments and combine them to create one larger unit. The city has not objected to this, and merely requires a notification to the Department of Buildings and self-certification by an architect. This is not a major undertaking, and a buyer should not be discouraged from combining apartments as long as the board indicates that it will approve the combination and there is no change in the room count. Given the level of activity to date, boards normally approve the combination of apartments unless there is some larger problem.

I Want to Make Changes to the Apartment I'm Buying

When a buyer plans to make alterations to an apartment after the purchase, he or she must provide the cooperative corporation or condominium association with a scope-of-work letter describing the work to be performed. Depending on the extent of the improvement, the managing agent may determine that an alteration agreement is required. This agreement sets forth the terms and conditions under which the alteration may be performed, and it will normally require that the following documents be provided:

- Architectural plans and specifications
- Required city building permits
- Proper insurance certificates
- Copies of any applicable contractor licenses

Once this information is submitted to the managing agent, it is reviewed by the building's architect or engineer and then presented to the board for approval. Usually, no work may be performed until after this approval is obtained. All costs incurred by the board for professional services related to the alterations must be paid by the new apartment owner. In addition, it is customary for a security deposit to be provided to the building and held in escrow until the alteration is complete.

If you wish to obtain funds for the improvement by refinancing your property, you will be able to increase the principal amount of your loan up to the permissible maximum of $1,100,000 and still enjoy a tax deduction on this interest, as long as all the refinanced funds are applied to pay off the mortgage you replaced and the improvement to the property.

Most boards will not usually review or approve any alteration proposals until after the purchaser has been approved to buy an apartment. A buyer who wishes to ascertain what improvements a board would permit should seek out the building's superintendent to determine what kinds of alterations were approved in the past for other apartments.

There Are Not Enough Closets in the Apartment

Very few apartments in New York have adequate closet space. Developers get a better return on investment if they devote more space to the main living areas than to closets. What can a buyer do? Consider the following possible solutions:

- Many buildings offer homeowners storage bins in the basement. Ask if this is available in the building you are considering. There is often no additional charge, and the storage unit is rarely reflected in the purchase price.

- Identify spaces in which to build closets. For example, you can build a closet on either side of a wall, which can serve as anchors for custom shelving with lighting; or you can situate a wall unit in the space created between the closets. Use push-latch openers for a minimally intrusive look.

- If the wall with the closets backs another room in your apartment, add a second set of doors so that the storage can be accessed from both rooms.

- Use armoires to provide storage space with the finished look of furniture and the practical hanging storage of closets.

- Use platform furniture with drawers or cabinets under the cushions or mattresses. Many furniture stores offer beds and sofas that provide convenient and inconspicuous space to stow things.

· Hire a storage consultant. Some are amazingly creative at developing storage ideas for small apartments, and you can hire one to design and build storage space for you. Your real estate broker can probably give you a recommendation.

What Are Lofts, and Are They Good for Me?

In the early 1900s, New York City was a manufacturing town. Buildings were erected throughout the city for small businesses producing everything from women's blouses to paper clips. Many of these buildings are now obsolete for their original uses and have been recycled as housing. These spaces contain some amazing features: they normally have high ceilings, huge windows, open environments with exciting ornamentation and cast-iron finishings. Without question, some of the most incredible apartments I have ever seen have been loft apartments.

But there can be a downside to living in a loft. Many loft buildings are located in areas where there are limited neighborhood services (exceptions include SoHo and the Flatiron District). During evening hours, the streets are desolate, and there are few parks and other amenities. Few lofts have doormen, so loft living lacks the security and services provided in buildings that do. However, if you can live without these amenities, investigating loft apartments is a good idea.

What Is a Prewar Building?

The "war" in "prewar" is World War II, and the term *prewar* refers to buildings constructed during that era. What makes prewar apartments special to many buyers is the quality of construction, which many aficionados feel is a lost art. The walls between apartments are thick enough to ensure that sound stays within each unit. The floors are made of thick hardwood, often with distinctive patterns, and the moldings are large, ornamental and frequently made of solid oak or cherry, rather than the inexpensive pine used in today's construction projects. In addition, the exteriors have a sense of distinction and warmth. Many buyers say that prewar buildings "feel" like a home, while new construction feels cold and stark.

The disadvantages of prewar buildings are equally apparent — especially when the heat comes on and the radiator makes a knocking sound, or the shower staggers with bursts of hot and cold water. The plumbing is old, and the electrical system may be inadequate unless updated by the previous owner. Worse, these problems can be hard to identify in the process of buying an apartment, because to do so would require a full engineering report, which is cost-prohibitive. When you live in a prewar building, you can all but expect that from time to time there will be an assessment to upgrade some building component. As long as you build this into your mental plan, prewar apartments are wonderful places to live. They are in such demand that you may have to pay a premium to buy one.

What Are the Advantages and Disadvantages of a Brownstone?

The term *brownstone* is a misnomer used by brokers to refer to all small buildings approximately 20 or 25 feet wide, normally on a plot running 100 feet deep. Generally these properties are walkups and provide no doorman services. However, there are a number of wonderful features in brownstones. They normally contain the cheapest apartments and often have the lowest maintenance charges. Many of them have been divided into small studio and one-bedroom apartments and are situated on tree-lined streets that offer a relatively safe, quiet existence. Some brownstones are partitioned into larger apartments that include rear gardens and duplexes. These sell extremely well because they afford a level of privacy close to that of a full townhouse. Brokers often use the term *townhouse* to refer to a building with a frontage of 16 to 25 feet that is frequently used as a single-family dwelling but is also commonly subdivided into apartments. Thus, a broker might refer to an apartment in a "brownstone" or a "townhouse" and mean the same thing.

The downside of brownstones is that they rarely have elevators. The owners on the fourth and fifth floors may find themselves in great physical shape in a year or two but somewhat discouraged about the resale value of their apartments. An additional problem is hiring competent management. Most of these buildings are handled by small management companies that provide minimal services. In addition, the superintendent is frequently part-time, which means he or she may not be around when needed.

What Does It Mean to Be in a Historic District?

New York has many neighborhoods that are so charming that you wish you could preserve the aesthetics forever. Each building seems like a reference to an age long past. The beauty of these neighborhoods requires ongoing vigilance to ensure that the wonderful architectural style is preserved and that the unique character of each neighborhood is sustained. New York City has sought to protect the best of these neighborhoods by designating historic districts. Under the strict rules associated with this designation, no building may be altered, demolished or restored without a thorough and vigorous review by the New York City Landmarks Preservation Commission.

Many buyers love historic districts; they believe these neighborhoods offer greater peace and tranquility, and they are pleased that the area's ambience is protected from change. However, some buildings in landmark areas are caught in limbo. They are not economically viable in their current form, yet they cannot be materially altered because of the Landmarks Preservation Commission's restrictions. The result is that sometimes they become eyesores to the neighborhood. If a building seeks to make improvements, it does so at its own peril: the improvements will probably be exorbitantly expensive, since they must replicate historic details that are all but impossible to recreate without the services of highly skilled artisans. History can be a very expensive commodity to maintain. If you are the owner of an apartment in a landmark building, bear that in mind as you question the size of the next assessment.

What Is the J-51 Tax Abatement/Exemption Program?

New York City offers a special program called the *J-51 tax program* to encourage renovation of residential properties for qualified rehabilitation costs, consisting of a tax abatement for a term of years and an exemption for the increased value of the property for an additional length of time. In large measure, condominiums in most areas of New York City are no longer qualified to take advantage of this program, though in some cases tax benefits have not yet expired on properties that participated in the program at an earlier point in time. The amounts of the exemption and the abatement have varied from time to time.

What Is the 421a Tax Program?

In order to encourage new construction, New York City created the *421a tax program*, which offered developers a partial exemption for property taxes under certain circumstances. For buildings built prior to 2008, the program was effectively a 10-year phase-in of the property tax at 20% every two years. For areas above 110th Street in Manhattan and selected areas in the other boroughs, the program was for 25 years, with an abatement period of 21 years followed by a phase-in of four years. Since 2012, new projects in Manhattan have been excluded from the program, though there are many areas in the outer boroughs where the program is actively used. A particularly exciting component is the 80/20 program, which offers a substantial abatement of 25 years in exchange for approximately 20% of the building as affordable housing. A buyer who sees a low rate of real estate tax on the Schedule A pricing in the prospectus should presume that the building is a participant in a 421a program. The prospectus should contain full disclosure of the phase-in term, as well as a tax opinion letter fully describing the program and the rights of all owners to participate in the tax abatement. Make sure you compute the full real estate tax on your unit and what will happen to your monthly cost after the phase-in period is complete.

What Is an 80/20 Building?

New York State's Housing Finance Agency offers developers low-rate, tax-exempt financing in exchange for the developer allocating 20% of the housing units to low- and moderate-income tenants (defined as tenants earning no more than 50% of the area median income). Many new construction projects have been built under this plan, and developers have found it a highly effective means to create excellent housing for both owners and renters. There has been no controversy about any of these properties, and indeed they are often among the most desirable properties to be found.

What Is an 'AIR' Building?

A number of years ago, the city set up a special program in certain areas where there were loft apartments: the "artist-in-residence" or "AIR" program. It is intended to give special protection to artists by designating their right to live and work in these special buildings. The rules demand that the artist be in full-time pursuit of his or her occupation. The program has been notoriously abused, and large numbers of AIR apartments are bought and sold without the occupants meeting the program requirements.

The degree of noncompliance has become so severe that most brokers believe the law has become unenforceable. That may be true, but there are no guarantees. It is common for prospective buyers to sign a waiver in which they acknowledge that the apartment they are buying is an AIR apartment, and that they waive their rights in the event that the building must enforce the terms of the program against them.

There is currently an active movement in New York City to rezone AIR districts, due to the widespread belief that the AIR restrictions have become obsolete. Thus, a party interested in properties meeting this qualification should make sure to check the current status of the law.

What About Asbestos, Lead and Mold?

Asbestos still exists in pipe insulation in many residential buildings. While removing asbestos may appear to be a prudent thing to do, many contractors discourage removal and recommend that asbestos be encapsulated, a procedure wherein the pipes are enclosed in drywall. Removal is very expensive, and even then dangerous filaments can remain in the apartment for a long time afterward.

Congress passed legislation requiring sellers and real estate brokers to provide buyers of homes built before 1978 with an information packet about the hazards of lead in the home, titled "Protect Your Family from Lead in Your Home." You should read this packet, which can be found at www.epa.gov/lead/pubs/leadpdfe.pdf, in order to properly understand the risks.

New York City enacted a law in 2004 mandating that for buildings built before 1960, the landlord must perform a lead test in any apartment where a child under the age of seven resides. If lead is found, the landlord must remove all contamination using prescribed remediation procedures. The law exempts cooperative and condominium units that are occupied by the owner. It does not exempt apartments if they are rented. An investor-owner should be aware that the reporting requirements and liability risks are considerable, and that it makes sense to ensure the apartment is not lead-contaminated prior to renting to a family with young children. In the event that there is lead risk, remediation should be performed only by a lead abatement specialist. Under no circumstances should the walls be scraped or sanded without special precautions to reduce the risk of generating airborne lead filaments.

While a special rider to the contract of sale requires that the seller affirm that he has no knowledge of lead risk in the apartment, there is no requirement that he perform a test or make any representations absent specific knowledge. The new law is causing older cooperatives and condominiums to revise their requirements for permitting sales. In more and more buildings, sellers will be compelled to perform a lead test and all remedial work as a condition of transferring the apartment. The cost of this remedial work is generally estimated to be $10,000 to $15,000. Given this change in the law, families with young children may find it increasingly difficult to obtain approval of a purchase if the possibility of lead contamination exists (although it is possible that federal fair housing laws may be violated by excluding such prospective tenants). My general recommendation is that if you buy an apartment built prior to 1960, you should assume that there is lead contamination. You should seek the assistance of a lead abatement expert, and you should perform the remedial work.

To learn more about lead hazards and the specifics of the new law, visit the website for the New York City Coalition to End Lead Poisoning (www.nmic.org/nyccelp.htm) or the website for the New York City Department of Housing, Preservation and Development (http://www.nyc.gov/html/hpd/html/homeowners/lead_paint.shtml).

There has always been controversy about mold, though no laws exist that specifically address this issue. Mold can form on any damp surface in an apartment. However, there are literally thousands of types of molds, and only a rare few are dangerous. Thus, there is currently no reasonable way that protection can be afforded to a buyer's satisfaction. The best thing to do is to look for bubbling in paint, which is an indication of moisture that may lead to mold. In most instances, visible mold can be easily cleaned. One expert has described the situation by saying that "we could drive a truck through what we don't know about mold, and the best thing to do in dealing with the problem is to use common sense." Common sense says to get a bottle of bleach and clean the area unless other indications warrant further investigation.

What About Bedbugs?

Considerable attention has been paid recently to the problem of bedbugs. Under New York City law, a condominium or cooperative apartment that is infested with bedbugs must be remedied by the apartment owner, and it is the duty of the seller to disclose to any buyer the existence of bedbugs in the apartment. In *Zayas v. Franklin Plaza* (881 N.Y.2d 368 (2009)), the court found that a cooperative was responsible for maintaining a building in good condition, and that a building that failed to protect against bedbug infestation was responsible for damages incurred by any shareholder (outside of the cost of exterminating within the apartment).

As a general rule, the buyer should make sure he or she has a right to visit the premises prior to closing on the apartment, at which time all appliances should be checked to ensure they are in good working order, and a review should be performed to make sure there is no damage to walls as a result of the seller's move. During this time, you might consider having an exterminator inspect the apartment. If the apartment is infested, an exterminator can generally remedy the situation within a couple of days, but you should delay the closing for obvious reasons.

Epilogue

The world of residential real estate in New York City has dramatically changed. However, this is not new — change seems to be the only constant. Since I started Bellmarc years ago, great changes have taken place. Back then, the city was crime-ridden. The trains were covered with graffiti. Times Square was an eyesore and an embarrassment to many New Yorkers. We were actually losing housing stock. More apartments were being abandoned than being built.

I recall using index cards to maintain information about properties. In those days, brokers would advertise their listings in the newspapers or leave hand-written flyers in a building's laundry room. Then, in the 1990s, computers became the latest hot thing, followed by the Internet in 2000. Now both are essential. Salespeople wonder what will be the next advancement — virtual salespeople? Virtual companies?

Oddly, the role of the real estate salesperson has become more important to most buyers and sellers. The overabundance of information hasn't solved the problem of how to buy an apartment in New York — it has only created the new challenge of utilizing the information to make an effective decision.

The role of the salesperson has changed from information accumulator to information definer. We are now called upon to analyze, compare and interpret. We are asked to create sophisticated marketing products on a moment's request that only a few years ago were significant undertakings. A good salesperson is a teacher and a student: teaching the customer about his choices and learning more about his needs. It is a wonderful endeavor. It is a rewarding career.

Every salesperson feels a thrill at finding the right home for a buyer or achieving a price agreement for a seller. We have helped each do something that is significant in their lives. We have made a difference.

APPENDIX I

Charts and Tables

Estimated Cooperative Closing Costs

The Buyer

Mortgage-Related Fees (If Financing)

Appraisal fee . . . . $ 450 *and up*

Credit report fee . . . . $ 75
approximate

Mortgage points . . . . $ 1,000
1% to 2% of loan, if any, (based on $100K loan)

Bank underwriting fee . . . . $ 350 *and up*

Bank legal fees . . . . $ 750 *and up*

UCC filing fee . . . . $ 100

Miscellaneous Expenses

Co-op board application . . . . $ 500

Buyer's attorney . . . . $ 2,500
approximate

Managing agent credit report . . . . $ 150

Move-in deposit . . . . $ 1,000
refundable in most cases

Move-in fee . . . . $ 300

UCC lien search . . . . $ 250

Lead paint disclosure . . . . $ 50

Prepaid expenses . . . . ([1])
[1] maintenance charge through end of month

"Mansion tax" . . . . ([2])
[2] 1% of sale price; applies to sales of $1 million or more

Estimated Cooperative Closing Costs

The Seller

New York City transfer tax filing fee .... $ 50
plus...

Sales under $500K .... 1% *of sale price*

Sales over $500K .... 1.425% *of sale price*

New York State transfer tax .... 0.4% *of sale price*

Seller's attorney .... $ 2,500
approximate

Co-op flip tax .... $ (¹) *if any*
*¹calculated as a percent of sale price, profit
or cost per share; varies by building*

Stock transfer tax .... $ 0.05 *per share*
computed by number of shares

UCC-3 .... $ 100

Mortgage pick-up/payoff fee .... $ 100 *to* $500

Managing agent fee .... $ 650
processing fees

Move-out deposit .... $ 1,000
refundable in most cases

Move-out fee .... $ 500

Estimated Condominium Closing Costs

The Buyer

Mortgage-Related Fees (If Financing)

Appraisal fee .... $ 400 *and up*

Credit report fee .... $ 75
   approximate

Mortgage tax
   Sales under $500K .... **1.8%** *of loan amount*
   Sales over $500K .... **1.925%** *of loan amount*

Mortgage points .... $ ([1]) *if any*
   [1]*1% to 2% of loan*

Bank underwriting fee .... $ 400 *and up*

Bank legal fees .... $ 750 *and up*

Application fee .... $ 500 *per application*

Miscellaneous Expenses

Condo board application .... $ 500

Buyer's attorney .... $ 2,500
   approximate

Condo credit report .... $ 75
   approximate

Move-in deposit .... $ 1,000
   refundable in most cases

Move-in fee .... $ 250

Title search and insurance .... $ ([2])
   [2]*$0.5% to 0.8% of sale price*

Recording charge .... $ 200 *to* $750

Title closer fee .... $ 150 *to* $250

Prepaid expenses .... $ ([3])
   [3]*common charges through end of month plus*
   real estate charges for up to six months

"Mansion tax" .... ([4])
   [4]*1% of sale price; applies to sales of $1 million or more*

Estimated Condominium Closing Costs

The Seller

New York City transfer tax filing fee ....$ 50

plus...

Sales under $500K..................................   1% *of sale price*

Sales over $500K .... 1.425% *of sale price*

New York State transfer tax......................... 0.4% *of sale price*

Seller's attorney ....$ 2,500
   approximate

Mortgage pick-up/payoff fee.........................$ 300 *to* $500

Managing agent fee...................................$ 650
   processing fees

Move-out deposit ....$ 1,000
   refundable in most cases

Move-out fee ....$ 500

Title charges...$ 150 *to* $250

Debt Service Payment Table — Per Thousand

(to fully amortize a principal balance at a given rate of interest over a term of 30 years

Interest Rate (%)	Per Month ($)	Per Year ($)
2.00	3.70	44.40
2.25	3.82	45.84
2.50	3.95	47.40
2.75	4.08	48.96
3.00	4.22	50.64
3.25	4.35	52.20
3.50	4.49	53.88
3.75	4.63	55.56
4.00	4.77	57.24
4.25	4.92	59.04
4.50	5.07	60.84
4.75	5.22	62.64
5.00	5.37	64.44
5.25	5.32	63.84
5.50	5.68	68.04
5.75	5.84	70.08
6.00	6.00	72.00
6.25	6.16	73.92
6.50	6.32	75.84
6.75	6.49	77.88
7.00	6.65	79.80
7.25	6.82	81.84
7.50	6.99	83.88
7.75	7.16	85.92
8.00	7.34	88.08
8.25	7.52	90.24
8.50	7.69	92.28
8.75	7.87	94.44

Debt Service Payment Table (Continued)

Interest Rate (%)	Per Month ($)	Per Year ($)
9.00	8.05	96.60
9.25	8.23	98.76
9.50	8.41	100.92
9.75	8.59	103.08
10.00	8.78	105.36
10.25	8.96	107.52
10.50	9.15	109.80
10.75	9.33	111.96
11.00	9.53	114.36
11.25	9.71	116.52
11.50	9.91	118.92
11.75	10.09	121.08
12.00	10.29	123.48

Tax Rates

Federal Income Tax Brackets for 2013

Bracket	Single ends at	Married, Joint Filers ends at	Head of Household ends at
10%	$8,925	$17,850	$12,750
15%	$36,250	$72,500	$48,600
25%	$87,850	$146,400	$125,450
28%	$183,250	$223,050	$203,150
33%	$398,350	$398,350	$398,350
35%	$400,000	$450,000	$425,000
39.6%	$400,000+	$450,000+	$425,000+

The capital gains rate is 15% unless the taxpayer's taxable income exceeds $400,000, in which case the rate is 20% if the holding period is less than five years, and 18% if it exceeds five years. (There are exceptions to this rule; e.g., for low-income taxpayers in the 15% bracket, the rate is 10% based on a holding period of one year.)

For depreciable property, the amount of recaptured depreciation on a sale is taxed at 25%.

The Medicare surcharge tax would apply for passive income exceeding $200,000 for individuals and $250,000 for married couples. This is an additional tax of 3.8% on the excess amount.

New York State and New York City Tax Rates

New York State Tax Rates for 2013

Tax Rate	Single ends at	Married, Filing Jointly ends at
6.85%	$200,000	$300,000
7.85%	$500,000	$500,000
8.97%	$500,000+	$500,000+

New York City Tax Rates for 2013

Tax Rate	Single ends at	Married, Filing Jointly ends at
3.591%	$50,000	$ 90,000
3.648%	$500,000	$500,000
3.876%	$500,000+	$500,000+

Standard Operating Expenses for Various Condominium and Cooperative Properties in New York City

(in thousands)

	10 units	50 units	100 units	200 units
Real estate tax	$125	$625	$1,200	$1,800
Debt payment	30	225	400	700
Payroll	18[1]	500[2]	650[3]	780[4]
Payroll tax	2	52	65	78
Pension and welfare	180	215	260	312
Workers comp	2	8	12	15
Gas	10	45	50	70
Heating	35	65	150	200
Water and sewer	8	35	70	90
Building supplies	6	18	33	50
Repairs & maintenance	24	80	140	200
Elevator maintenance	10	21	40	40
Insurance	15	45	54	100
Management	10	45	55	80
Legal	5	5	10	24
Accounting	6	9	13	14
Other professional	2	6	6	6
Corporation tax	15	15	15	15
Office administration	8	10	14	30
Total expenses	$511	$2,024	$3,237	$4,604

[1] No doorman

[2] Full-time doorman, one super

[3] Full-time doorman, one super, one porter

[4] Full-time doorman, one super, one handyman, two porters

APPENDIX 2

Worksheets

Rent vs. Buy Analysis

Part 1: Analysis of Monthly Effect

Section I: Rent Alternative

Rent for the apartment $_____(A)

Section II: Tax Liability

Description of Payment (Annual)	Gross Amount	Percent Deductible	Tax-Deductible Amount
Maintenance	$_____	_____%	$_____
Debt payment	$_____	Interest portion	$_____
Total	$_____ (B)		$_____

Federal tax rate   _____%

State & local tax rate   *plus* _____%

Total tax rate[1]   *equals* _____%

Computed tax effect $_____(C)

Section III: Rent vs. Buy Comparison

After-tax ownership cost *(B minus C)* $_____(D)

After-tax monthly cost *(D divided by 12)* $_____(E)

Rent vs. ownership: monthly cost *(A minus E)* $_____(F)

Therefore:

The purchase of an apartment is less/more expensive than a comparable rental by _____ per month.

[1]*Net of federal tax effect*

Rent vs. Buy Analysis

Part 2: Analysis of Investment Return

Section I: Investment

(1) Invested funds $_____

(2) Investment yield   _____%

(3) Yearly investment return $_____

(4) Tax on investment income (rate _____%) $_____

Net after-tax return $_____(A)

Section II: Homeownership

(1) Purchase price of home $_____

(2) Rate of inflation/appreciation   _____%

After-tax yearly appreciation benefit[1] $_____(B)

Relative yearly benefit (B minus A) $_____

Therefore:

The economic return on an investment in the home offers a more/ less favorable return than an alternative investment by _____ (before transaction costs).

[1]In the event of a sale, the proceeds will be tax-free because current tax laws exempt up to $250,000 in profit from taxation for individuals, or $500,000 per couple.

Evaluating the Primary Motivators

Location

What is your minimum location requirement?

___ **10.** Overlooking Central Park, near world-renowned buildings and landmarks

___ **9.** Internationally prestigious, residential, near Central Park or overlooking a park

___ **8.** Exceptionally beautiful and charming residential street, near a park or river

___ **7.** Quiet and charming residential street

___ **6.** Commercial or residential street without notable features, with good demand

___ **5.** Commercial or residential street with growing potential and active buyer interest

___ **4.** Emerging area with few local services, restaurants, etc.

___ **3.** Minimal aesthetics, less convenient to transportation and shopping

___ **2.** Street with low market demand

___ **1.** No preference

Building

What is your minimum building requirement?

___ **10.** Internationally recognized, architecturally significant, high-end services, top condition

___ **9.** Excellent local reputation, architecturally significant, high-end services, top condition

___ **8.** Very good local reputation, great amenities, at least two lobby attendants

___ **7.** Doorman, good-quality amenities

___ **6.** Doorman, average amenities

___ **5.** Either an intercom, top condition or a doorman, needing renovation

___ **4.** Low- or mid-rise, intercom, average condition

___ **3.** Low- or mid-rise, intercom, condition issues

___ **2.** Low- or mid-rise, intercom, substantial renovations needed

___ **1.** No preference

Air

Are there any layout elements that are critical to you?

___ Formal dining room

___ Eat-in kitchen

___ Alcove studio

___ Maid's room

___ Spacious entry

___ Separation between master and other bedrooms

___ Other _____

Light

Is there a minimum floor that you require?

___ No preference

___ Third floor and above

___ On or above the ____ floor

View

What is the minimum direct view you require out of the living room?

___ **10.** Sweeping views of Central Park and grand cityscape views

___ **9.** Grand cityscape views with river and/or park

___ **8.** Grand cityscape views without a river or park

___ **7.** Basic skyline views, basic river views or beautiful courtyard views

___ **6.** Street views into buildings but bright

___ **5.** Street views into buildings, moderate light (middle floor)

___ **4.** Street views into buildings, limited light or basic courtyard views

___ **3.** No views but bright

___ **2.** No views, moderate light

___ **1.** No preference

Space

What is the minimum amount of space you desire for the following rooms?

Living room _____ × _____

Master bedroom _____ × _____

Secondary Amenities

Are there secondary elements that are important to you?

___ Garage in building

___ Fireplace

___ Health club

___ Pool

___ Laundry room

___ Terrace/outdoor space

___ Pets

___ Washer/dryer

___ Prewar building

___ Specific neighborhood(s) _____

___ Other _____

Evaluating the Overall Cost of an Apartment

(A) Cash Down Payment

Non-borrowed cash you want to use to purchase
an apartment $_____

(B) Cost Per Month

Compute your ideal monthly payment below:

Reported monthly income $_____

Coverage rate   × 45%
  as defined by all banks

Maximum monthly debt payment   *equals* $_____

Total of other debts you currently pay   *minus* $_____

Cash available for covering the monthly cost
of your home   *equals* $_____ (A)

Mortgage $_____
  assume 75% of the purchase price

Monthly interest factor for ____ % = _____
  see debt service payment table on page 135

Monthly mortgage payment   *equals* $_____ (B)

Available for monthly housing cost[1]   *(B minus A)* $_____

[1]Maintenance for a cooperative; common charges and real estate taxes for
a condominium. The average maintenance charge for the type of property
you are looking for can be ascertained by going to Bellmarc.com and clicking
on Survey Our Inventory. The system will then display by type of property
and price category the average monthly cost for that type of apartment.
For a cooperative it shows the maintenance charge; for a condominium it
shows the monthly common charges and the real estate tax allocation to the
apartment.

Comparison Analysis of Selected Apartments

	Buying Formula	Selected Apartments		
		A	B	C
Address	_____	_____	_____	_____
Location grade	____	____	____	____
Building grade	____	____	____	____
Air qualities	____	_____	_____	_____
Light				
View grade	____	____	____	____
Minimum floor	____	____	____	____
Space				
Living room sq. ft.	____	____	____	____
Master bedroom sq. ft.	____	____	____	____
Secondary factors	____	____	____	____
Price	_____	_____	_____	_____
Monthly charge[1]	_____	_____	_____	_____
Cash down	_____	_____	_____	_____
Cash per month	_____	_____	_____	_____

[1]For co-ops use maintenance payment; for condos use common charges and real estate taxes.

Personal Tax

The following is a generic form showing the structure used for personal income tax returns. It is useful for understanding the underlying framework behind tax terminology and application. It is not to be construed as a complete and accurate form for tax-filing purposes.

Total cash received for the year $_____

Less changes in assets, liabilities and other
non-income items:

    Loans received   *minus* $_____

    Return of loans provided   *minus* $_____

    Insurance proceeds received on losses for which
    you suffered damages   *minus* $_____

    Gifts received   *minus* $_____
    may be subject to separate gift tax filings

                   = GROSS INCOME $_____

Less Tax-Exempt Income:

    Tax-exempt income received
    (e.g. tax-exempt interest or dividends)   *minus* $_____

    Deferred-income programs
    such as IRAs or 401(k)s   *minus* $_____

        = GROSS INCOME SUBJECT TO TAX $_____

Less deductions for adjusted gross income (AGI)

    Business-related expenses   *minus* $_____

    Investment-related expenses   *minus* $_____

        = ADJUSTED GROSS INCOME (AGI) $_____

Less itemized deductions of personal expenses:

    Interest deductions relating to primary and
    vacation homes as permitted   *minus* $_____

    Real estate tax deductions on primary and
    vacation homes as permitted   *minus* $_____

    Personal deductions
    (e.g. charitable contributions, medical expense
    allowances)   *minus* $_____

State income tax liability   *minus* $_____

Personal exemptions for dependents   *minus* $_____

                  = TAXABLE INCOME $_____

Multiplied by applicable tax rate   _____%

        = TAX BEFORE TAX CREDITS $_____

Less tax credits $_____

         = FEDERAL TAX LIABILITY $_____

Glossary

12 MAT Index: Stands for *12-Month Average Treasury Index.* This is a 12-month average of the one-year U.S. Treasury rates used for one form of a monthly adjustable mortgage. Since it is based on historical experience, this index lags current interest rates.

12-Month Average Treasury: A type of adjustable rate mortgage whose payment varies monthly, based on an index consisting of the monthly United States Treasury bill rate.

421a tax program: A tax abatement program for newly constructed buildings that reduces the real estate taxes on the property for a designated period of time. The degree of reduction is based on the location of the property and the date the building was actually constructed.

accountant's opinion letter: A letter generated by an accountant after performing an audit review on a cooperative corporation or condominium association. This letter expresses the accountant's opinion about whether the financial statement fairly presents the financial position of the entity. If there are any material issues, they would appear in this opinion letter. The date of the letter is the final date of the accountant's examination of the books of the company or association.

adjustable-rate mortgage: A loan secured by real estate that has a varying interest rate and payment based on a short adjustment period (normally one month, six months or one year). The adjustment is dependent on the variation in a benchmark index, usually the LIBOR rate.

adjusted sale price: The price on the contract less all selling costs recognized and permitted under the Internal Revenue Code.

affirmation (New York State disclosure requirements): A written statement made by an agent affirming his position and representation to a party to a proposed or actual transaction. An agent will use an affirmation, which requires two witnesses, if he is unable to obtain signed consent from the party he represents on a New York State disclosure statement.

all-equity cash purchase: A property transaction in which the buyer pays only with personal funds, and does not rely on financing.

amendment: In the course of converting a building to homeownership, the sponsor may alter the information contained in the prospectus, including his offering price, by filing an amendment to the offering plan. Amendments may also occur after the date of conversion if there is additional relevant information, including new offers made to tenants still in occupancy, and to provide pertinent financial disclosure information about the sponsor or material investors.

amortization: The periodic payment of principal on a liability (including a mortgage), or the write-off of a nondepreciable asset over a scheduled term of years.

annual percentage rate (APR): A figure that is intended to represent the full cost of all elements associated with obtaining a mortgage in a single formula. The APR is a useful device for making comparisons between mortgage products.

appraisal: The evaluation of a property's value by a licensed expert (an *appraiser*) on its price, assuming a ready, willing and able buyer, and a seller without any external forces compelling a sale. The appraised value is used by a bank to determine the lending limit on a given property.

appraisal pool: A group of participating appraisers who subscribe to participate as members of a bank's selected group. Only members within the pool can perform appraisals associated with loans being underwritten by the bank.

appraiser: An expert responsible for evaluating the worth of a selected property. See *appraisal*.

assessment: An extraordinary payment called for by the board of directors of a cooperative corporation or condominium association for the purpose of making a capital improvement, or to provide some other essential service for which funds in the reserve account are inadequate.

assessment, property: A tax valuation levied on a property from the county assessor, which is used as a basis for levying real estate tax.

asset: Something you own that has value.

at risk: Under the United States Internal Revenue Code, an owner of investment property either must be personally responsible for the indebtedness on real estate, or the debt must be issued by a financial institution, in order for the full purchase price of the property to qualify as the tax basis in determining depreciation.

back-end ratio: A measure used by banks to determine whether a prospective borrower is qualified for a loan. The ratio is determined by the projected cost of owning the home, including the yearly cost of the proposed home loan plus all other annual debt payments, divided by the borrower's reported income. Normally banks look for a percentage that does not exceed 45%.

balance sheet: An accountant's statement that outlines a building's Assets, Liabilities and Equity at a specific point in time. Also known as a *statement of financial position*.

balloon mortgage: A mortgage that matures with a balance still owed at the end of the term.

black book: See *prospectus*.

board approval: A condition in the standard cooperative sales contract requiring that the buyer obtain approval from the board of directors of the cooperative corporation as a prerequisite to completing the sale.

boot: In a like-kind exchange transaction, any cash or cash-equivalent payment (including mortgages) will be considered separate to the transaction and may be subject to tax even though the parties engaged in a property exchange. Boot is the amount of recognized gain in a like-kind exchange.

bridging: A strategy used by investors in considering the appreciation potential of a property. The investor will look for an area of malaise that is bordered by two vibrant neighborhoods. The area of malaise is the "bridge" between the two strong neighborhoods and is considered a good prospect for appreciation.

brownstone: A brownish-reddish sandstone often used for building exteriors. It has been generally used by real estate brokers to refer to a type of property, normally a walkup of four to six stories with a frontage of 20 to 40 feet.

business judgment rule: The guiding principle used by New York State courts in gauging the liability of a co-op or condo's board of directors. According to this rule, the board of directors cannot be held legally liable for the consequences of its actions if it can be shown to have made those actions in good faith and with good judgment.

buydown: A payment made by a borrower to a bank for the purpose of reducing the interest rate on a loan.

buyer's broker: A broker who represents the buyer in effectuating a purchase. Normally, in residential real estate transactions, the buyer's broker shares the commission paid by the seller with the listing broker.

buying formula: A list of the essential criteria that are involved in a buyer's purchasing decision. By creating a buying formula, a buyer can compare different properties to each other in order to choose the apartment that best fits his or her desires.

bylaws: The rules by which the cooperative corporation operates, including those regulating elections, officers and authorizations.

cap: see *capitalization rate.*

capitalization rate: The rate of return on a property, measured as a ratio of the property's net operating income compared to its perceived value to the investor (required rate of return) or its market value (return on investment). Investors use cap rates as a quick means of defining an asset's relative value compared to other alternatives.

capital gain: The seller's gain on the sale of an asset used in a trade or business or for investment, including real estate. This gain is taxed at varying rates depending on whether the asset was held for more or less than one year. If less, then the gain is taxed at ordinary rates. If more than one year, the rate is 15%; if the taxpayer's income exceeds $400,00 it is 20%. If more than five years, the rate is reduced to 18% under most circumstances.

carrying-cost rule: A rule used by banks to evaluate borrowers for loans. It gives the maximum percentage of a borrower's income that the bank will find acceptable to carry the loan and related housing costs. This rule is used in conjunction with the debt-to-equity ratio.

co-brokerage: An arrangement between two brokerage firms to share a commission. Normally it is used when one broker is the seller's exclusive listing agent and the other broker represents the buyer.

collateral: The security put up in exchange for a loan, which can be taken by the bank if the loan goes unpaid.

commitment letter: A letter issued by a bank that legally binds it to provide funds, subject to written terms and conditions.

common charges: The monthly sum levied by a condominium to cover the cost of maintaining the common areas and services.

condominium: A building in which ownership has been partitioned into unit interests. Each apartment owner receives a unit deed.

condops: In legal terms, a condominium in which one of the condomium units is owned by a cooperative corporation. However, brokers also use the term to refer to a cooperative that has flexible entry and renting requirements similar to those found in a condominium.

conforming loan: A mortgage issued within the framework of Fannie Mae guidelines in terms and amount.

construction concession: A payment made by the seller to the buyer for the purpose of funding improvements to the property. It is commonly used as a means of adjusting the sale price without reducing the stated price on a contract of sale.

contingent liability: An obligation incurred when a predefined event causes one party to have a claim against another.

contract vendee sale: A transaction in which a seller transfers beneficial rights — including the right of possession and obligations of ownership — to the purchaser, and agrees to close at a future date under definite terms. Ownership can be transferred for tax purposes prior to the transfer of title.

conversion: A change in ownership status. For example, rental housing may be converted to co-op or condo ownership. Such changes must conform to guidelines determined by the laws of New York State.

cooperative: A building owned by a corporation in which each apartment is allocated shares of stock as well as a proprietary lease.

coverage rate: The level to which the income of the buyer is "covering" (paying for) the cost of owning and carrying the property that the buyer proposes to purchase. Also known as the *housing cost ratio*.

deal sheet: A written delineation of the material terms of a real estate transaction that is prepared by real estate brokers on behalf of their clients and submitted to attorneys for the preparation of a formal contract. Also known as a *term sheet*.

debt factor: see *interest rate factor*.

debt service: The cost of carrying a loan (usually through monthly payments), including the payment of interest and principal.

debt-to-equity ratio: A rule used by banks requiring that a borrower invest a minimum amount of equity cash (usually 10% to 25% of the purchase price) as a condition to obtaining a mortgage. This rule is used in conjunction with the carrying-cost rule to determine how much money a bank will lend.

debt-to-income ratio: The percentage of income allocated to pay the borrower's cumulative debt, including potential mortgage payments and apartment carrying costs. Typically this percentage cannot exceed 45% for home loans. Also known as the *housing cost ratio*.

deep leverage: Applies to financing that exceeds 80% of the purchase price of the property. These loans are commonly granted at 90% of the purchase price. Also known as *heavy leverage*.

default: An act performed by either the buyer or seller that breaches the contract of sale and permits a claim for damages.

deficiency amount: In the event of a short sale or a foreclosure, the amount the bank actually receives as compared to the amount owed.

deposit: The amount of cash given to the seller's attorney at the time the contract is signed by the buyer. It is typically held in escrow and is subject to the successful completion of the contract by the parties.

depreciation: The expensing of the original cost of an asset, plus any qualified improvements, over its scheduled life as defined by the Internal Revenue Code. Depreciation deductions are permitted only for assets held for the production of income or used in a trade or business. The current term for depreciating residential real estate is 27.5 years.

depreciation recapture: See *recapture.*

direct deal: A transaction that is undertaken directly by the seller without the use of a broker. However, brokers also utilize the term to designate a transaction where there is no other broker involved in the deal.

disclosure form (New York State): A form required by the State of New York in which the real estate broker discloses his or her relationship with the buyer and/or seller in a real estate transaction.

double-declining balance depreciation: A depreciation technique whereby the asset is divided by its useful life, and this sum is doubled. Thereafter, in each succeeding year the accumulated depreciation is deducted from the original asset value to recompute depreciation for the succeeding period. It is not available for real estate, but it is permissible for tangible personal property.

down payment: The amount of non-financed cash invested in a property.

dual agency: A transaction in which the buyer and seller are both represented by the same real estate broker. In this case, consent must be obtained from both parties to the transaction.

equity: The difference between what something is worth and any loans secured by that asset (e.g., the value of a property less the outstanding mortgage).

equity credit line: Generally referred to by banks as a "HELOC" (Home Equity Line of Credit). It is a second mortgage secured by an owner's residence that affords the borrower the ability to borrow and repay funds up to the designated amount of the credit line. The interest on the credit line is generally tax-deductible up to a maximum credit line of $100,000.

escrow: A sum of money held by one person in trust for another for the purpose of assuring performance under an agreement. Normally, in a residential real estate sale, the attorney for the seller is the escrow agent for the deposit money securing the deal until closing.

escrow agreement transfer: See *contract vendee sale.*

exclusive-agency agreement: An agreement between a broker and a seller designating the broker as the seller's sole agent for the purpose of selling his or her property. This agreement does not preclude the owner from effectuating a sale on his own.

exclusive listing agent: The broker acting as the sole representative of the seller in promoting a property for sale or rent, and then in negotiating agreeable terms for a transaction on behalf of the seller. This party is a fiduciary to the seller. Also referred to as the *seller's broker.*

exclusive-right-to-sell agreement: An agreement between a broker and a seller designating the broker as the seller's sole representative for the purpose of selling property. In contrast to an exclusive-agency agreement, under an exclusive-right-to-sell agreement, a commission is due to the broker even if the apartment is sold directly by the owner.

expression of interest: An indication of interest in a property shown by a prospective buyer. A broker can communicate an expression of interest as a form of negotiation with a seller or seller's broker, in order to create a basis for developing a subsequent offer.

Fannie Mae guidelines: A set of rules formulated by Fannie Mae that outline the necessary conditions to qualify for a loan that Fannie Mae will accept. Fannie Mae guidelines are effectively used by all banks as necessary conditions for obtaining a loan.

FICO score: A score determined by credit agencies that reflects your creditworthiness and ability to support a loan. FICO scores are used by banks to evaluate prospective borrowers.

financial motivators: The defining economic criteria behind a buyer's decision to purchase an apartment. These consist of the cash down payment, which is the amount of money needed to close on the sale, and the monthly cost, which is the amount needed to pay the mortgage and common or maintenance charges on an ongoing basis.

financing loan: A loan secured by personal property. The stock and lease of a cooperative corporation constitute such personal property, and a loan secured by these instruments is referred to as a financing loan. Real estate brokers generally refer to these financing loans as mortgages because they operate in the same manner, even though technically they are not.

financing contingency: Refers to the buyer's right to obtain a bank loan as a condition to completing the transaction. This is evidenced by a commitment letter from a bank promising to provide the agreed-upon funds. In the event that a commitment letter cannot be obtained, the buyer may cancel the contract and have his contract deposit returned.

fixed-rate mortgage: A loan secured by real estate that has a fixed interest rate and payment amount for the term of the loan (normally 15 or 30 years).

flip: The immediate resale of a property following its purchase. Typically, this is done opportunistically as a means of generating a profit.

flip tax: A levy issued on the transfer of ownership by a cooperative corporation or condominium association against either the buyer or seller.

foreclosure: A legal procedure implemented by a lender against a borrower to recapture real property (or a security interest in the case of a cooperative) secured for a loan.

for sale by owner: A situation in which an owner seeks to market his or her property without the aid of a real estate broker. See *open listing*.

front-end ratio: The percentage of a buyer's income that is allocated to cover monthly housing expenses, including mortgage payments and apartment carrying costs. This ratio is distinguished from the back-end ratio, which evaluates what percentage of a buyer's income goes toward paying all his or her debts, including housing debts. Real estate brokers use the front-end ratio to make a quick evaluation of whether a buyer is capable of supporting a home loan, and cooperative boards use it as one gauge to determine whether the buyer is financially qualified to live in an apartment.

fully indexed rate: An interest rate applied to an adjustable-rate mortgage that is calculated by adding a margin to an exisiting index rate (often the LIBOR index).

funding contingency: A provision added to the standard contract for sale that conditions the transaction on the bank actually providing at the closing the funds promised in the commitment letter.

heavy-leverage loan: Financing provided to a buyer who seeks to make a deposit of less than 20%. Normally brokers associate heavy leverage with 90% financing, which is typically used only for condominium apartment purchases. Also known as a *deep-leverage loan*.

house rules: Building rules regulating the conduct and responsibilities of homeowners as they affect the building's common areas and services.

housing cost ratio: See *debt-to-income ratio*.

implied mortgage: The amount of mortgage that a purchaser may be able to obtain given his or her income and financial resources.

income statement: The presentation of funds earned and funds expended for a defined period of time, usually a year. Also known as a *statement of operations*.

insider rights: Special rights offered to tenants occupying apartments in a building in the process of converting to a co-op or condo, giving them the exclusive right to buy their apartments for a limited period of time, normally at a discounted price.

installment sale: A property sale in which the purchaser pays the purchase price over a period of years. The seller recognizes gain for tax purposes by the proportion of the profit (determined by the profit divided by the net sale price of the asset) received on each payment as it is received.

interest rate cap: The maximum change in interest rate in any given year or over the term of the loan in an adjustable-rate mortgage.

interest rate factor: the payment amount, as expressed in either monthly or yearly terms, to pay off a loan at a given rate of interest for a given length of time. See the Debt Service Payment Table on page 135 for the interest rate factors for 30-year loans.

interest rate spread: The differential between the retail interest rate charged to a borrower and the wholesale rate accepted by Wall Street when acquiring home mortgage loans. The spread represents profit to the bank.

interest-only loan: A loan that requires the borrower to pay only the interest amount for a certain term, after which time the entire balance of the loan must be repaid. Also known as a *standing mortgage*.

J-51 tax program: A New York City program giving tax breaks for the substantial rehabilitation of an existing property. The program provides for an abatement of tax using a formula based on the level of improvement, and an exclusion from additional tax due to the change in use of the property.

jumbo loan: A mortgage issued in an amount exceeding the threshold stipulated under Fannie Mae regulations for a conforming loan.

land contract sale: See *contract vendee sale*.

land lease: A contract through which a building and other land improvements are rented for a term of years. At the end of the lease term, the right of possession is extinguished and reverts back to the landowner. At that time, the owner loses any remaining equity interest in the property.

landmark: The designation given to a building or neighborhood that is under New York City protection for purposes of preservation.

Landmarks Preservation Commission: A city governmental agency assigned responsibility for recommending properties and neighborhoods to be landmarked and ensuring that landmarks are properly preserved.

letter of adequacy: A letter (usually issued by a managing agent) found in the offering plan of a building converting to cooperative or condominium ownership, affirming that the income and expenses, as expressed in the proposed budget, are adequate to cover the costs of running the building. This expert evaluation is required by New York State law.

letter of reasonable relationship: A letter issued by an expert (usually a real estate broker) affirming that the allocation of shares or unit-percentage interest in a cooperative or condominium conversion is rational and reasonable in accordance with New York State law.

liability: A debt you owe or a claim against you.

LIBOR: Stands for *London Interbank Offered Rate*, which is the interest rate offered by a specific group of London banks for U.S. deposits.

LIBOR is a common index used as a benchmark for adjusting mortgage interest rates in adjustable-rate mortgages.

like-kind exchange: An exchange of similar property, as defined in the Internal Revenue Code, that can be performed without recognition of taxable gain at the time of transfer.

limited-liability company: A form of organization that is similar to a partnership in that recognition of income and expenses flows directly through to the owners for tax purposes (without a corporate tax), but that still permits insulation from liability similar to that of a corporation.

listing: The term used by brokers for an apartment for sale after it has been publicly posted by the broker.

listing broker: The broker who represents the interests of the seller in the sale of his or her property. Also known as a *seller's broker*.

maintenance: The monthly charge levied on owners by a cooperative corporation to cover the building's operating costs, real estate taxes and the debt service on the building's underlying mortgage.

mansion tax: A New York State tax of 1% of the selling price levied on the buyer of any residence costing in excess of $1,000,000.

Martin Act: The New York State law regulating the conversion of properties to cooperative or condominium ownership. Also referred to as Sections 352-eee and 352-eeee of New York State's General Business Law.

minimum upset price: In a property auction, a base price that must be reached before the property can be sold. Any price above the minimum will be accepted by the seller.

mortgage: A loan secured by real estate.

mortgage banker: An institution that performs services similar to those of a mortgage broker. However, a mortgage banker is also legally permitted to lend its own funds.

mortgage broker: A real estate professional who represents an array of banks seeking to issue mortgages. The mortgage broker meets with a customer, assists with the application and facilitates the mortgage process on behalf of the borrower and the bank. The mortgage broker is usually paid a fee by the bank for working with residential mortgage applicants. These relationships are generally referred to as *correspondent lending programs*.

negative amortization: Occurs when a loan permits the borrower to make a payment that is less than the full amount required to cover the interest charge on the open balance, and the shortfall is added to the mortgage principal.

negative pledge: Occurs when the condominium places restrictions on the unit deed and trust agreement, restricting the right of an owner to finance a condominium unit for more than a specified amount.

net worth: Your assets less your liabilities.

nonrecourse financing: Loans for which the borrower is not personally liable. These loans are collateralized exclusively by the property being financed, which can be seized if the borrower defaults.

notes to the financial statement: Addenda that detail any pertinent information expressed in a building's income statement and balance sheet. These notes are intended to provide greater clarification of the building's financial affairs.

official offer: The formal written offer for a property that a buyer's broker submits to a seller's broker. The official offer contains the material terms of the deal and a personal financial statement of the borrower, as well as a preapproval letter from the bank if financing is being used in the purchase. Email is an accepted means of communication for an official offer.

offering plan: See *prospectus*.

open listing: An apartment for sale for which the owner has not signed an exclusive agreement with a real estate broker. Many brokers may represent the seller, or the seller can promote the property independently. See *for sale by owner* listing.

operating profit: Revenues less operating expenses before debt service and other non-operating expenses. The operating profit expresses the real cost of operating the property and is used by an investor to identify the potential return on investment of the asset.

original-acquisition financing: The funds borrowed at the time a property is acquired. The Internal Revenue Service normally permits the borrower to take a deduction for interest on this mortgage, as long as the loan is obtained within 90 days of closing. If the loan is obtained subsequent to this threshold date, the interest is generally not deductible.

overassessment: Each year the City of New York issues an assessment of valuation for all real property, which is then the basis for its yearly tax levy. When a property's assessed value exceeds its fair market value, it is called an overassessment. The property owner has a right to appeal this overassessment in court in order to reduce the valuation and resulting tax. This process is called a tax certiorari proceeding.

owner-paid (OP): Refers to instances when the landlord of a property agrees to pay the real estate broker a commission for finding a ready, willing and able tenant to rent his property.

passive loss: A loss generated by investment real estate when real estate is not the taxpayer's primary business. Loss in excess of income may not be fully recognizable for tax purposes in the year it was incurred.

perfecting a loan: When a loan is issued against personal property, it is recorded in the county clerk's office against the name of the borrower. The recording process perfects a security position against the collateral.

personal property: All property that is not physically attached to real estate is designated in the contract of sale as personal property. Depending on the circumstances, transferred personal property must have a bill of sale and is subject to sales tax.

phantom gain: A sale of real estate in which income is recognized for tax purposes but little or no money has actually been received. This can occur when the property's basis has been depreciated below the property's mortgage amount.

piggyback loan: A loan that is added onto a primary mortgage in the purchase of a home. This is a form of heavy leverage, and is effectively a second mortgage encumbering the property.

points: Payment made to a bank as consideration for issuing a mortgage, usually based on a percentage of the loan amount.

portfolio lenders: Regional banks and financial institutions that offer financings and mortgages at terms different from Fannie-Mae-conforming loans.

preapproval letter: A letter issued by a bank approving the buyer for a loan on a specific property, subject to an appraisal and verification of submitted documents.

preliminary offering plan: A notification to tenants in a building of the sponsor's intention to convert the building to unit ownership. Each tenant will receive a preliminary offering plan which will have red lettering on the front cover of the prospectus book advising that the book is merely a notification of the sponsor's intention to convert the property and not an offer to purchase. Also referred to as a *red herring*.

pre-qualification letter: A letter issued by a bank advising a prospective borrower that the bank will lend a specified amount based on a satisfactory appraisal of the property and the verification of income and expenses.

prewar: A building that was built prior to World War II.

primary motivators: The primary aesthetic criteria that a buyer should use in order to evaluate apartments. These include the qualities of location, building, air, light and space.

private mortgage insurance (PMI): An insurance policy associated with heavy-leverage loans. This type of insurance, which is arranged by the bank and paid for by the borrower, guarantees the payment of bank debt for loans exceeding conventional debt levels (80% or more) in the event the borrower defaults.

procuring cause: The duty of a broker under New York State law to engage in developing an agreement between a ready, willing and able buyer and an accepting seller on the material terms of the deal. The broker has a duty to effectuate the transaction, not just to show the apartment.

profit exemption: Current tax rules permit the profit on the sale of a primary residence to be tax-exempt for up to $250,000 for an individual, or $500,000 for a married couple.

proprietary lease: The lease issued by a cooperative corporation to each tenant-shareholder prescribing his or her right to occupy a specific apartment and his or her general obligations as an owner and tenant.

prospectus: A document issued by a sponsor in the process of converting a building to cooperative or condominium ownership. It is intended to provide full disclosure of all relevant facts associated with evaluating an investment in the property. Also referred to as an *offering plan* or *black book.*

purchase money mortgage: A loan from a seller to a buyer in order to effectuate a transaction that is secured by the property.

qualified mortgage: The amount of financing a borrower can obtain from a bank after ensuring that he or she meets the bank's lending criteria.

real estate owned: When a bank takes ownership of a property as a result of a loan foreclosure, it is defined by the bank as "real estate owned" or more commonly as a "REO" property, and is managed by a separate department within the bank.

recapture: When investment real estate has been depreciated for tax purposes, the gain on the sale includes a *recapture* of the previously written-off depreciation as gain. In certain cases, this can result in a tax liability that exceeds the cash received (see *phantom gain).*

recognition letter: A letter from the cooperative corporation's board of directors recognizing the secured rights of a lender to the shares of stock and the proprietary lease on a specific apartment.

recording: Registering the ownership, lien or claim of a party to a specific parcel of real estate with the local county.

red herring: See *preliminary offering plan.*

rental: The possession, but not ownership, of a property for a limited duration of time under defined terms and conditions.

restraint of alienation: An attempt in a deed to restrict the right of transferability of a property. This is illegal under New York State law, and a condominum cannot directly restrict the right of a condominium owner from selling his property. Condominum plans therefore normally provide for a right of first refusal as a means of protecting the condominium from undesirable purchasers by permitting the condominium to step into the contract signed by that buyer and accept the terms of that contract.

right of first refusal: A condition contained in many condominium master deeds that permits the board to review any party seeking to purchase or rent an apartment and to refuse the applicant if it so desires. If the board refuses the applicant, it must thereafter purchase or rent the apartment under the same terms and conditions stipulated in the contract.

right-of-first-refusal waiver letter: A letter issued by the condominium association waiving any claim the condominium may have to purchase the property subject to a contract. Normally banks require a waiver letter as a condition to issuing a mortgage, and failure to obtain the letter is a cloud on the title of the condominium apartment.

schedule A: A list in the offering plan of all the apartments being sold in a newly constructed building or one that is undergoing conversion. It presents allocated shares or unit percentage interest, room count and other material cost elements, including the projected maintenance charge and the tax-deductible portion of the maintenance.

schedule B: Documentation in an offering plan that represents the projected cost of operating a cooperative or condominium during its first year of operation.

Section 421a: A New York City tax program intended to stimulate new construction by permitting a phase-in of the real estate tax over a period of years.

secondary factors: Other features and amenities relating to an apartment that play a role in the buyer's decision, in addition to the primary motivators of location, building, air, light and space. The secondary factors should only be relevant if the buying formula for the primary motivators has been satisfied.

seller's broker: See *listing broker.*

short sale: An agreement between a borrower and a bank whereby the bank accepts less than the full outstanding balance due on the loan upon the transfer of the property. It is generally applicable where the owner of a property is in financial difficulties and is seeking the assistance of the bank to resolve the payoff of the loan where its principal amount exceeds the value of the property.

single-family property: A building, such as a house, that consists of a single residence.

sponsor: The party initiating the conversion of a property from single ownership to cooperative or condominium ownership.

standing mortgage: See *interest-only loan*.

statement of financial position: See *balance sheet*.

statement of operations: See *income statement*.

subject to financing: A clause in the contract of sale for a cooperative apartment stipulating that the agreement is conditioned upon the buyer's obtaining financing from a financial institution in an agreed-upon amount.

subordinate lien: When a claim, encumbrance or lien is filed against a property, its right to receive payment is based on the date it was filed (unless otherwise expressed in the document). Accordingly, any lien placed after another lien will be paid only after the other lien is fully satisfied, and is therefore subordinate to it.

super jumbo loan: A loan exceeding $1,100,000.

teaser rate: A very low initial rate of interest that is offered by banks to borrowers. This rate is then increased after a certain duration to a standard rate of interest. Teaser rates are appealing because they give the borrower greater financial flexibility to move in and fix up a new home at the beginning of the loan term.

tenancy in common: An ownership arrangement whereby multiple residents jointly own a property and allocate apartments to each owner. There is no offering plan filed with the New York State attorney general's office for a tenancy in common.

tenant-shareholder: An owner of a cooperative apartment.

term sheet: See *deal sheet*.

three-way triangular exchange: In a like-kind exchange, the tax code permits a special arrangement under which a property can be sold at one time and the proceeds put in escrow until another property is found within a defined timeframe. Thereafter, the taxpayer can still qualify for like kind-exchange tax treatment upon the purchase of this third property.

time value of money: A financial technique in which money is viewed as having interest value and any purchasing decision is considered in light of the implied interest value benefit. Thus, present value is the current value of future cash inflows at a given interest rate, while future value is the projected value of cash inflows at a specified point in the future.

townhouse: A single-family dwelling with a usual frontage of 16 to 25 feet. Townhouses are generally three, four or five stories in height, and are frequently partitioned into multiple apartments. In such cases, brokers refer to them as "townhouse apartments" or "brownstone apartments."

UCC-1: When a party takes a loan against his cooperative shares, a financing statement is filed against his name in order to "perfect" the bank's rights against this collateral. The UCC filing is a constructive notice to all parties of the bank's rights against the borrower and the property.

UCC-3: A filing to terminate a recorded UCC-1 once the obligation to the bank is satisfied.

UCC filing fee: The fee required to submit a UCC filing against another party. This filing perfects the right of the lender against the borrower against any claims by other parties at a subsequent date.

UCC lien search: A search performed by an attorney or title company to identify any claims against a given party that the transaction may need to satisfy.

underlying mortgage: A mortgage obtained by a cooperative corporation and secured by the building. This underlying mortgage is generally paid off over time by all the tenant shareholders as part of their monthly maintenance charge.

unique risk: Specific risks associated with the purchase of a specific property, as distinct from general market risk.

unit owner: The party who owns a cooperative or condominium apartment.

unrelated business taxable income (UBTI): Investment income generated from property held in a pension plan in which there is a mortgage, which is subject to a special federal tax. The property ownership is allocated between the cash investment and the mortgage, and all gain allocable to the mortgage portion is subject to UBTI tax.

unsold shares: Shares of stock in a cooperative corporation transferred to the sponsor at the completion of the conversion process, for those apartments that were not sold to tenant insiders or investors. The sponsor normally gets special rights to rent and/or sell these shares (representing specific apartments) without board approval.

Index

U

V

W

Z